Women in
Trollope's Palliser Novels

Nineteenth-Century Studies

Juliet McMaster, Series Editor
University Professor
University of Alberta

Consulting Editor:
James Kincaid
Professor of English
University of Colorado, Boulder

Other Titles in This Series

The Character of Beauty in the Victorian Novel	Lori Hope Lefkowitz
Carlyle's Life of John Sterling: *A Study in Victorian Biography*	Robert Keith Miller
Victorian Word-Painting and Narrative: Toward the Blending of Genres	Rhoda L. Flaxman
Reading Middlemarch: *Reclaiming the Middle Distance*	Jeanie Thomas
Disruption and Delight in the Nineteenth-Century Novel	Cathy Comstock
Ruskin and Italy	Alexander Bradley
The Religious Dimension of Jane Austen's Novels	Gene Koppel

Women in Trollope's Palliser Novels

by
Deborah Denenholz Morse

Copyright © 1987
Deborah Denenholz Morse
All rights reserved

Produced and distributed by
UMI Research Press
an imprint of
University Microfilms, Inc.
Ann Arbor, Michigan 48106

Library of Congress Cataloging in Publication Data

Morse, Deborah Denenholz, 1949-
Women in Trollope's Palliser novels.

  (Nineteenth-century studies)
  Bibliography: p.
  Includes index.
  1. Trollope, Anthony, 1815-1882—Characters—Women.
2. Trollope, Anthony, 1815-1882. Palliser novels.
3. Women in literature. I. Title. II. Series:
Nineteenth-century studies (Ann Arbor, Mich.)
PR5688.W6M67   1987   823'.8   87-21497
ISBN 0-8357-1847-6 (alk. paper)

British library CIP data is available.

*To my mother
and to the memory of my father*

Am I not doing it all for him?

Glencora, *The Prime Minister*

Contents

Acknowledgments *xi*

Introduction *1*

1 *Can You Forgive Her?:* The Real Self versus the Ideal Woman *7*

2 The "Phineas" Saga: The Terms of Equality *39*

3 *The Prime Minister:* The Cost of Civilization *85*

4 Glencora's Legacy: Mary, Mabel, and Isabel as Spiritual Daughters in *The Duke's Children* *119*

Conclusion *137*

Notes *141*

Bibliography *155*

Index *159*

Acknowledgments

I began this book in 1978. Life intervened dramatically in the form of two beautiful children, Evan and Lucy, and later, a full-time teaching position. I am only now completing the work I began nine years ago. Many people have helped me along the way. I would like to thank my mother, Elizabeth Denenholz, who gave me inspiration, love, and—not least—funding, and my mother-in-law and father-in-law, Letty and Howard Morse, who provided me with affectionate counsel and childcare. My sister, Cynthia Denenholz, and my brother, David Denenholz, have been wise counselors even in the dark watches of the night. Barbara Shwom and Deborah Robbins once again proved their devoted friendship by not only reading the entire manuscript but also criticizing my ideas via the mail and over the telephone, and right beside me at the computer. Rick Ryan and Carol Sklenicka spent many hours editing the manuscript, and many more hours discussing ideas while watching children. My advisor, Christopher Herbert, a brilliant critic and a wonderful friend throughout the years I studied at Northwestern, deserves credit for introducing me to Trollope's fiction. Bill Heyck and Larry Evans gave the original manuscript a careful reading at all its stages. Jeanne Brand typed the first version of chapter 4. All illustrations used in this study are reproduced by gracious permission of the Robert H. Taylor Collection of the Firestone Library at Princeton University. Mark Farrell, curator of the collection, was very generous and helpful, advising me on the illustrations and agonizing with me about which to choose. Juliet McMaster spent a good deal of time with me on the telephone while looking through first editions of Trollope's novels, all the while describing illustrations that she thought might complement my text. I also would like to thank her for her judicious reading of my manuscript. Nina Auerbach, John Halperin, James Kincaid, and Jane Nardin also read the manuscript, and to them I am thankful both for their generosity and for their astute commentary. To Joan Sterns I owe thanks for her help not only with this book, but also with many other aspects of my research and teaching.

Janet Dunleavy and Jean Hagstrum have unfailingly given me support over the years. To Bliss Carnochan, I am grateful because he taught me to work at something I love. To all those who cared for my children while I wrote this book—

especially the people at Plymouth Children's Center, Irene Langheinrich, Azin and Nakhostin Spantman, and Marie Werner—I give heartfelt thanks. My writing group—Alice Gillam-Scott, Carol Sklenicka, and Bill Van Pelt—gave me much-needed criticism in the last stages of preparing the manuscript. My friend and running partner, Pat Goldstein, has listened patiently to my ideas throughout many four-mile runs.

Finally, I would like to thank my husband, Charles Morse, who not only has been infinitely patient with a seemingly endless task, but who also has provided excellent literary criticism for many years.

Introduction

Patricia Thomson wrote in *The Victorian Heroine: A Changing Ideal* (1957) that "it was on reading Trollope that Victorians must have felt their ideal of wifely submission was in its finest hour" (111). In a book published the same year, Rebecca West wrote that "Trollope was a feminist" (167). While few serious critics of Anthony Trollope's novels would now agree with Thomson, many would call West's assessment an overstatement. Carolyn Heilbrun decides in *Toward A Recognition of Androgyny* (1973) that Trollope leaves unquestioned the masculine assumptions of his culture in his "conventional world" (57). While Heilbrun states that there is not a passage "which does not betray the gender of its author" (77), a recent critical work by Rajiva Wijesinha which is especially concerned with Trollope's attitudes toward courtship and marriage indicates a diametrically opposed view in its title, *The Androgynous Trollope* (1982). In between these two extremes—Trollope as male chauvinist and Trollope as feminist—critics commenting on Trollope's treatment of women are divided into two camps: those who insist upon his essential conventionality, and those who, while concentrating upon other aspects of his work, note in passing that there are elements in his depiction of women that seem discordant with conventional images of Victorian femininity. The issue of Trollope's attitude toward women is far from being resolved.

Michael Sadleir began the controversy with his statement that Trollope, acquiescing to the cultural assumptions of his times, was the "Voice of an Epoch" (13). Assuming Trollope's conventionality, Sadleir claimed that Trollope's ideal maiden is "modest of mien, low-voiced . . . claiming nothing of equality, she achieves supremacy" (382-83). Since Sadleir, critical opinion asserting the conventionality of Trollope's women is epitomized by Mario Praz, who wrote thirty years after Sadleir that "Trollope's novels are designed to encourage gentle, modest, not very passionate girls" (271). Still more recently, A. O. J. Cockshut focuses on Trollope's undisturbed vision of his society's dictates for men and women: "Trollope's assumption of polarity of sexual roles . . . with its manifold implications about contrasting roles in the family, in work and in society, was for Trollope simply an obvious assumption of common sense" (152). The most provocative recent critic who argues for Trollope's essential conventionality is

George Levine, who admits Trollope's "complicated and sensitive but thoroughly masculine perception of the difficulties of being a woman in so arbitrarily constructed a society" (10), while he simultaneously identifies "that special angle from which Trollope sees with cynical warmth" which "reduces reality for any woman to marrying and having two children and being honest with an honest husband" (15).[1]

Critics who deal peripherally with some aspect of Trollope's unconventional treatment of women—his sympathetic, psychologically intricate depiction of female character or his recognition of women's sexuality—are more centrally concerned with other aspects of Trollope's art. Most notable among these commentators on Trollope are Robert Polhemus, Ruth apRoberts, James Kincaid, R. C. Terry, Juliet McMaster, Shirley Letwin, and Christopher Herbert. A recent critical study by Bill Overton, *The Unofficial Trollope* (1982), challenges the idea of Trollope's conventionality more directly: it posits the existence of two Trollopes, a conventional "official" self and a subversive "unofficial" self. However, Overton's suggestive comments upon Trollope's attitude toward women are not expanded upon. Another recent critical work, *Corrupt Relations* (1982), by Richard Barickman, Susan MacDonald, and Myra Stark, focuses more centrally on Trollope's ambivalent presentation of Victorian sexual relations. However, Trollope is only one of four Victorian novelists (the others are Dickens, Thackeray, and Collins) discussed in the work, and its examination of his novels is necessarily cursory.

I am interested in duality and conflict in Trollope's vision of Victorian womanhood, and therefore my work connects with Overton's study, and with the work of Barickman, MacDonald, and Stark. However, my study differs from these critiques in its central focus. I am most concerned with the intricate ways in which Trollope's fiction embodied the tensions generated by the Victorian "Woman Question" debate. In particular, I examine Trollope's ambivalent relation toward the often contradictory ideals for Victorian womanhood which were at the heart of the "Woman Question" controversy. This study investigates the subtle manifestations of Trollope's disquiet with his culture's assumptions about Woman's "nature and mission." His conflict between affirmation and subversion manifests itself in a variety of ways: disruption of traditional narrative structure, ambiguous characterization, tension between narrative intent and resolution, between characterization and narrator's commentary, or between text and illustration.

I have chosen to deal only with the five Palliser novels which form the series as it was originally envisioned by Trollope: *Can You Forgive Her?*, *Phineas Finn*, *Phineas Redux*, *The Prime Minister* and *The Duke's Children*.[2] (Although I will on occasion allude to that anomalous work now included in modern versions of the Palliser series of novels, *The Eustace Diamonds*, it is not a part of my critique.)[3] Nowhere else in Trollope's work is the conflict between belief in the prevailing cultural myths about ideal femininity and subversion of those same myths given as sustained a presentation. Some of Trollope's unconventional women figure prominently in several of the novels. The stories of Lady Laura and (to a lesser extent) Violet are told in both *Phineas Finn* and *Phineas Redux,* while Marie Goesler's tale, which begins in *Phineas Finn,* extends throughout the rest of the series. The central woman in the novels is of course Glencora, who is introduced as an unhappily married bride in *Can You Forgive Her?* Her story continues even after her death in the Duke's—and Trollope's—retrospective, *The Duke's Children.* She is Trollope's most extended characterization of a Victorian woman not only in the Palliser novels, but in all his tremendous corpus. Other sympathetic characterizations of intelligent, strong women who challenge prevailing myths about Victorian femininity are prominent in every Palliser novel: Alice Vavasor and Arabella Greenow in *Can You Forgive Her?;* Adelaide Palliser in *Phineas Redux;* Emily Wharton in *The Prime Minister;* Isabel Boncassen, Lady Mabel Grex and Mary Palliser in *The Duke's Children.* In the stories of all these women Trollope expresses his own conflicting reactions to the Victorian "Woman Question."

Trollope's sympathetic depiction of these untraditional female characters is only one form his disquiet with Victorian society's core myths about womanhood takes. Another central manifestation of his critique is the alteration of narrative conventions that embody the conventional view that feminine fulfillment lies only in love and marriage.[4] The structure of the conventional romantic courtship plot is broken in every novel, and there are elements that qualify perfect closure in each novel's comic resolution.[5] From Alice's cloying admission of John Grey's omnipotence in *Can You Forgive Her?* to Mabel Grex's bitter dispossession in *The Duke's Children,* Trollope never allows us to feel that all is well for Victorian womanhood.

Amid a welter of conflicting feminine ideals, the form the "Woman Question" debate took for Trollope was an ongoing fictional dialectic between belief in and subversion of Victorian ideals for womanhood. The problem of "redundant women" in Victorian England is perhaps the clearest example of Trollope's divided mind on a major nineteenth-century social issue which figured prominently as a part of the "Woman Question" debate. The term "redundant" (i.e., unmarried) women referred to the great surplus of women—especially middle-class women—in mid-century Britain.[6] The chief reason usually given to explain the disproportionate number of women to men was male—especially middle-class male—emigration. But middle-class women were at least in part "redundant" because men of their class were marrying late, or not at all. The ideal of the nonworking middle-class girl who could not help bring money into the family paradoxically forced many men of this class to get along without wives, who were "expensive luxuries."[7]

Trollope's ambivalent stance on the "redundant woman" question is characteristic. His sympathy with the plight of single women is evident in novels as different as *Miss Mackenzie* (1865) and *The Belton Estate* (1866). Although *Miss Mackenzie* contains Trollope's happiest and most fulfilled old maid, Miss Todd (introduced in *The Bertrams* [1859]), the heroine's lonely life of spinsterhood happily ends when she marries the loyal, stolid John Ball. Clara Belton, the heroine of *The Belton Estate,* declares, "'I think it would be well if all single women were strangled by the time they are thirty' with a fierce energy that absolutely frightened her aunt" (chapter 8). Trollope portrays Clara's frustration at being a poor, unmarried woman of twenty-five with nothing in particular to do now that death has absolved her of the feminine role of nursemaid to her demanding father, but she finds complete fulfillment in marriage to the worthy, passionate Will Belton.

In the Palliser novels, the same dichotomy exists between sympathy with the single woman and certainty that her answer lies only in marriage. In *Phineas Finn* (1869), for example, the issue of "redundant" women is treated sympathetically in the characterization of Aspasia Fitzgibbon, although Trollope portrays her unhappiness in her single state. In the same novel, Augusta Baldock's answer to spinsterhood is to enter a nunnery. Any solution to the "redundant woman" problem other than marriage is not given serious treatment. Violet jokes, for instance, about her aunt's "Female Protestant Unmarried Women's Emigration Society" (*Phineas Finn,* chapter 41), although 20,000 Victorian women did in fact emigrate to the colonies in order to work and be self-supporting (Hammerton, "Feminism and Female Emigration," 53).

In his own life, Trollope's closest woman friend was the American feminist, Kate Field (Snow, 117–28), who never married. But characteristically, while Trollope respected and indeed encouraged Kate's education, he urged her to marry and discouraged her advocacy of professional careers (especially lecturing) for women. As he tells her in a February 1877 letter, women "are unfitted because they are wanted elsewhere;—because in such pursuits a man is taken from his home, and because she is wanted at home."[8] Trollope's vision of spinsterhood is perfectly expressed in Glencora's declaration about the unmarried Parisian female operatives in *Can You Forgive Her?:* "it was a great shame, and they ought all to have husbands" (chapter 68). As H. L. Mencken's *Quotations* uncomfortably reminds modern readers, it was Trollope who wrote (in *North America* [1:chapter 18]): "The best right a woman has is the right to a husband." Palliser's precise explanation to Glencora that the 150,000 Paris female operatives must work because of the "redundancy of the female population" (chapter 68) does not convince her.

Yet Trollope, like Palliser, admired women workers, as he illustrated in his story, "The Telegraph Girl" (1877), and his essay, "The Young Women at the London Telegraph Office" (1877).[9] He simply felt that they ought to have a chance to marry and have children. Trollope is probably thinking of England rather than France when he has Glencora outrage Palliser's rational mind by remarking that "she saw a great many men walking about who, she was quite sure, had not wives of their own" (chapter 68). Trollope would most likely concur with W. R. Greg, who stated in an 1862 *National Review* article entitled "Why Are Women Redundant?" that the solution to the "redundant woman" problem is not career training but earlier marriage, female emigration to the colonies, where wives are "clamored for"—and male premarital celibacy (quoted in Helsinger, Sheets, and Veeder, 2:139).

Trollope's divided mind on the question of England's redundant women—his sympathy for them, but his conviction that the answer to their difficult position in

Victorian society was marriage rather than professional careers—is also expressed in the two types of spinsters he characteristically portrays in his novels. The first type, the man-hating militant feminist, is better known: it is expressed in caricatures of dry, ridiculous spinsters from the "Republican Browning," Wallachia Petrie, in *He Knew He Was Right* (1869) to Olivia Q. Fleabody and the Baroness Bannman (who jumps at the chance to marry) in *Is He Popenjoy?* (1878) and the apostate feminist Francesca Altifiorla in *Kept in the Dark* (1882), who unsuccessfully pursues the domineering Sir Francis Geraldine. The other type of old maid—the self-reliant, kind spinster—is less discussed. There is a varied gallery of characterizations of her, from the energetic, rosy-cheeked Miss Todd in *The Bertrams* and *Miss Mackenzie* to the stoic, intelligent Priscilla Stanbury in *He Knew He Was Right*. Older confirmed spinsters also tend to be gently treated by Trollope. He respects the old-fashioned virtues of honesty and integrity represented variously by Monica Thorne in *Barchester Towers* (1857), Miss Marrable in *The Vicar of Bullhampton* (1870), Jemima Stanbury in *He Knew He Was Right,* and Aunt Rosina in *Ayala's Angel* (1881).

Finally, Trollope's ambivalent attitude toward the "redundant" woman problem is evident in the combination of disdain and sympathy with which he portrays husband-hunters like Georgiana Longstaffe in *The Way We Live Now* (1875), Arabella Trefoil in *The American Senator* (1877) and—to a much lesser extent—Arabella and Camilla French in *He Knew He Was Right*. On one hand, the aggressive, mercenary Georgiana Longstaffe and Arabella Trefoil, who paint their faces, are uncomfortably like aristocratic versions of Eliza Lynn Linton's "Girl of the Period," whom the lower-middle-class Arabella and Camilla French embody. On the other hand, Trollope seems to agree with Henry James, who wrote in his review of Linton's essay: "it is a very dismal truth that the only hope of most women, at the present moment, for a life worth the living, lies in marriage, and marriage with rich men or men likely to become so, and that in their unhappy weakness they often betray an ungraceful anxiety on this point."[10]

Trollope's sympathy for husband-hunting women is of course greatly qualified.[11] Despite the chance of happiness he holds out for Arabella at the end of *The American Senator,* she *is* exiled to Patagonia in her marriage. Trollope writes of her: "Will such a one as Arabella Trefoil be damned, and if so why? Think of her virtues; how she works, how true she is to her vocation, how little there is of self indulgence, or of idleness. I think that she will go to a kind of third class heaven in which she will always be getting third class husbands" (*Letters,* 2:710–11).

If Trollope passes harsh judgment on Arabella, his sympathy with the plight of the old maid in his society is nevertheless shown when he deliberately has Georgiana Longstaffe's lament that she will be "nothing" if she does not marry echo his favorite heroines—from the self-effacing Dorothy Stanbury of *He Knew He Was Right* (who embodies the very opposite qualities of the "Girl of the Period," represented in the French sisters) to the witty Violet Effingham in *Phineas*

Finn. But Trollope's sympathy with his society's "redundant" women, however genuine, never shades into an affirmation of spinsterhood as a fate for Victorian womanhood that might be as desirable and fulfilling as the roles of wife and mother. There are no heroic old maids in Trollope. None of his spinsters are pioneers like the emigrant Mary Taylor (friend of Charlotte Brontë).[12] Trollope's emigrant heroine is, significantly, a married woman, Gertrude Tudor in *The Three Clerks* (1858), who helps her erring husband find redemption for his sins. There are no old maids in Trollope like Florence Nightingale, Frances Mary Buss, Dorothea Beale, Frances Power Cobbe or Christina Rossetti—each an innovator in her own area of work.[13] If Miss Todd is modelled on Cobbe,[14] it is significant that Trollope transforms the intellectual feminist journalist into a kindly surrogate mother figure, a kind of philanthropist who operates only in the private sphere. Trollope's only spinster heroine, Lily Dale, is ultimately portrayed as perverse (if not masochistic) and self-involved, for all her charm. Trollope tired of her before his readers did, and finally viewed her as something of a "female prig" (*Autobiography*, 150). For Trollope, it is a defeat when, at the end of *The Last Chronicle of Barset* (1867), Lily identifies her social role forever with the initials "O. M."[15] But some Victorian women were trying to transform the vision of the "redundant woman," to see opportunity where their society saw failure.

If Trollope's perception of Woman's role was limited, it was much more elastic than that of most of his contemporaries. Trollope's definition of women's rights was an egalitarian marriage. But in the context of a culture in which ideal women were supposed to deny much of what a natural human being might feel and express, Trollope's vision of a relation between two intelligent, sexual beings who were equals within their private union of Man and Woman is subversive.

1

Can You Forgive Her?:
The Real Self versus the Ideal Woman

Anthony Trollope portrays the character and career of Lady Glencora Palliser (née Lady Glencora McCluskie, and later Duchess of Omnium) more fully than those of any other woman in all of his novels. Glencora figures most prominently in the six books known as the Palliser novels. However, her history begins in one of the novels of the Barset series, *The Small House at Allington* (1864), and she also appears briefly in *Miss Mackenzie* (1865), written immediately after *Can You Forgive Her?*. Trollope traces Glencora's history from her passionate, thwarted romance with the dashing scrapegrace, Burgo Fitzgerald, and her subsequent arranged marriage with the dull but respectable statesman, Plantagenet Palliser (*The Small House at Allington* and *Can You Forgive Her?*), through the account of her drawing-room political aspirations in *The Prime Minister,* to the story of her influence upon her family even after her death (*The Duke's Children*). Glencora's story is a record of frustrated self-realization, an account of an intelligent, spirited Victorian woman who struggles with the constraints imposed upon her by her society's ideals for women.

The narrative framework of Glencora's story images its unconventionality. Instead of ending in marriage as the proper consummation of true love, her tale begins, in *Can You Forgive Her?*, with a history of her coercion into marriage with Plantagenet Palliser—a man she does not love—and her persistent desire for her former lover, Burgo Fitzgerald. Her story is continued in each of the novels of the Palliser series, but I shall concentrate on three: *Can You Forgive Her?, The Prime Minister,* and *The Duke's Children*. It is in these three books that Glencora's struggle for self-realization is most fully chronicled.

Moreover, the stories of the other women in these books tend to complement Glencora's narrative, because each, in some guise, depicts rebellion against prescribed female roles, efforts at independent action and creation of a self apart from traditional feminine ideals. In *Can You Forgive Her?*, the story of Glencora is framed by the tale of Alice Vavasor's search for selfhood, embodied in her vacillations between her two suitors, John Grey and George Vavasor; it also ramifies beyond this, accented by the stories of both George's sister, Kate, and his former mistress, Jane, who suffer under patriarchal domination. In *The Prime Minister,* Glencora's failed bid for political as well as social power, her attempt to "be written of in memoirs, to make a niche for herself in history" (chapter 28), is counterpointed by Emily Wharton's struggle to define herself apart from the Fletcher-Wharton clan through her marriage to the outsider, Ferdinand Lopez, only to discover that her husband wants to re-create her in accordance with those very ideals of feminine passivity she was trying to escape. In *The Duke's Children,* in which the action takes place after Glencora's death, her life is imaginatively extended through the lives of three women of the next generation: Lady Mary Palliser, her daughter; Lady Mabel Grex, the first love of her elder son, Silverbridge; Isabel Boncassen, the American girl Silverbridge marries. Through her daughter, Glencora is vicariously fulfilled, because Mary consummates her passion for Tregear (an idealized Burgo) in marriage, a victory she achieves by resisting the Duke's authority, confounding his conventionally patriarchal expectations of feminine behavior. Isabel Boncassen, eventually Silverbridge's wife, represents the greatest range of possibilities Trollope can imagine for a spirited, intelligent Victorian woman; however, it is significant that she is an American, and therefore an outsider. Through both Mary's and Isabel's marriages, Glencora's dream of love is symbolically realized, for they both wed lively, handsome men who have integrity and purpose, uniting much of what is best in both Burgo and Palliser. Finally, Lady Mabel's story is a more tragic version of Glencora's, describing the possible desolation of this society's women, bound both by Victorian culture's feminine ideals and by its often contradictory code of respectability and materialistic ethic. While Glencora experiences sustained marital dissatisfaction, she also comes to care deeply for her husband, and with her characteristic versatility, she tries to find compensations in her intimate involvement with her children, in the career of political hostess, and in the management of others' romantic affairs. Tragically, the beautiful, articulate Mabel is left with "no other affairs" (*The Duke's Children,* chapter 77) than her isolation and her dispossession. And although Glencora's restless attempts at vicarious gratification are ultimately unsatisfactory, she does step outside the boundaries of the conventional wife-mother role, while Mabel is finally driven to enact another Victorian female part, living with her paid companion, Miss Cassewary, as "two old maids together" (*The Duke's Children,* chapter 77).

Critics have argued about the significance of Trollope's title, *Can You Forgive Her?,* ever since Henry James's testy dismissal in his 1865 *Nation* review: "The question is, Can we forgive Miss Vavasor? Of course we can, and forget her, too, for that matter. What does Mr. Trollope mean by this question?" (quoted in Smalley, 249–50). The answers to James's question vary from critic to critic. Juliet McMaster interprets the title's question to refer to the behavior of a jilt. She focuses on Alice's inability to distinguish between words and things, between theory and practice, as the reason behind this behavior (*Palliser Novels,* 25–26). James Kincaid decides that the title's question refers to Alice's "independent exercise of will'' (186). Richard Barickman, Susan MacDonald, and Myra Stark cite the narrator's description of Alice as "filled with some undefined idea of the importance to her of her own life,'' concluding that "it is for this that he chiefly asks us to forgive her'' (42). Shirley Letwin views Alice's error as that of associating passionate love with frenzy and madness, with irrationality, and it is for this mistake that she must be forgiven (142). Bill Overton thinks that the title refers to Alice's jilting of Grey, but that it is meant to be ironic, since Alice "has to maintain her independence against a man who is all too self-assured,'' and "it's in this way that the jilting is to be understood—a jilting that will make for a stronger relationship between them'' (101).

However, most essentially, the title is a question about the Victorian ideal of female purity. It refers most directly to Alice Vavasor, who has "sinned'' against canons of feminine purity by accepting an offer of marriage from a man she doesn't love, George Vavasor, while she is still in love with the man she jilted, John Grey. Moreover, when the title is considered in this light, its meaning ramifies beyond Alice's problem, to include virtually all the women's stories in the book.

The title's question can also be interpreted as referring to Glencora's thoughts of adultery, and even to her longing for her former lover, Burgo, after she is married to Palliser. The question is also implicitly asked of the prostitute Burgo Fitzgerald twice meets, to whom Glencora is compared, and of George's abandoned mistress, Jane, for whom he once betrayed Alice. In the low-comedy subplot of the novel, the question also applies to the gay widow Arabella Greenow, whose independence and obvious sexuality belie Victorian ideals of childlike passivity and angelic purity.

Trollope's examination of the title's question creates a tension between the narrator's seemingly literal interpretation and the ironic overtones the title slowly assumes as not only Alice, but all the novel's young women are characterized sympathetically. By the end of the book, when we have seen the ordeals not only Alice and Glencora, but also Kate and George's mistress, Jane, experience, the question posed by the title seems ironic. The implicit question one asks might well be, "Can you forgive him?'' The "him'' could be any of the men in the novel: John Grey, for failing to give credence to Alice's aspirations; Plantagenet Palliser, for marrying a woman he doesn't love, and then ignoring her emotional needs; George Vavasor, for assuming all male prerogatives in this patriarchal society, while manipulating his women (Alice, Kate, Jane) through the ideal of feminine self-sacrifice; Burgo Fitzgerald, for his ultimate willingness to sacrifice Glencora, realizing that he will eventually mistreat her if she becomes his mistress, that he will be unable to view her as other than a "fallen'' woman when "all women should cease to acknowledge her; when all men would regard her as one degraded and dishonoured'' (chapter 50).

The ambivalence Trollope apparently feels about the ideal of feminine purity is reflected in the tension between the sympathetic characterizations of women wrestling with the strictures their society imposes upon them, and the resolutions of all the novel's plots. Alice's story, as well as Arabella Greenow's, ends with the comic resolution of marriage, while Glencora's story closes with the birth of an heir. Moreover, as I shall discuss later, there are tensions manifested within the conventional endings themselves.

The ambivalence in Trollope's attitudes is also reflected in his fictional structure, which is a variation on the conventional "two suitor" narrative framework. The fictional construct Trollope uses in *Can You Forgive Her?* is analyzed in Jean Kennard's critical work, *Victims of Convention*. In her book, Kennard examines the literary convention she labels "the convention of the two suitors" (10-11). Kennard is interested in the fundamentally sexist nature of this fictional formula, in which a central female character is courted by two men, the exemplary or "right" suitor and the unscrupulous or "wrong" suitor. The heroine's choice of the "good" suitor defines her acceptance of the qualities embodied in him and her rejection of the qualities embodied in the "wrong" suitor. The two lovers are thus touchstones of the heroine's developing maturity. All three of Trollope's plots in *Can You Forgive Her?* use this narrative structure, but each diverges from it in a significant way. Glencora's story differs in two crucial particulars: her story begins after, not before, her marriage, and marriage to the "worthy" lover, Palliser, constitutes a denial of self rather than self-realization. Alice's story also breaks away from the conventional "two suitor" pattern, in "mad" switches from the worthy lover (John Grey) to the wild one (George Vavasor) in search of fulfillment.

Trollope introduces Arabella Greenow with the history of her reputation as a flirt, which leaves her still unmarried at thirty-four, and of her rebellion against her father and brothers, whom she had offended "by declining to comply with their advice at certain periods of her career." Eventually Arabella represses her strongly sexual nature and marries Mr. Greenow who "was an old man, and was very old for his age; but the whole thing was quite respectable, and there was, at any rate, no doubt about the money" (chapter 7). She exchanges many casual admirers who are not earnest suitors for Mr. Greenow, although the narrator makes it pretty clear that her husband is no longer capable of being a real lover. Moreover, the narrator's emphasis on the male Vavasors' approval of Arabella's "respectable" marriage—a union in which there is no passion, but there is "no doubt about the money"—clearly suggests the patriarchal ideals by which Arabella has temporarily had to abide in order eventually to gain power through the inheritance of her husband's money. Finally, Arabella is presented as far less mercenary than her father and brothers. While she is married to Greenow, she is a "pattern wife," and her husband "considered himself to be the happiest old man in Lancashire," and after her husband's death, "in her prosperity she quite forgave the former slights which had been put upon her by her relatives" (chapter 7).

Arabella's story begins immediately after her aged husband's death, when she embarks as a widow upon a new life of freedom and sexual possibility. As in Glencora's and Alice's stories, the disrupted narrative convention images the dislocation of conventional attitudes about women in relation to courtship and marriage. The widow Greenow breaks the traditional pattern by marrying the "wild" man, not the "worthy" one. Moreover, she certainly does not recognize her "better self" in Bellfield; her choice is sensual rather than moral. Finally, Arabella chooses a weak man whom she can master, rather than the conventional male whose superior strength and knowledge mark him as the master. It is significant that Trollope dares this reversal only in the comic subplot, where its subversiveness is immediately undermined.[1] In the two main plots of the novel, both Alice and Glencora ultimately choose the "worthy man," although both their experiences (and the parody of the worthy man in Cheeseacre) tend to qualify the novel's resolution.

When we first meet Glencora, she is already married to the "worthy man," Plantagenet Palliser, a man "whose dry nature realized neither the delights nor the dangers of love" (chapter 43). The aristocratic statesman Palliser is a man to whom the respectability of his wife is important, who "especially wished that she should be discreet and matronly; he feared no lovers, but he feared that she might do silly things—that she would catch cold,—and not know how to live a life becoming the wife of a Chancellor of the Exchequer" (chapter 43). In contrast, Glencora's former lover, the "beautiful" profligate, Burgo Fitzgerald, is "laughing to scorn the rules which regulate the lives of other men" (chapter 18). The choice Glencora has been compelled to make between the two men is the context of her introduction into the narrative, and it is crucial to Trollope's portrait of her. Burgo Fitzgerald has just been introduced into the story; his first action is to ride a horse to death in a foxhunt, recklessly forcing the poor animal to leap to his death. Immediately thereafter, on the next page of the novel, the history of Burgo's love affair with Glencora is recalled.

This description is reminiscent of the scene in *Anna Karenina* in which Vronsky rides Frou-Frou to her death, breaking her back, and the implications are similar: with these men, there is certain destruction for the women whose sense of romance or passion dares them to flout societal convention.[2] Immediately juxtaposed against the graphic image of Burgo's probable treatment of her, however, is the story of Glencora's abandonment of her love for him, and her marriage to Palliser, the man she is compelled to accept by her powerful elders. She is in the process of being coerced in the first scene in which we see her, in which "sundry mighty magnates, driven almost to despair at the prospect of such a sacrifice" (chapter 18), force Glencora to relinquish her love rather than her fortune. During the course of the novel, Glencora repeatedly recurs to this central act of repression; her story details her struggle to realize some sense of self despite her former subjugation to her relatives.

The passage also emphasizes the similarity of Burgo's sacrifice of his horse, upon which he relies, to his expectation that Glencora will sacrifice both her respectability and her money for him:

> Then came poor Burgo! Oh, Burgo, hadst thou not have been a very child, thou shouldst have known that now, at this time of the day,—after all that thy gallant horse had done for thee,—it was impossible to thee or him. But when did Burgo Fitzgerald know anything? Poor noble beast, noble in vain! To his very last gasp he had done his best, and had deserved that he should have been in better hands. His master's ignorance had killed him. There are men who never know how little a horse can do—or how much! (Chapter 17)

The result of Glencora's obedience to her relatives is that she loses what little self-esteem she has. In a conversation at the Palliser country home, Matching, Glencora describes her feelings of self-hatred to Alice, who has unwittingly alluded to Glencora's betrayal of her love for Burgo. Alice has been describing her own inability to "transfer my affections quite so quickly as that" to Jeffrey Palliser, Plantagenet's cousin, after separating herself from John Grey, "a man whom I certainly did love truly":

> It was exactly what Glencora had done. She had loved a man and had separated herself from him and had married another, all within a month or two. "It is an unmaidenly thing to do, certainly," said Lady Glencora very slowly, and in her lowest voice. "Nay, it is unwomanly; but one may be driven. One may be so driven that all gentleness of womanhood is driven out of one. I did not propose that you do it as a sudden thing. . . . I did it suddenly. I know it. I did it like a beast that is driven as its owner chooses. I know it. I was a beast. Oh, Alice, if you knew how I hate myself!" (Chapter 20)

It is the only time I can recall when Glencora speaks slowly; she is, as she tells Alice, "one of those who like talking, as you'll find out" (chapter 22). She is trying to define carefully the ideals for women according to which she has failed; she begins by labelling her actions as "unmaidenly," progresses to calling them "unwomanly," and then laments her loss of "all gentleness of womanhood." Through Glencora, we see the psychological damage wrought by the approval of passivity in women, by the ideal of woman as docile, obedient child.[3] Glencora likens this acquiescence to that of an animal, finally, and we are reminded that Burgo, too, it seems, would have driven Glencora, as he did his horse, "as its owner chooses."

What Glencora describes as "an unmaidenly thing to do" has, of course, been dictated by those very pillars of propriety who are supposed to uphold all the conventional cultural assumptions about Woman's purity. Spoken after her last passionate kiss with Burgo, when all danger of elopement with him is over, Glencora's later words make it clear that those who wish to control women with the weapon of respectability give expedient interpretations of the feminine purity ideal:

> "But why have I been brought to such a pass as this? And as for female purity! Ah! What was their idea of purity when they forced me, like ogres, to marry a man for whom they knew I never cared? Had I gone with him—had I now eloped with that man who ought to have been my husband—whom would a just God have punished worst,—me, or those two old women and my uncle, who tortured me into this marriage?" (Chapter 67)

Glencora's images of her role in the marriage contract stress her impotence and her victimization; she refers to herself as "tortured" by ogres. Glencora clearly realizes that she has been used by her family and society as a chattel.[4] As she bitterly tells Alice, "We talk with such horror of the French people giving their daughters in marriage, just as they might sell a house or a field, but we do exactly the same thing ourselves. When they all come upon you in earnest, how are you to stand against them? How can any girl do it?" (chapter 22). This speech reverberates forward to the story of Glencora's daughter, Mary, who is able to answer her mother's question with her own sturdy resistance to her father's coercion.

However, Glencora's subjugation and her consequent sense of self-loathing should be seen in the context of a novel in which all the young women, victimized by men, think that they are worthless. Robert Polhemus has pointed out the parallels between Glencora and the prostitute Burgo twice meets, illustrating the vulnerability and exploitation of all women in Victorian society, no matter what their social class (*Changing World,* 106–8). George Vavasor, of course, is the great oppressor of women, exploiting three women mercilessly. He betrays his first engagement to Alice, undermines her subsequent betrothal to John Grey, takes Alice's money, and verbally abuses her. He continually uses Kate to do his bidding, and when she rebels, he uses both threats and physical violence against her. He seduces Jane, alienating her from her family and her class, and then abandons her after a three-year liaison. (To these women may be added the invalid heiress, Miss Grant; George engages himself to her without loving her, but she dies before the marriage.) There is a triad of women's roles here which is particularly Victorian: Alice, the moneyed, respectable woman, suitable for marriage and motherhood; Kate, the totally devoted, serviceable spinster sister; Jane, the "fallen" woman. George's association with Romanticism has been frequently noted, most recently in Donald Stone's book *The Romantic Impulse in Victorian Fiction,* although the link between this sham romanticism and the repression of women has been largely ignored.[5]

Glencora's expressions of self-hatred are echoed in Alice's expressions of her unworthiness for John Grey, in Kate's exclamations of her negligibility, and in Jane's ineffectual lamentations to the man who has seduced and abandoned her. Not Glencora only, but also Alice and Kate—indeed all the women Trollope describes in the world of *Can You Forgive Her?*—are vulnerable because men have the institutionalized power in Victorian society.

Moreover, the precarious identities of Glencora, Alice, and Kate are due in part to the inadequate parental care they have received, in particular the lack of maternal care. Glencora and Kate are orphans. Alice's mother dies in childbirth after committing one significant act of rebellion: marrying against her family's wishes. Glencora is perceived by her relatives chiefly as an heiress before her marriage, and as the mother of future dukes afterwards. Alice is first under the care of her Sabbatarian aunt, Lady Macleod, and then she is sent away to boarding school in France, "a comitatus of her relatives having decided that such was to be her fate" (chapter 1). After seven years in Aix-la-Chapelle, Alice tries to live with her aunt again, but finds they are incompatible, so she then sets up housekeeping with her worldly, self-indulgent father, who prefers club life to the company of his lonely daughter. Kate has focused all her energy and affection on her brother, who in turn is interested only in her support of his interests. Her plaintive question echos throughout the novel: "How is it that I can never get up any interest about my own belongings?" (chapter 31). Her only other male relative, her grandfather, tells her: "You are a good girl, Kate—I wish you had been a boy, that's all." Kate's answer is pointed: "If I had, I shouldn't perhaps have been here to take care of you" (chapter 53).

These women are given very little loving parental care, but they are, nevertheless, perceived as children by those who wish to manipulate them. The ideal of Woman as compliant child becomes a subtle means of control, even a weapon of oppression. Indeed, a central image of Glencora's subjugation is that of the child. The euphemistic phrase Glencora's duennas, Mrs. Marsham and Mr. Bott, use about her is that she is "very young," meaning she might be headstrong and passionate. The insidious side of the ideal of "woman as child" is exposed when Glencora's youth is used to exact obedience in the most significant decision affecting her life. However, the mistake Glencora's watchdogs make is to think that she will continue to be malleable, and that they can exact childlike obedience from her. Glencora is determined to take her prerogatives as a married woman along with her liabilities, and she refuses to obey anyone but her husband, performing that duty with the spirit of insurrection scarcely concealed. Part of Glencora's rebellion consists in showing that a woman is not a child, but an adult. Glencora's skirmishes with Mrs. Marsham and Mr. Bott are a kind of reenactment of the conflict in which Glencora was defeated by her grand relatives—only this time, Glencora wins. "Tortured" into her marriage, she now fervently tells Alice that "there's one thing I have made up my mind about. I will not be persecuted" (chapter 43). Glencora's defense of Alice in her first "battle" with Mrs. Marsham demonstrates her ability to fight with her tongue, when Alice would simply retreat:

> But Lady Glencora would not let her go.
> "Nonsense, Alice," she said. "If you and I can't fight our little battles against Mr. Bott and Mrs. Marsham without running away, it is odd. There is a warfare in which they who run away never live to fight another day."
> "I hope, Glencora, you do not count me as your enemy?" said Mrs. Marsham, drawing herself up.
> "But I shall—certainly, if you attack Alice. Love me, love my dog. I beg your pardon, Alice; but what I meant was this, Mrs. Marsham; love me, love the best friend I have in the world."
> "I did not mean to offend Miss Vavasor," said Mrs. Marsham. (Chapter 43)

By this time, Glencora has learned to use her childishness as a weapon: "She's a nasty old cat," said Lady Glencora, as soon as the door was closed; and she said these words with so droll a voice, with such a childlike shaking of her head, with so much comedy in her grimace, that Alice could not but laugh" (chapter 43). Even Glencora's allusion to the nursery rhyme about "Dr. Fell" when referring to Mr. Bott indicates her confiscation of "childish" things as armament against those she sees as her oppressors.

Palliser himself practices marital tyranny in playing the role of the parent lecturing or reprimanding Glencora as he would a child. Palliser's ideal image of a submissive wife clashes resoundingly, of course, with Glencora's real nature. During the husband's comic attempt to lecture his wife about the British Constitution, "Lady Glencora yawned, and strove lustily, but ineffectually, to hide her yawn in her handkerchief" (chapter 42). Palliser first punishes her by announcing that he will, after all, come to bed late (with the obvious implications). He then tries to impose both Mrs. Marsham and Mr. Bott upon her, and to deny her the company of her own friend, Alice:

> She felt that he was hard to her, and unreasonable, and that he was treating her like a child who should not be allowed her own way in anything. She had endeavoured to please him, and having failed, was not now disposed to give way. . . .
> "I wish you would let me have my own way in this. Of course I cannot have very much to say to Mrs. Marsham, who is an old woman."
> "I especially want Mrs. Marsham to be your friend," said he.
> "Friendships will not come by ordering, Plantagenet," said she.
> "Very well," said he. "Of course, you will do as you please. I am sorry that you have refused the first favour I have asked you this year."
> Then he left the room, and she went away to bed.

But Lady Glencora "resolved upon rebellion," and she does ask Alice (chapter 42). Indeed, Glencora must be prepared to fight for even the seemingly most trivial of self-assertions, such as her desire to go out among the Priory ruins (chapter 27). It is not accidental that this scene of rebellion is enacted directly after Lady Midlothian's visit to Matching, made with the purpose of compelling Alice Vavasor to renew her engagement to John Grey, for the sake of the family's respectability. Alice has been neglected by her august relative heretofore, and will brook no interference in her affairs. Glencora, who is forced to discuss Alice's conduct with Lady Midlothian after Alice leaves the room, is struck both by the importance Lady Midlothian attaches to an affair that cannot possibly have a material effect upon her, and by Lady Midlothian's seeming amnesia about Glencora's own love affair with Burgo Fitzgerald, which that austere matron rigidly opposed:

> And Lady Midlothian, as she insisted on the absolute iniquity of Alice's proceedings, almost startled Lady Glencora by the eagerness of her countenance. Lady Midlothian had been one of those who, even now not quite two years ago, had assisted in obtaining the submission of Lady Glencora herself. Lady Midlothian seemed on the present occasion to remember nothing of this, but Lady Glencora remembered it very exactly. "I shall not give it up," continued Lady Midlothian. (Chapter 26)

In light of the fact that Lady Midlothian has made a highly respectable marriage with a dissolute nobleman from whom she is now separated, her position and her propriety are all she has, and her life is devoted to maintaining them. But there is more to her persistent meddling than this: as she has suffered in order to do what has seemed proper, she abhors any rebellion from the feminine code of respectability.

On the evening of the day upon which Alice resists Lady Midlothian's authority, Glencora asserts her own independence by going out among the Priory ruins, in defiance of her duennas and her spouse. In the moonlit ruins, in a scene evocative of Romantic associations, her act resonates beyond a winter evening's stroll into a rebellion against her entire reality, as she reverts to her love for Burgo, and her thoughts about the coming visit to Monkshade, his aunt's house, where she will meet him. It is a poignant scene, in which the reasons for Glencora's desperate unhappiness are made clear. She is an affectionate, sexual woman, but her feeling about her marriage is "icy coldness." In her confessions to Alice about her continued love for Burgo, Glencora's accents of despair overwhelm Alice's attempt to soothe her by repeating respectable homilies:

> "Glencora, do not speak like that. Do not make me think that anything could tempt you to be false to your vows."
> "Tempt me to be false! Why, child, it has been all false throughout. I never loved him. How can you talk in that way, when you know I never loved him? They browbeat me and frightened me till I did as I was told;—and now;—what am I now?"
> "You are his honest wife. Glencora, listen to me." And Alice took hold of her arm.
> "No," she said, "no; I am not honest. By law I am his wife; but laws are liars! I am not his wife. I will not say the thing that I am. When I went to him at the altar, I knew that I did not love the man who was to be my husband. But him,—Burgo,—I love him with all my heart and soul. I could stoop at his feet and clean his shoes for him, and think it no disgrace!" (Chapter 27)

But perhaps Glencora's most startling speech about her passionate nature occurs later during this walk among the ruins, as Alice tries to dissuade her from going to Monkshade:

> "Alice, look here. I know what I am, and what I am like to become. I loathe myself, and I loathe the thing that I am thinking of. I could have clung to the outside of a man's body, to his very trappings, and loved him ten times better than myself!—ay, even though he had ill-treated me,—if I had been allowed to choose a husband for myself. Burgo would have spent my money,—all that it would have been possible for me to give him. But there would have been something left, and I think that by that time I could have won even him to care for me. But with that man. . . . (Chapter 27)

There are several prominent features in these passages. First, Glencora's insistence on her false identification as Victorian wife, when she actually feels as if she is a whore, her demand that one's identity should be based on the correlation of role and feeling, brings into question the validity of rigidly defined roles and ideals for women. The confusion of role, the fact that the "honest wife" feels like a fallen woman, implicitly poses the reverse possibility: the fallen woman could feel like an honest wife, even though she is perceived as a whore. The second significant characteristic of the passages is the self-hatred Glencora professes, and the third aspect is her vision of love as self-sacrifice. There is an implicit critique of the Victorian ideal of "woman as martyr"[6] in these speeches that so obviously link the willingness to deny one's self with self-hatred. The self-abasing images with which Glencora describes her love indicate that a desire for punishment in part motivates her passion for Burgo: "I could stoop at his feet and clean his shoes for him. . . . I could have clung to the outside of a man's body, to his very trappings, and loved him ten times better than myself!—ay, even though he had ill-treated me."

However, despite her craving for love, it is also evident from this speech that Glencora measures Burgo's possibilities and the depth of his love for her fairly accurately. As Trollope states in a later chapter, in which Glencora ponders her fate, agonizing over whether she should run away with her lover: "As to Burgo, I doubt whether she deceived herself much as to his character." And although she considers undertaking the role of moral teacher[7] to Burgo, Glencora knows that as a "fallen" woman, she can no longer hope to rescue her lover:

> She knew also that whatever chance she might have had to redeem him, had she married him honestly before all the world, there could be no such chance if she went to him as his mistress, abandoning her husband and all her duties, and making herself vile in the eyes of all women. Burgo Fitzgerald would not be influenced for good by such a woman as she would then be. . . . But, as I have said before, she did not count herself for much. What though she were ruined? (Chapter 58).

It is, rather, in her assessment of her husband's possibilities that, luckily for Glencora, her imagination falls short.

Glencora is punished for her moonlit exploit indirectly, through Alice, who can be attacked by both the duennas and by Mr. Palliser more easily than can Glencora herself. Again Glencora is treated like a child by her husband, who blames Alice for "taking" his wife with her, as if Glencora is a child who would obey her friend's command as she would that of a parent. The next morning, the punishment Alice receives is informed by another feminine ideal, that of the "perfect lady as delicate invalid":[8]

> Mr. Bott was particularly anxious. "The frost was so uncommonly severe," said he, "that any delicate person like Lady Glencowrer must have suffered in remaining out so long."
> The insinuation that Alice was not a delicate person, and that, as regarded her, the severity of the frost was of no moment, was very open, and was duly appreciated. . . .
> "I hope you do not consider Lady Glencora delicate," said Alice to Mr. Palliser.
> "She is not robust," said the husband.
> "By no means," said Mrs. Marsham.

> "Indeed no," said Mr. Bott. Alice knew that she was being accused of being robust herself, but she bore it in silence. Ploughboys and milkmaids are robust, and the accusation was a heavy one. (Chapter 28)

The accusation, obviously, is that Alice is not a lady, and Trollope's comic scene, in which his sympathies are clearly with her, elucidates the method by which this ideal can be used as a weapon of sexual persecution, enclosing women within their homes—and within male conceptions of their proper nature.

Another aspect of the vision of the perfect Victorian lady is the ideal of the leisured "ornament of society,"[9] woman as symbol of her husband's success and status, the incarnation of her family's respectability and their claim to gentility. Trollope criticizes this ideal by having that role enacted by a woman whom the narrator obviously derides, the Marchioness of Hartletop (previously Lady Dumbello, in *The Small House at Allington,* née Griselda Grantly):

> Very beautiful she was, and one whose presence at their houses ladies and gentlemen prized alike. She never said silly things, like the Duchess, never was troublesome as to people's conduct to her, was always gracious, yet was never led away into intimacies, was without peer the best-dressed woman in London, and yet gave herself no airs;—and then she was so exquisitely beautiful. Her smile was loveliness itself. There were, indeed, people who said that it meant nothing; but then, what should the smile of a young married woman mean? . . . she knew the ways of high life, and what an exigeant [sic] husband would demand of her, much better than poor Glencora. She would have spoken of no man as a baboon with a bristly beard. She never talked of the long and the short of it. She did not wander out o' nights in winter among the ruins. She made no fast friendship with ladies whom her lord did not like. She had once, indeed, been approached by a lover since she had been married,—Mr. Palliser himself having been the offender,—but she had turned the affair to infinite credit and profit, had gained her husband's closest confidence by telling him of it all, had yet not brought on any hostile collision, and had even dismissed her lover without annoying him. But then Lady Hartletop was a miracle of a woman.
>
> Lady Glencora was no miracle. (Chapter 49)

While the ironic tone of this passage is evident, a close analysis of its mode of ridicule is beyond the scope of this essay. For our purposes, however, it is worth especially noting a few things. First, the ornamental aspect of the Marchioness is stressed: she is "exquisitely beautiful," and her "presence," suggesting an inanimate statue, is "prized." She is valued as a lovely object, and her cold perfection (like that of Merdle's wife, the "Bosom," in *Little Dorrit*) is a symbol of her husband's status. (Readers of the Barsetshire series know that Griselda Grantly was raised to be an ornament of society; however, when Griselda has in fact become an aristocrat, her mother, the Archdeacon's wife, is saddened by the grand but cold daughter she has created.) Second, the narrator clearly prefers the fallible humanity of Glencora. Finally, male hypocrisy is lampooned in the form of the offending lover, Palliser, now the "exigeant [sic] husband," demanding respectability.

Indeed, in this passage as well as throughout *Can You Forgive Her?*, Trollope defines a new ideal for women in describing Glencora, who "was not softly delicate in all her ways; but in disposition and temper she was altogether generous. I do not know that she was at all points a lady, but had Fate so willed it, she would have been a thorough gentleman'' (chapter 49). Trollope is judging Glencora by traditional male standards, by her wit, integrity and courage, rather than by her delicacy or moral purity, the essential qualities of the Victorian lady. Trollope's novels are greatly concerned with defining the idea of the gentleman, which embodies an intricate, distinctive morality; he is unconventional in creating a woman who could have been a ''thorough gentleman,'' and who therefore embodies that complex moral life. Moreover, this sympathetic approval is given to a woman who is potentially ''fallen,'' who not only contemplates but talks to her friend about becoming an adulteress, although she can only speak of that damned state of Victorian womanhood as being ''under the protection of another man, and she would become—what she did not dare to name even to herself'' (chapter 43).

However, Glencora's thoughts of adultery are neither convincingly condemned by the narrator, nor sentimentalized either through his comments or through Glencora's own passionate outbursts. The narrator's ambivalence is epitomized by this sentence: 'She might be very ignorant about the British Constitution, and, alas! very ignorant also as to the real elements of right and wrong in a woman's conduct, but she was no fool'' (chapter 43). The very structure of the sentence in which the narrator laments Glencora's dubious credentials as a moral teacher undermines his criticism: Mr. Palliser is implicitly chided in the opening phrase, ''She might be very ignorant about the British Constitution,'' which refers to the comic scene previously alluded to, in which he tries to educate her while she stifles a yawn, after which he attempts to tyrannize over her. In the closing phrase, ''she was no fool,'' the narrator commends Glencora's intellect. Moreover, the entire sentence is couched in a plethora of words praising Glencora's sensitivity to human character and criticizing her husband's ''obtusity'' in this respect.

However, the narrator's most heretical position, which implicitly questions the pure nature supposedly qualifying woman for her special mission as moral teacher, is expressed in his insistence on a woman's purity as contingent rather than inherent:[10]

> It has often been said of woman that she who doubts is lost,—so often that they who say it now, say it simply because others have said it before them, never thinking whether or no there be any truth in the proverb. But they who have said so, thinking of their words as they were uttered, have known but little of women. Women doubt every day, who solve their doubts at last on the right side, driven to do so, some by fear, more by conscience, but most of them by that half-prudential, half-unconscious knowledge of what is fitting, useful, and best under the circumstances, which rarely deserts either men or women till they have brought themselves to the Burgo Fitzgerald state of recklessness. Men when they have fallen even to that, will still keep up some outward show towards the world; but women in this condition defy the world, and declare themselves to be children of perdition. Lady Glencora was doubting sorely; but, though doubting, she was not as yet lost. (Chapter 49)

Moreover, Glencora's decision to remain with Palliser undermines conventional notions about woman's purity because it is presented as a complex moral dilemma, dramatized as a slow, accretive realization on her part about the possibilities of her own nature within an uncongenial reality. After her last passionate encounter with Burgo, Glencora says about the possibility of elopement with her former lover: "I am beginning to know myself by degrees. As for running away with him . . . Mr. Palliser is quite safe. He need not try to coax me to remain" (chapter 47).

Trollope's ambivalence toward the purity ideal is also manifested in Glencora's repeated bitter ruminations and exclamations to Alice about the damned state of the fallen woman, while at the same time exposing the hypocrisy of the elders who prostituted her in marriage:

> Of course it would have been my own destruction. I'm not such a fool as not to know that. Do you suppose I have never thought of it;—what it would be to be a man's mistress instead of his wife? If I had not I should feel myself to be loathsome, and as it were, a beast among women. But why did they not let me marry him, instead of driving me to this? And though I might have destroyed myself, I should have saved the man who is still my husband. (Chapter 62)

Glencora's lessons in self-denying feminine ideology greatly influenced her attraction to Burgo. She knows "Burgo to be a scapegrace, and she liked him the better on that account" (chapter 19), a statement that implies more than the old adage that every woman is a rake at heart. As Glencora says, with Burgo, "though I might have destroyed myself, I should have saved the man who is still my husband."

But it is not by self-sacrifice on Glencora's part only that the marriage will be saved, but by mutual sacrifice. In response to Glencora's relinquishment of Burgo, Palliser gives up his chance to be Chancellor of the Exchequer, the office he has tirelessly worked to attain. This process of accommodation rather than marital tyranny is rewarded with fertility, Glencora's longed-for pregnancy. Viewed symbolically, until the husband could become responsive to his wife's nature, until he realizes his love for her, their union could not be fertile. The crucial scene of realization for Palliser occurs only after Glencora admits her love for Burgo Fitzgerald and her desperate sense of worthlessness because she thinks she is barren, unable to bear Palliser the heir for which—along with her fortune—she knows he has married her. For the first time, Palliser shows that he values Glencora for herself, rather than as the future mother of his heir: "I would rather have you for my wife, childless,—if you will try to love me,—than any other woman, though another might give me an heir. Will you try to love me?"

Surely this is an explicit comment on the inadequacy of the feminine ideal of self-sacrifice, and the richer possibilities in mutual giving between marital partners. And yet, Trollope is too honest in his perceptions about the power and freedom allowed to men versus the limitations forced upon women in his culture to view even this magnanimity in more than personal terms; the freedom allotted to men is so much greater than that assigned to women that, while Trollope commends the husband as having "behaved very well," he qualifies this praise in the same breath by saying: "but then, he had his own way in everything. Lady Glencora did not behave very well,—contradicting her husband, and not considering, as, perhaps, she ought to have done, the sacrifice he was making on her behalf. But then, she had her own way in nothing" (chapter 68).

Trollope records all the moments on the European trip in which Glencora tries to have her way, a "way" opposed to conventional standards of propriety. What she wants, she tells Alice, is "something to live for,—some excitement" (chapter 68). She defines her predicament, the dilemma of an intelligent, passionate Victorian woman who wants to be her real self, not someone else's ideal:

> "Do you know, there are moments when I almost make up my mind to go headlong to the devil,—when I think it is the best thing to be done. It's a hard thing for a woman to do, because she has to undergo so much obloquy before she gets used to it. A man can take to drinking, and gambling and all the rest of it, and nobody despises him a bit. . . . Now I have plenty of money,—or at any rate, I had,—and I never got my fling yet. I do feel so tempted to rebel, and go ahead, and care for nothing." (Chapter 68)

But Glencora can only gesture at insurrection: waltzing madly with Burgo at Lady Monk's ball, constantly baiting her husband, gambling one gold coin in the casino at Baden, wishing to be swept down the Rhine like the swimmers she sees from the hotel balcony in Basle.

In terms of narrative convention, Glencora's pregnancy is a resolution, ending her rebellion and riveting her identity in the role of mother. As the narrator comments about both Alice's and Glencora's ambitions: "One was to become a wife and the other a mother, and that was to be their fate after each had made up her mind that no such lot was to be hers" (chapter 77).

One of the criticisms levelled at Trollope in George Levine's controversial article on *Can You Forgive Her?*, in which he argues that Trollope "unquestionably accepted the conventions he inherited" (5), is that the conclusion to the Palliser story is utterly conventional, because the plot is "comfortably encased within a narrative which provides just that satisfactory conclusion that Trollope imagined his audience required" (26-27). However, Levine is missing the ambivalent undercurrents beneath the surface harmony, the tensions against the overt sense of complete fruition and reconciliation in the Palliser marriage.

Certainly, at first glance, Glencora does seem wholly fulfilled. And nowhere does this satisfaction seem to be more pronounced than in the final chapter of the book, in which she and Alice admire the new baby while talking about Glencora's experience of motherhood. Indeed, Trollope chose this scene for one of M. E. Taylor's illustrations; the drawing depicts both women seated, Glencora cradling the baby in her arms while Alice looks on admiringly from over Glencora's shoulder.[11] The drawing is captioned with Glencora's words to her son: "Yes, my bonny boy,—you have made it all right for me." However, the scene which Taylor crystallizes into a tableau representing conventional feminine aspirations is, in truth, a vindication of Glencora's struggle for identity. The very line Trollope chooses as his caption is spoken by Glencora in telling Alice about the ordeal of aristocratic motherhood in a patriarchal society, in which male children are the inheritors of titles and property:

> "Oh, Alice,—if you could have known? Your baby may come just as it pleases. You won't lie awake trembling how on earth you will bear your disgrace if one of the vile weaker sex should come to disturb the hopes of your lords and masters;—for I had two, which made it so much more terrible"....
> "It's all right now, dear."
> "Yes, my bonny boy,—you have made it all right for me."

Her comments about the importance of producing a male child give resonance to her own struggles with the imbalance of sexual power in Victorian society. Ironically, Glencora can wield influence only by giving birth to an heir, and thereby strengthening the patriarchal society which oppresses her. As she tells Alice: "I shall dare to assert myself, now." Moreover, in the midst of her happiness, Glencora twice recalls the self-hatred that she has felt since making this marriage, and in this way Trollope maintains a tension against the comic resolution of Glencora's story. Immediately after telling her husband about her pregnancy, she says to Alice: "I won't deny that I am very happy. It seemed as though I were destined to bring nothing but misery to everybody, and I used to wish myself dead so often. I shan't wish myself dead now" (chapter 72).

The second time Glencora harks back to her past despair is during her walk in the Priory ruins on the eve of Alice's marriage (chapter 79), an occasion imbued with symbolic meaning. The manner in which the scene is introduced recalls the past conflict between the Pallisers (in which Alice had such a prominent role as scapegoat), when Glencora insisted upon walking in the Priory ruins in the moonlight because it was an appropriately romantic scene in which to think and talk of Burgo (chapter 27). Palliser "sternly" discouraged that former walk, and punished Glencora through Alice, as we have seen. The narrator remarks upon this second walk in the ruins: "Whether Lady Glencora would have been allowed to walk through the ruins so late as half-past eight in the evening if her husband had been there may be doubtful, but her husband was away and she took this advantage of his absence." Although Glencora's inclination to evade her husband's authority is still much in evidence, this walk in the ruins is not an act of rebellion, but of remembrance.

Juliet McMaster has written insightfully of the tendency of Trollope's characters to return to a significant place in order to gain a sense of closure to an important phase of experience. She states that "there is a kind of ritual which the characters themselves are sometimes aware of in this retracing of steps. They go

"Yes, my bonny boy,—you have made it all right for me."
(Illustration by E. Taylor)

back in time as well as in space, they face their past selves, they exorcise a ghost, they sometimes succeed in making a new start" (*Palliser Novels,* 192). Although McMaster does not discuss this particular scene, her comments shed light on both Glencora's desire to walk again among the ruins with Alice, and Trollope's purpose in having her do so.

While they stroll among the ruins, Glencora again confides to Alice: "I used to lie in bed and wish myself dead, and make up my mind to drown myself—if I could only dare" (chapter 79). The language Glencora uses echoes almost exactly the very words she uses to Palliser in the scene in which, after Lady Monk's ball, Glencora tells her husband of Burgo's plan to elope with her, and of her desperate unhappiness because she not only loves Burgo and not Palliser, but she also cannot produce an heir for her husband: "What matters it whether I drown myself, or throw myself away by going with such a one as him, so that you might marry again, and have a child? I'd die;—I'd die willingly. How I wish I could die! Plantagenet, I would kill myself if I dared" (chapter 58). Glencora's recurrent thoughts of drowning herself evoke her opposite wish, expressed to Alice on the balcony at Basle, that she, like the male swimmers below, could be joyfully swept down the river. Trollope's imagery suggests that in this society, women are encouraged to long for self-obliteration, while men are allowed an exhilarating freedom.

When Glencora says to Alice, "I used to lie in bed," her phrase explicitly locates the source of her self-hatred. For her, the marriage bed has engendered only guilt: guilt because of her sexual frustration, her desire for a man who is not her husband, and her inability to produce a child. Judging herself by the ideal of the angelic, sexless Victorian wife-mother, Glencora has perceived herself as worthless. Now she does, at last, manifest one aspect of the ideal by bearing a child, but the history of her oppression is immanent in what seems at first to be a conventionally simple resolution to her story, and the critique of feminine ideals, indicating Trollope's ambivalence about them, is inherent in the novel's conclusion.

This tension between the struggle for self-realization and societal expectations of women closely links the story of Alice Vavasor to that of Glencora. The central ambivalence in Alice's story is between the sympathetic rendering of an intelligent, upper-class Victorian woman's search for fulfillment and the overt approval that seems to be given to a conventional resolution in which she capitulates to the "mastering" of the proper suitor. Trollope uses the convention of the "two suitors" in an even more conscious and explicit way than he does in Glencora's story, introducing Alice's lovers as "John Grey, the Worthy Man" and "George Vavasor, the Wild Man." Indeed, since the Alice plot is the first to be presented, it is here that Trollope sets up the convention that the other two plots will imitate. It is, then, worthwhile to look again at Jean Kennard's book, *Victims of Convention,* in connection with Alice's story. Kennard discusses the conflict between this literary convention and the "more modern concept of female maturity that develops during the 19th century" (11). The traditional expectation is that Alice will choose the "worthy man." As Kennard states: "For her, maturity lies in learning that her ideals are fantasies, that happiness lies in approximately the male reality and in denying much of what had seemed to be herself" (14). This accurately describes the overt intention of Trollope's novel and the import of its resolution; Alice explores and rejects the false romance of George Vavasor, and finds happiness in the "mastering" of the gentlemanly John Grey. However, that conventional structure is undermined in several ways which suggest its inadequacy to the problems raised in *Can You Forgive Her?*. In her brief discussion of Trollope's Barsetshire novel, *Doctor Thorne* (the only Trollope novel she examines), Kennard states that Trollope characteristically "avoids" structural problems by "clinging to an older notion of women," but in truth, it is his realistic depiction of Victorian women trapped within societal conventions that causes the ending of this novel to jar with the preceding narrative. Moreover, as I noted earlier in this essay, Alice's shuttling back and forth between her two suitors breaks the usual pattern in which the woman is courted by both suitors, eventually choosing the "worthy" man.

Indeed, at the outset of her story, Alice is already engaged to the "worthy" man, John Grey, a fact announced dramatically by the narrator in a two-sentence paragraph at the close of chapter one: "And now for my fact. At the time of which I am writing she was already engaged to be married." (This statement seems reductive somehow, and sets up a tension even in the first chapter between the importance of Alice's personal history, and the conventional narrative assumption that what is really significant is the courtship plot, as if all other "facts," all knowledge about Alice, pales in comparison to the fact of her engagement.) We later learn of her previous engagement to the "wild man," George Vavasor, to whom she reengages herself after breaking with Mr. Grey. She breaks her engagement with Vavasor again, and becomes betrothed a second time to Grey, whom she marries in the penultimate chapter of the book. All this switching about, this dramatic altering of literary convention, indicates its inability to contain the realities about sexual relations that Trollope perceived. The disrupted courtship pattern images a disturbance in the sexual relations of Victorian life.

Another way in which Alice Vavasor's story reflects its author's ambivalences about current feminine ideals of his culture, aside from the altered literary convention, is in the ambivalence evident in the presentation of Alice's character. Juliet McMaster has discussed Alice's morbid, masochistic psychology, apparently created by the loss of her mother at Alice's birth, her neglectful father, and the Sabbatarian aunt, Lady Macleod, who raises her, all circumstances that would be likely to engender guilt (*Palliser Novels*, 20–23). The first of these influences, the fact that Alice (like Glencora, and Alice's cousin Kate) is motherless, helps us to understand Alice's complex character, and her often seemingly perverse reactions to both her suitors. Since Alice's mother dies at her birth, the central feminine source of identity is absent from her life. The primary inheritance the daughter very likely would have is guilt, which would probably be deepened by the evangelical influence of her surrogate mother, Lady Macleod.

However, if we examine Alice's mother's history, which Trollope relates in the very first paragraph of *Can You Forgive Her?*, we discover another probable influence on her identity in her maternal heritage. Alice's mother, Alice Macleod, "gave great offence to all her friends by her marriage," was ostracized by her family, and died in childbirth a year after the wedding. Alice is named after and thus identified with her mother, who is both rebel and victim: she defies familial authority in choosing her mate for herself, and dies a uniquely female death. (In light of her mother's history, we comprehend more fully why the term "respectable," spoken approvingly by one of those very relatives about Alice's marriage to John Grey, "galls" Alice [chapter 2]). Moreover, Alice inherits not only her mother's name and a legacy of resistance to patriarchal power, but also her mother's money, which enables her to be independent of her family's dictates once she comes of age. She escapes from the constricted custody of Lady Macleod, shares household expenses on an equal basis with her father, while acknowledging no paternal supervision, and she rejects out-of-hand the meddling in her affairs of her august relative, Lady Midlothian: "'I will endure no interference,' said Alice, 'either from persons who are friends or who are not friends'" (chapter 26).

A central ambivalence in the novel emerges when one compares the narrator's explanations of Alice's problems, such as, "all her troubles and sorrows in life had come from an overfed craving for independence," and the fact that, in the context of the pain and ruin women undergo in the novel because of their dependence on the power of men, Alice's defensive need to be independent begins to take on an increasingly rational cast as a stance for a Victorian woman. Trollope seems both to depict her rebellion sympathetically, as an understandable effort to create an identity, and to treat her struggle for independence as a delusion which must be cured by marriage to the right suitor. A key to this contradiction lies in the presentation of "the worthy man," John Grey.

Critics have disagreed sharply about John Grey. James Kincaid is among those who view him negatively, labelling him as a man of "bland public perfection," a man of "pure surface and public language" (179, 184). Richard Barickman, Susan MacDonald, and Myra Stark also dislike Grey, stating that his "love" and "suburban placidity" mask "condescending mastery" and a refusal to give credence to Alice's feelings (51, 214). On the other hand, Juliet McMaster calls him "the appropriate hero of the novel, in refusing to let words betray him into a contradiction of essence," the confusion both Alice and Glencora manifest (*Palliser Novels,* 35). Shirley Letwin, who is concerned with defining the idea of the gentleman in Trollope, agrees with McMaster's assessment of Grey, viewing him as a perfect gentleman, a kind of Trollopian hero. In rejecting him, Alice "was in fact converting an entirely congenial reality into an illusion worthy of romantic agony" (143). George Levine agrees that Grey is a "perfect gentleman," but argues that "from the woman's point of view, to be a gentleman is to be at best a benevolent tyrant" (14). Bill Overton, arguing against Levine's assessment of Trollope's art as enforcing a "worldly wisdom of acquiescence in social convention," points out Grey's ability to change and to compromise, ultimately to come round to Alice's way of thinking and make the decision to enter politics, after opposing this career for the entire novel (100–101).

What, then, is the "truth" about the presentation of John Grey's character? Or is his character presented so ambiguously that one can make an argument for all these interpretations? More to the point of our discussion: what is it Alice is rebelling against, and is whatever she is trying to escape embodied somehow in John Grey, or is it—as the narrator insists—a creation of her own imagination?

Part of the answer to these questions lies in an attention to the narrator's repeated insistence on Alice's inability to perceive the depths of the spirit underlying the equanimity of Grey's manner. Again and again, Alice rebels against an apparent self-assurance which is, as Letwin astutely analyzes it, the integrity of Trollope's perfect gentleman:

> She did not doubt his love, but she believed him to be so much the master of his love,—as he was the master of everything else, that her separation from him would cause him no uncontrollable grief. In that she utterly failed to understand his character. Had she known him better, she might have been sure that such a separation now would with him have carried its mark to the grave. Should he submit to her decision, he would go home and settle himself to his books the next day; but on no following day would he be again capable of walking forth among his flowers with an easy heart. He was a strong, constant man, perhaps overconscious of his own strength; but then his strength was great. (Chapter 11)

Several critics have misinterpreted Grey's character because they have overlooked this discrepancy between the depths of Grey's feeling and his placid manner. To reiterate the point that Alice "utterly failed to understand his character" in this respect, she favorably compares the "passion" of her other suitor, the counterfeit romantic George, to Grey's air of calm:

> She looked up into his face, but it was still serene in all its manly beauty. Her cousin George, if he were moved to strong feeling, showed it at once in his eyes,—in his mouth, in the whole visage of his countenance. He glared in his anger, and was impassioned in his love. But Mr. Grey when speaking of the happiness of his entire life, when confessing that it was now at stake with a decision against him that would be ruinous to it, spoke without a quiver in his voice, and had no more sign of passion in his face than if he were telling his gardener to move a rose tree. (Chapter 15)

The irony of this passage is heightened when the "impassioned" George flips a coin to decide whether he will propose to Alice. To give this comparison between the two men further point, there is an implicit reference to the difference between Alice's love for Grey, and Glencora's for Burgo, upon which the narrator comments: "With all the fuss that Lady Glencora made to herself,—with all the tears that she had shed about her lost lover, and was so often shedding,—with all her continual thinking of the matter, she had never loved Burgo Fitzgerald as Alice Vavasor had loved Mr. Grey" (chapter 19).

Glencora is, of course, very different from the villainous George, but she is like him in her romantic display of feeling, her extravagant expression, as Alice's sense of decorum, restraining the expression of deep feeling, is akin to Grey's. (After her break with Grey, when Alice receives George's letter proposing marriage, although Alice is with Kate, the narrator comments that she does not show "that anything had occurred to disturb her tranquility. . . . Alice said no word of her own letter" [chapter 31].) The narrator, contrary to Alice, stresses Grey's ability to mask his feelings from others, and he sees this, at least at first, as a part of his strength of character. The effect of this passage is heightened by Alice's reflection before she writes her letter telling Grey of her engagement to Vavasor that "he also is not passionate" (chapter 32): "I have said that he read Alice's letter with an agony of sorrow; as he sat with it in his hand he suffered as, probably, he had never suffered before. But there was nothing in his countenance to show that he was in pain" (chapter 36).

Grey is indeed at his country estate, but this is definitely not the "suburban placidity" of Barickman, et al., nor Kincaid's man of "pure surface." However, in a much later passage, the narrator, again noting that Grey's manner belies his true feelings, indicates that great strength can harden into intransigence. This comment occurs right after Palliser has unsuccessfully tried to convince Mr. Grey to give up his retired way of life and to run for Parliament: "But though he spoke with an assured tone, he was shaken, and almost regretted that he did not accept the aid which was offered to him. It is astonishing how strong a man may be to those around him,—how impregnable may be his exterior, while within he feels himself to be as weak as water, and as unstable as chaff" (chapter 74).

Finally, a later passage illuminates Grey's own, perhaps subconsious, knowledge that his unbending attitudes have contributed to Alice's actions, rationalizing their apparent contrariness:

> He was not a man prone to be talked out of his own way of life. . . . Alice had also wanted him to go into public life, but he had put aside her request as though the thing were quite out of the question,—never giving a moment to its consideration. Had she asked him to settle himself and her in Central Africa, his manner and mode of refusal would have been the same. It was this immobility on his part,—this absolute want of any of the weakness of indecision, which had frightened her, and driven her away from him. He was partly aware of this; but that which he had declined to do at her solicitation, he certainly would not do at the advice of anyone else. So it was that he argued the matter with himself. Had he now allowed himself to be so counselled, with what terrible acknowledgements of his own faults must he not have presented himself before Alice? (Chapter 74)

What terrible acknowledgments indeed! Perhaps he *has,* as Alice has accused him, treated her efforts to make him understand her needs as the ideas of an imbalanced mind. As Alice answers when Grey recommends a "change of air" for her "malady": "Yes; you treat me as though I were partly silly, and partly insane; but it is not so. The change you speak of should be in my nature, and in yours." Perhaps he *has* considered any resolve of Alice's to be "the petulance of a child" (chapter 11). Perhaps he *has* been at least partly responsible for making Alice a jilt.

Implicit in this "perfect gentleman's" treatment of Alice, which at first seems so appropriate, is a critique of the assumptions engendered by cultural ideas about Victorian womanhood. Grey's prescription for Alice's ailments is informed by a belief in the delicate nature of a woman's constitution. His expectation that Alice will sometimes act in a childlike manner is colored by the ideal of "woman as capricious child." Finally, his reliance on her passivity, on her willingness to bend to his will—however benign—is based in part on the ideal of "woman as obedient child."

Thus, while it is clear that Alice mistakes Grey's manner to be the entire man, it is this very habit of strength which has become a kind of immobility, a mastery against which she struggles. Alice's mind has been, as Grey tells her, "twisted by false impressions" (chapter 15), and she does to a degree misjudge both her suitors, as the narrator continually points out; these things make Alice's vacillations seem to be a problem of perception, and they cause her rebellion to appear to be a delusion, as McMaster and Letwin have argued. But Alice is rebelling against something real.

John Grey *is* Trollope's perfect gentleman, as Letwin has said, and yet, in his character inheres a critique of the feminine ideals even the most admirable Victorian men relied upon. The reality he offers Alice is not, as Letwin states, an "entirely congenial" one, because it is his reality, not hers. The narrator insists upon the "perfect equality" (chapter 10) of Grey's love for Alice, but in fact, his gentlemanliness conceals a rigidity that precludes true equality:

> She could not bring herself to hint to him that his views of life were so unlike her own, that there could be no chance of happiness between them, unless each could strive to lean somewhat towards the other. No man could be more gracious in word and manner than John Grey; no man more chivalrous in his carriage towards a woman; but he always spoke and acted as though there could be no question that his manner of life was to be adopted, without a word or thought of doubting, by his wife. When two came together, why should not each yield something, and each claim something? (Chapter 3)

Indeed, Grey's first letter to Alice is almost a paradigm for a Victorian gentleman's hopes to have Ruskin's "queen" for his "garden": "God bless the mistress is what I now say, and send her home, to her own home, to her flowers, and her fruit, and her house, and her husband, as soon as may be, with no more of those delays which are to me so grievous, and which seem to me to be so unnecessary. That is my prayer" (chapter 3).

It is a poignant letter, graceful and gentlemanlike, not only in its frank and poetic expression of love and longing for Alice, but also in its trusting acceptance (expressed previously in the letter) of Alice's proposed companion for her Swiss tour, her former fiance, George Vavasor. But Alice's seemingly perverse response is an urge to separate herself from Grey, a guilty rebellion. As her justification for these inappropriate feelings, she concentrates on her moral inadequacy, on her unangelic nature, knowing that "she, full of faults as she knew herself to be,—how could she hope to make happy a man perfect as he was!" (chapter 3). Later Alice again echoes these words when she wishes, "Oh, that he were less perfect" (chapter 11). Significantly, when George first sees Alice after her engagement to Grey, he intuitively senses that to tell Alice that she is "not the angel I had supposed" but "the same woman I had once loved" will tap all the doubts Alice has about her own self-worth: "Was she not telling herself daily,—hourly,—always,—in every thought of her life, that in accepting Mr. Grey she had assumed herself to be mistress of virtues which she did not possess? Had she not, in truth, rioted upon brandy, till the innocence of milk was unfitted for her?" (chapter 5).

However, her own inability to live up to the angelic ideal, to be Grey's "gleam of something better that is to come hereafter" (chapter 11), is only part of the reason that she revolts against his request. In truth, she senses dominion in his perfection. Alice fears being relegated to Ruskinian female domestic sphere, as she surely would be at Nethercoats. She wants instead to be a part of the male sphere of business, the world of politics: "'Why should he be unhappy in London?' she said, as she went back to the letter. 'Why should he pretend to condemn the very place which most men find the fittest for all their energies? Were I a man, no earthly consideration should induce me to live elsewhere'" (chapter 3).

Although Letwin argues that Alice doesn't really even like London, and that her vehement preference is a myth, the issue is actually that she wants a say in the decisions that will affect her entire future as Grey's wife. It is poignant at this point to recall Alice's mature definition of hoped-for mutuality in her love for Grey, in which "love meant a partnership, in which each partner would be honest to the other, in which each would wish and strive for the other's welfare, so that thus their joint welfare might be insured" (chapter 1). However, Grey assumes hegemony over decision-making:

> On this very point she had left him. He had never argued the matter with her. He had never asked her to argue with him. He had not condescended so far as that. Had he done so, she thought that she would have brought herself to think as he thought. She would have striven at any rate, to do so. But she could not become unambitious, tranquil, fond of retirement, and philosophic, without an argument on the matter,—without being allowed even the poor grace of owning herself to be convinced. If a man takes a dog with him from the country up to town, the dog must live a town life without knowing the reason why;—must live a town life or die a town death. But a woman should not be treated like a dog. "Had he deigned to discuss it with me!" Alice had so often said. "But no; he will read his books, and I am to go there to fetch him his slippers, and make his tea for him.". . . But all her misery had been brought about by this scornful superiority to the ordinary pursuits of the world,—this looking down upon humanity. (Chapter 63)

However, in the resolution of Alice's story, in which she succumbs at last to Grey, she relinquishes her authority to pronounce upon his actions; judging herself by the canons of female purity, she calls herself "a fallen creature" who has "no longer a right to such thoughts" (chapter 74). This scene of self-excoriation, in which she not only submits to but exults over Grey's "mastery,"[12] undermines the legitimacy of her cause for rebelling. The tone is almost cloying after reading Alice's angry words in the passage just quoted:

> And there must now, she acknowledged, be an end to her pride,—to that pride which had hitherto taught her to think that she could more wisely follow her own guidance than that of any other who might claim to guide her. She knew now that she must follow his guidance. She had found her master, as we sometimes say, and laughed to herself with a little inward laughter as she confessed that it was so. (Chapter 74)[13]

As Overton has noted, there is a counterbalance to the conventionality of this ending in Grey's decision to go into Parliament (101), but it is significant that he "is shaken in his quiescent philosophy" (chapter 77) by a man, Palliser; moreover, although he asks Alice's de facto opinion about the decision, when she enthusiastically concurs, the narrator's comment is that "he was not so perverse as to be driven from his new views by the fact that Alice approved them" (chapter 77).

And yet, there are also contradictions within this apparently conventional ending. The very setting Trollope chooses for his proposal scene—a churchyard—suggests that an intrinsic part of this union must be death—not literal, but figurative death:

> The church is immediately over the lake, and round the church there is a burying-ground, and skirting the burying-ground there are cloisters, through the arches and apertures of which they who walk and sit there look down immediately upon the blue water, and across the water upon the frowning menaces of Mount Pilate. It is one of the prettiest spots in that land of beauty; and its charm is to my feeling enhanced by the sepulchral monuments over which I walk, and by which I am surrounded, as I stand there. Up here, into these cloisters, Alice and John Grey went together. I doubt whether he had formed any purpose of doing so. She certainly would have gone without question in any direction that he might have led her. (Chapter 74)

This description illustrates what John Kleis calls "Trollope's skill in using setting for psychological investigation" (1409). It seems that there is more going on here than the ancient linking of sex with death. It is difficult not to sense that Alice's capitulation to Grey is portrayed as a kind of death of her independent self, and both martyrdom and the abdication of responsibility are suggested by the looming Mount Pilate. Indeed, Alice's initial response to Grey's "demand" that she marry him, when she sits "silent beneath his gaze, with her eyes turned upon the tombstones beneath her feet," seems to support this view. Moreover, when Grey embraces Alice as she still remains silent, "she shrank from him, back against the stonework of the embrasure." Even as she admits that "You win everything—always," Alice "still shrank from his embrace." The intimations of death in the imagery of the setting are augmented by Alice's resistance; she seems instinctively to realize that once she is physically possessed by Grey, something of her identity will die. This suggestion is intensified by Trollope's description of Grey's

"How am I to thank you for forgiving me?"
(Illustration by E. Taylor)

response: "'In winning you I have won everything.' Then he put his face over her and pressed his lips to hers." The phrase "put his face over her" perhaps suggests more than a posture for kissing; Trollope's words convey a sense of the obliteration of identity, a figurative effacement.

Against the vision of Alice and John Grey in the churchyard must be set Taylor's illustration depicting Alice's wedding, captioned "Alice and her Bridesmaids." It is difficult not to view this highly conventional illustration as straining against the text rather than harmoniously imaging it. After her tortured courtship and painful acceptance of Grey, this vision of Alice in her conventional moment of womanly glory appears incommensurate to her troubled experience, in the same way that the picture of Glencora fulfilled in motherhood (with Alice leaning over her shoulder looking at the baby, who symbolizes her own possible future cares now that she is to be married) suggests that all of Glencora's misery was easily cured by giving birth to a male child. Alice's wedding tableau, portraying her in her new identity, sweet-faced and expectant in her last moments of virginal girlhood, cannot but seem ironic rather than celebratory when viewed in the light of Alice's pain.

The narrator's concluding question after Alice had accepted Grey in the churchyard—"I wonder whether he was made happier when he knew that no other touch had profaned those lips since last he had pressed them?"—tries to resolve the issue of Alice's purity, but this query seems wholly out of alignment with the rest of this profoundly disturbing scene. His implication that the real issue is Grey's state of mind rather than Alice's tormented resistance blithely ignores the psychological dynamics of the scene he has just described. The narrator's question suggests that because Alice's sacred purity has not in truth been "profaned," everything is really just fine—while at the same time he reiterates the word "pressed" to describe Grey's proprietary kiss, a word which connotes imprinting and uncomfortably reinforces the image of Grey re-making Alice's identity. Finally, the word "profaned" also tends to remind us of the sacred, its opposite, and to point up the implicit image of John Grey as God: "He, possessed of power and force infinitely greater than hers, had left her no alternative but to be happy . . . She knew now that she must yield to him,—that his power over her was omnipotent. She was pressed by him as in some countries the prisoner is pressed by the judge,—so pressed that she acknowledged to herself silently that any further antagonism to him was impossible."

Trollope may intend that the narrator's conventional commentary should seem almost absurdly less subtle than the experiences he relates. As Frank O'Connor astutely commented, "His favorite device is to lead his reader very gently up the garden path of his own conventions and prejudices and then to point out that the reader is wrong. This is not very like the behavior of a typical mid-Victorian gentleman" (168). In other words, the conflict between Trollope's story itself and the narrator's apparent view of that story may be a deliberate strategy Trollope uses to force his readers to confront their own prejudices.

*Alice and her bridesmaids
(Illustration by E. Taylor)*

The disparity between the narrator's commentary and the events of the narrative itself is evident not only in the proposal scene, but also in the rest of Alice's story. This tension accents the incompatibility of the logic of the narrative and that of the novel's resolution. In answer to the question, "What should a woman do with her life," the narrator offers the conventional advice: "Fall in love, marry the man, have two children, and live happily ever afterwards" (chapter 11). Obviously, this traditional dictum is in tension with the actual presentation of Alice's rebellion against Grey, in which her questioning of this conventional fate seems valid.[14] In addition, the narrator's focus on the purported central theme of the noble jilt—his effort to justify Alice's ostensible breach of feminine purity because her actions were motivated by conscience—is undermined by Alice's authentic desire to have an identity of her own, the true motivating force behind her jilting of Grey. Indeed, the narrator switches wildly back and forth between condemnation of Alice's desire for independence and apologia for her actions. Alice has been "mad with a vile ambition" that leads her to betray the ideal of feminine purity, to lose "that wondrous aroma of precious delicacy, which is the greatest treasure of womanhood"; however, although she has "sinned against her sex" (chapter 37), her sin is mitigated by the nobility of her self-sacrificing intentions:

> But there was in it [Alice's love] an amount of self-devotion which none of those near to her had hitherto understood,—unless it were that one to whom the understanding of it was of the most importance. In all the troubles of her love, of her engagements, and her broken promises, she had thought more of others than of herself,—and indeed, those troubles had chiefly come from that self-devotion. She had left John Grey because she feared that she would do him no good as his wife—that she would not make him happy; and she had afterwards betrothed herself for a second time to her cousin, because she believed that she could serve him by marrying him. (Chapter 69)

The close examination we have made of Alice's thoughts about her engagement to Grey belies the narrator's rationale for her jilting, his insistence that her behavior was entirely motivated by the pure feminine ideal of self-sacrifice, and that she is thus worthy of forgiveness. (A woman's longing for freedom is, by implication, an impure motive, a "vile ambition.") There is more truth to the assertion that in each of her engagements to George, Alice is inspired by self-denial. When Alice thinks of her first passion for George, she defines it in terms of the exaltation of self-sacrifice, when love was "a total abnegation of self" (chapter 1). In her second engagement to her cousin, she is actuated by a more prosaic sense of duty, coupled with the low self-esteem which is the corollary emotion to this kind of self-sacrifice, of the same nature as Glencora's when she bows under to her family's will that she marry Palliser. She thinks of this engagement as the key to reconciling George and her grandfather, as a means of helping George in his political career, and as a way to make George a glory of the House of Vavasor:

"If I can do him good why should I not marry him?" In that had been the chief argument which had induced her to return such an answer as she had sent to her cousin, "For myself, what does it matter? As to this life of mine and all that belongs to it, why should I regard it otherwise than to make it of some service to some one who is dear to me?" (Chapter 34)

Alice's embracing of self-sacrifice pales, however, before that of George's sister, Kate, in whom the devotion to her brother's life is coupled with a self-hatred that is, as Kincaid declares, fueled by her guilty love for her brother, for which she seeks "to satisfy her guilt by becoming nothing" (186).[15] Her wish for self-destruction recalls Glencora's thoughts of suicide:

"I've been often curious to consider what sort of husband would suit you, but I've had few thoughts about a husband for myself. The truth is, I'm married to George. . . . If George ever married, I should have nothing to do in the world;—literally nothing—nothing—nothing! . . . But I'd give up all, everything, every hope I have, to see you become George's wife. I know myself not to be good. I know myself to be very bad, and yet I care nothing for myself." (Chapter 6)

Indeed, the vision of Kate that we carry with us at the end of the novel is not so much that of the self-reliant spinster depicted at the close of *Can You Forgive Her?,* freed by George's disappearance and her grandfather's legacy, but that of the distraught woman on the fells who has just had her arm broken by the brother she adores, when she at last defies him (chapter 56). Taylor draws one of her finest illustrations for this scene; every detail, from Kate's disheveled hair and lined eyes to the thorny branches about her on the barren, wintry fells contributes to the atmosphere of despair. The scene resonates with the memory of two previous walks taken by Alice and Kate to that very spot on the moors, Swindale Fell: the first when Alice told Kate that she had broken her initial engagement to George (recalled in chapter 31), and the second, three years later, when Alice tells Kate that she has re-engaged herself to him (chapter 31). During the second walk, Kate recalls how she "screamed in my sorrow," when Alice told her of her decision to sever herself from George, while her joy at Alice's new engagement to George impels her to exclaim, "'I will so love this place. I hated it before.' And then she put her face down upon the boulder-stone and kissed it." As she sits a third time upon Swindale Fell—this time alone, abandoned by the violent, abusive George—Kate's defeated posture serves as a kind of frieze depicting the position of exploited Victorian womankind, literally battered and thrown to the ground as recompense for all her self-sacrifice.

Finally, Alice and Kate are associated with Jane, George's mistress for three years, for whom he seems to have broken faith with Alice during their first engagement. Jane is sympathetically portrayed as a victim, and the only chapter in which she appears, starving, is heart-wrenching. As a "fallen" woman, she is of course outside the pale of Victorian society; in contrast, George Vavasor has recently been an M.P. and is heir to a squire. George exploits her as he has all the women in his life, and the ideal of feminine self-sacrifice that has served as a tool of oppression

Kate
(Illustration by E. Taylor)

in all his relationships with women operates even now, in Jane's extremity. She offers to "slave" for him, and when he rejects her and threatens suicide, she denies her urgent hunger in deference to his melodramatic gesture, leaving quietly (chapter 76). As she creeps away to further degradation, the narrator's complacent advice to "fall in love, marry the man, have two children, and live happily ever after" resounds in the reader's memory.

2

The "Phineas" Saga: The Terms of Equality

In the "Phineas" novels, which follow *Can You Forgive Her?* in the Palliser series, Glencora's story recedes into the background. She is still a strong presence when she appears, in both *Phineas Finn* and *Phineas Redux,* but the women who are central in these novels are the hero's loves: Lady Laura Standish, Violet Effingham and Madame Max Goesler. The stories of these women are not only important in their own right, but they also set the stage for our understanding of Glencora's development later in the series when she again becomes the central female character in the Palliser saga. In *The Prime Minister,* we read the story of her efforts to enter the political sphere with the memory of Laura, Violet and Madame Max fresh in our minds. In Trollope's sympathetic depiction of these strong, articulate women as they decide for or against Phineas, Trollope discloses his uneasiness with the feminine ideals against which women are conventionally measured.

Trollope demonstrates this uneasiness by juxtaposing the fate of Lady Laura with that of Violet and Madame Max. Phineas's first English love, Lady Laura, comes to grief in her attempt to influence the male sphere of politics through a loveless marriage to a rich man, while the other two women marry the men they love, but insist upon equality in their marriages. Lady Laura's story is the tragedy of a highly gifted woman whose husband seeks to quell her powerful nature because it does not coincide with his conventional image of a sober Christian wife. In contrast, the marriage of Violet and Chiltern and that of Madame Max and Phineas are two of the most successful marriages in the entire Palliser chronicle, rivalled only by the happy promise of Isabel's marriage to Silverbridge in *The Duke's Children.* In each of these marriages, a strong, witty, passionate woman is mated with a man who appreciates these unconventional qualities, and who is himself a sensitive and sexual man. The fulfillment that these women find in contrast to Lady Laura's frustration suggests that Trollope's solution to the problems raised by the "Woman Question" is marital equality.

Trollope clearly did not arrive at that solution without some hesitation. A comparison of the resolution of *Phineas Finn* with *Phineas Redux* suggests the possibility that between 1867, when Trollope finished *Phineas Finn,* and 1871, when he completed *Phineas Redux,* his disquiet with the ideals for Victorian womanhood had become more pronounced. In *Phineas Finn,* one way that Trollope manifests his ambivalence toward these feminine ideals is in the conflict between his admiration for the forceful, independent women in the novel—Lady Laura, Violet, Madame Max, Glencora—and his ultimate allegiance to the little Irish girl, Mary Flood Jones, who is preeminently characterized by her "sweet, clinging feminine softness" (*PF,* chapter 68).[1] Trollope plays out this conflict in the character of his hero, Phineas, who is caught between the attractions of these sophisticated women and Mary's simple adoration, which he chooses at the end of *Phineas Finn.* In contrast, at the conclusion of *Phineas Redux,* Phineas at last marries the most independent woman of all, Madame Max Goesler. Trollope says in *An Autobiography* that *Phineas Finn* and *Phineas Redux* "are, in fact, but one novel, though they were brought out at a considerable interval of time and in different form" (265). The difference between the endings of the two works, however, suggests that perhaps in the "considerable interval of time" between the publication of *Phineas Finn* and its sequel, Trollope's reservations about Victorian ideals for woman had deepened.

Another indication of Trollope's disquiet with his culture's feminine ideals lies in the rupture of the traditional courtship plot that is evident in the stories of Lady Laura, Violet, Madame Max, and —in *Phineas Redux*—of Adelaide Palliser. As in the stories of Glencora and Alice in *Can You Forgive Her?,* the broken structure of the courtship plot seems to reflect the imperfection of Victorian sexual relations. In this book, however, in the story of Madame Max, the unconventional courtship plot also suggests something more positive: a new view of woman as heroic suitor for the man she loves. In discussing the courtship plots of these women's stories, it is useful to refer again to what Jean Kennard, in her book, *Victims of Convention,* calls the "convention of the two suitors" (10–11). None of the love plots in either book follows the conventional pattern which Kennard describes, in which the heroine's maturity is marked by her rejection of the wrong suitor, who embodies her own bad qualities, and her marriage to the right suitor, whose good qualities she has learned to emulate.

Lady Laura is, indeed, confronted with two suitors: poor, young, handsome Phineas, who loves her, and rich, plain, middle-aged Mr. Kennedy, who does not love her, but who seems to like and respect her. In the conventional courtship plot, as Kennard tells us: "maturity is seen to consist of adjusting oneself to the real world, which is synonymous with becoming like the right suitor. The attainment of maturity wins the great reward, marriage to the right suitor, which provides a conclusion to the novel" (chapter 12).

Lady Laura's story is a tragic version of this prescription, a distorted mirror image of the happily-ever-after romantic comedy conventions. To begin with, neither suitor is cut to the pattern of the traditional worthy suitor who, like George Knightly in *Emma,* is a mentor to the woman he loves. With Phineas, the situation is explicitly stated to be the reverse. Laura muses out loud to Phineas: "I wonder whether you will be angry with me if I take upon myself the task of mentor" (chapter 8). Of course, she has already unofficially played this role, as he admits when he wonders, "And was it possible that a female Mentor should love her Telemachus,—should love him as Phineas desired to be loved by Lady Laura?" (chapter 14).[2] With Kennedy, the ideal of a male mentor is not reversed but rather grotesquely twisted. At first, Kennedy seems to be the pattern worthy man; as Lady Laura states: "I think, upon the whole, that is as good a man as I know" (chapter 14). It is only after the marriage that Kennedy is Laura's unwelcome mentor, as he tries to subdue her into being a dutiful Christian wife. Kennedy is the mentor as tyrant; Laura, far more intelligent than her rigid husband, ultimately decides to escape his bondage rather than submit to his rule.

Not only does Trollope make both of Laura's lovers fall short of the traditional worthy suitor ideal, but he further skews the "two suitors" convention by portraying neither of them as the conventional unscrupulous suitor. The insidious irony Trollope creates in Laura's story is that Kennedy is unworthy because he is narrow-mindedly scrupulous—hyperscrupulous—especially with regard to the duties of his wife. As Laura acridly describes him to Phineas shortly after her marriage, "He is a rigid martinet in all matters of duty" (chapter 17). As for Phineas, his rationalizations for loving the highly positioned Lady Laura might leave him open to the charge of opportunism,[3] but he is never an unscrupulous adventurer. He does love Laura and always acts honestly toward her, even when it causes him pain; he blurts out his love for her on the braes of Loughlinter even after she has told him of her engagement with Kennedy. Thus, in the original configuration of Laura's courtship plot, there is neither the conventional worthy suitor nor the conventional unworthy suitor. Lady Laura has greater stature than both her suitors.

The final irony in Laura's story is that Phineas becomes the worthy suitor as he matures throughout the course of the two novels. By the end of *Phineas Finn,* he learns the value of not having "sacrificed for money or social gains any of the instincts of his nature" (chapter 70), as Laura has. In *Phineas Redux,* when he is an innocent man on trial for murder, he learns the value of Madame Max's passionate belief in the goodness and truth of his nature, when many who have called themselves his friends think he is guilty. Phineas now recognizes fully the primacy of love,[4] expressed in Madame Max's heroic journey. It is, however, too late for Laura: when she finally realizes the depth of her love for Phineas, he no longer loves her. In this bitter version of the two suitors convention, Laura's "maturity" contains not "the great reward, marriage to the right suitor," but a humiliating separation from her husband in which she envisions "no escape, no hope, no prospect of relief, no place of consolation" (chapter 56), and a lonely widowhood during which she longs hopelessly for the man she once rejected, who has chosen another woman as his wife.

Trollope also subverts the convention of the two suitors in Violet's story. Violet has a quartet of suitors, not just two, as Trollope points out in the chapter entitled "Miss Effingham's Four Lovers" (*PF,* chapter 45). Her most respectable suitors, according to her guardian aunt, Lady Baldock, are Lord Fawn and Mr. Appledom. They are safe—that is, sexually nonthreatening—as the pastoral sweetness of their names indicates. As Violet comments, Mr. Appledom's "love fever, which is of a very low kind" (*PF,* chapter 45) is seasonal. The two lovers whom Violet takes seriously are Phineas and Lord Chiltern. The violent red lord, Chiltern, who is nearly outside the pale of respectable society even though he is heir to an earl, should—according to convention—be the pattern unworthy lover, like Burgo Fitzgerald or George Vavasor. But Chiltern is in fact the worthiest suitor for Violet, because he loves her most truly, and he is the man Violet at last accepts. When she does decide to marry him, she has learned not to emulate but rather to complement him. In a final twist of conventional structure, Violet breaks the engagement because Chiltern is offended by her self-assertiveness: she tells him that he should find a useful occupation. The lovers reconcile, and Chiltern—unconventionally following Violet's advice—promises to "work for you like a coal-heaver" (*PF,* chapter 73). Chiltern is as true as his word, and when we next see him, in *Phineas Redux,* he is hard at work as master of hounds in the Brake country.

Marie Goesler has three suitors: the old Duke of Omnium, the elder Mr. Maule, and Phineas. In her story, Trollope subverts narrative convention in nearly every possible way. There are two wrong suitors, the Duke in *Phineas Finn* and Maurice Maule in *Phineas Redux.* The far more important of these is the worn-out, selfish old Duke, who is not unscrupulous (as Maule is), but simply unworthy of the integrity, wit and beauty of Madame Max. However, in a rupture of the traditional pattern, *she* initiates the courtship with *him* to punish his initial rudeness to her; she befriends him, instructs him in proper manners, but rejects him when he proposes. In another break with the conventional pattern, Phineas, the right suitor, is courting another woman (Violet) for most of *Phineas Finn.* He is a friend rather than a suitor to Madame Max, and he seeks comfort, not love, from her. In the most untraditional twist of all, she proposes to Phineas anyway—and he rejects her. Phineas marries another woman (Mary) who subsequently dies, leaving him free again, and Madame Max spends the interlude of Phineas's marriage with the old Duke despite her refusal to marry him, nursing him until he dies. Phineas reaches maturity when *he* is educated to appreciate *Madame Max's* qualities of strength, loyalty and wisdom—a reversal of the conventional pattern, in which the woman is educated to appreciate the worthy man—and it is only then that they can marry. Finally, neither Phineas nor Madame Max is a conventional young lover when they decide to become man and wife; they are widowed and middle-aged, suggesting the difficulty of finding a union of equals in this society.

Finally, in the low-comedy subplot of *Phineas Redux,* Adelaide Palliser's story is a parody of the convention of the two suitors. Adelaide must choose between the lackadaisical but gentlemanly Gerard Maule, whom she inexplicably loves, and the energetic but ridiculous Mr. Spooner, who she feels is committing an unpardonable sin in presuming to address her at all. Maule is a parody of the unworthy lover—not unscrupulous, but simply not equal to Adelaide's intellect and energy. Spooner is a parody of the worthy lover, much like Cheeseacre in *Can You Forgive Her?*. He has solid material comfort and energetic purposefulness on his side, but he's bombastic and sexually unattractive—and, moreover, not quite a gentleman. In *Can You Forgive Her?*, every reader applauds when the widow Greenow rejects Cheeseacre (although Bellfield is no great prize) and the feeling is the same when Adelaide dismisses Spooner. Adelaide accepts, rejects, and then again accepts Gerard Maule, and—contrary to the conventional courtship plot—she changes her mind not because she is becoming more mature, but because her favored lover is selfish and lazy. For Adelaide, who is superior in every way to Maule, "the great reward, marriage to the right suitor" is dubious in itself, and can be effected only by getting the reluctant Maule to imitate Adelaide's good qualities, not by having her learn to emulate him, as in the conventional pattern. However, the final twist to the parody courtship plot is that a convenient legacy absolves either partner from having to exercise much mature judgment at all.

This overview of the disrupted structure of the traditional courtship plot points to an emphasis on the strength and intelligence of the female characters in *Phineas Finn* and *Phineas Redux*. Indeed, it is in his characterizations of the novels' women—especially of Lady Laura, Violet, and Marie Goesler—that Trollope's critique of his society's feminine ideals is most clearly manifested. Since Trollope himself states in his *Autobiography* that "Lady Laura Standish is the best character in *Phineas Finn* and its sequel, *Phineas Redux*" (265), I will discuss her tragic history first.

But in order to begin with Lady Laura Standish, one must also begin with at least a mention of Phineas's Irish love, Mary Flood Jones. The two characters are juxtaposed right from the beginning of the Phineas saga: Lady Laura is introduced into the narrative as Mary's opposite as Phineas and Mary engage in lovers' banter. As this introduction foreshadows, the two women continue to be contrasted throughout the novel, both in Phineas's mind and in Trollope's. Mary has been neglected by critics because Trollope gives her scant attention himself—which is of course part of the subversiveness of this work, since she is the embodiment of traditional womanly virtues. Mary is described as "a little girl . . . with the softest hair in the world . . . as pretty as ever she could be" (*PF,* chapter 2). Phineas finds her very sexually attractive, and so does Trollope:

> She was one of those girls, so common in Ireland, whom men, with tastes that way given, feel inclined to take up and devour on the spur of the moment; and when she liked her lion, she had a look about her which seemed to ask to be devoured. . . .[T]here are [some] girls to abstain from attacking whom is, to a man of any warmth of temperament, quite impossible. They are like water when one is athirst, like plovers' eggs in March, like cigars when one is out in the autumn. No one ever dreams of denying himself when such temptation comes in the way. (*PF,* chapter 2)

Adelaide Palliser
(Illustration by F. Holl)

Mary's attractiveness and other womanly virtues may have been sufficient to earn her young Phineas's love, but they are not sufficient to earn her a central role in the novel. Trollope indicates her subordinate role right from the beginning: while he entitles the chapter in which he tells the history of Lady Laura Standish with her own name (as he does for Violet Effingham and Madame Max Goesler), the chapter in which Mary is introduced into the narrative is entitled "Phineas Finn is elected for Loughshane" (*PF*, chapter 2) and not "Mary Flood Jones." Trollope indicates by this title that Mary is important to Phineas not in her own right, but because of her absorption in him. To Mary, Phineas is a hero. As she tells him: "You're a great man to me already, being in Parliament. Only think—I never saw a member of Parliament in my life before" (*PF*, chapter 2). In contrast, Lady Laura is "related to almost everybody who was anybody among the high Whigs" (*PF,* chapter 5); Phineas notes at one of her dinner parties that *all* the men are M.P.'s. Mary implicitly invites Phineas to be her mentor, and he responds to this inherently erotic situation enthusiastically, assuring her that "I'll explain it all to you when I come back, after learning my lesson." Of course, he intends to learn much of that lesson from *his* mentor, Lady Laura, a situation that Mary suspects:

> "Is Lady Laura pretty?"
> "She's about six feet high."
> "Nonsense. I don't believe that."
> "She would look as though she were, standing by you."
> "Because I am so insignificant and small."
> "Because your figure is perfect, and because she is straggling. She is as unlike you as possible in everything. She has thick lumpy red hair, while yours is all silk and softness. She has large hands and feet, and —"
> "Why, Phineas, you are making her out to be an ogress, and yet I know that you admire her."
> "So I do, because she possesses such an appearance of power. And after all, in spite of the lumpy hair, and in spite of large hands and straggling figure, she is handsome. . . . One can see that she is quite contented with herself, and intends to make others contented with her." (*PF,* chapter 2)

Phineas explicitly compares the two women to whom he is attracted. Mary's qualities are the conventional female ones of softness, diminutive prettiness, and self-effacing modesty, while Laura's cardinal attributes are those traditionally considered to be male: power and self-assurance. In a later passage, when Phineas is amidst the grandeur of Kennedy's estate, Loughlinter, far from the simple domesticities of Killaloe, he thinks of proposing marriage to Laura, and he implicitly compares her to Mary, who is "a girl who would confess . . . that love should be everything." Phineas realizes that Laura, in contrast, is "a woman who looked at the world almost as a man looked at it,—as an oyster to be opened with such weapon as she could find ready to her hand." Mary would remain content with the conventional feminine assignment to the sphere of the affections, but Laura "professed to have a care for all the affairs of the world. She loved politics, and could talk of social science, and had broad ideas about religion, and was devoted to certain educational views" (*PF,* chapter 14). Laura expresses this wish for immersion in the male sphere even in her adoption of masculine mannerisms: "she would lean forward when sitting, as a man does, and would use her arms in talking, and would put her hand over her face, and pass her fingers through her hair,—after the fashion of men rather than of women;—and she seemed to despise that soft quiescence of her sex in which are generally found so many charms" (*PF,* chapter 4).

Although Phineas desires Mary's soft womanliness, he admires Laura's strength, and it is clear from the narrator's comments that "she was worthy of admiration" (*PF,* chapter 4). Trollope sets up a choice for Phineas between two types of women: Mary, who will treat him as her superior because he is a man, and Laura, who wants to live on equal terms with men. Mary's more conventional femininity, preferred at first by Phineas, heightens the subversiveness of Lady Laura's characterization.

Laura's confident assumption of power stems in part from her unusual familial circumstances, as well as from her natural gifts and high social position. She is the only woman living in her father's household at the time we begin her story, when she is twenty-three years old. Because her mother has been dead for many years, and her sister is married and lives at St. Petersburg, Laura has been allowed to assume the position of sole mistress of the house at a young age. As Phineas notes:

> The point in Lord Brentford's character which had more than any other struck our hero, was the unlimited confidence which he seemed to place in his daughter. Lady Laura seemed to have perfect power of doing as she pleased. She was much more mistress of herself than if she had been the wife instead of the daughter of the Earl of Brentford,—and she seemed to be quite as much mistress of the house. (Chapter 4)

Despite her "perfect power of doing as she pleased," in the domestic sphere, Laura longs for something more: great political influence. But Laura is not a feminist; indeed, "that women should even wish to have votes at parliamentary elections was to her abominable, and the cause of the Rights of Women generally was odious to her" (*PF,* chapter 10). For Laura, there is no public solution to her lament that "a woman's life is only half a life, as she cannot have a seat in Parliament" (*PF,* chapter 6). She sees no other way to acquire political power than the conventional feminine one: marriage to a politically important man. So she marries the fabulously wealthy Kennedy—and escapes the lesser status that she would have if she married Phineas, the man whom she loves:

> She had married Mr. Kennedy because she was afraid that otherwise she might find herself forced to own that she loved that other man who was then a nobody;—almost nobody. . . . [I]n marrying Mr. Kennedy she had maintained herself in her high position, among the first of her own people,—among the first socially and among the first politically. But had she married Phineas,—had she become Lady Laura Finn,—there would have been a great descent. . . . She might, indeed have remained unmarried! But she knew that had she done so,—had she so resolved,—that which she called her fancy would have been too strong for her. She would not have remained unmarried. At that time it was her fate to be either Lady Laura Kennedy or Lady Laura Finn. (*PF,* chapter 55)

"You don't quite know Mr. Kennedy yet."
(Illustration by J. E. Millais)

The most striking element of this passage is the clarity with which it sets forth the dictates of respectability and the materialistic ethic, in particular the requirements of social prestige, which Laura remembers had seemed paramount to her at the time she accepted Kennedy.[5] Her situation is similar to that of other Trollopian heroines whose stories end in tragedy: Lady Mabel Grex in *The Duke's Children* or Julia Brabazon in *The Claverings*. But the indictment that Trollope makes in each of these situations is closer to home than simply a critique of society's values. In the tragic stories of each of these women, he specifically points to a failure in family relations. Most strikingly, none of these women have mothers, and Trollope seems to link this lack of maternal nurturing with the inability of each heroine fully to appreciate the power of love—until it is too late. James Gindin has written sensitively on this subject:

> All these women, incidentally, those who deliberately and frankly choose (or even almost choose) money over love, are the products of cold, unfeeling fathers and absentee mothers or dissipated fathers who squander their wealth, or relatives entirely indifferent to them. In other words, they have all, despite beauty and brains and birth, suffered from an inhumane environment. (Chapter 38)

Lady Mabel Grex, who is clearly victimized by her father and brother, is perhaps the most striking embodiment of this phenomenon, as we shall discuss in chapter 4 when we look at *The Duke's Children*. But Lady Laura's story also follows this pattern of choosing money over love. In strict fairness, Trollope does make it clear that "it was not Mr. Kennedy's money that had bought her. This woman in regard to money had shown herself to be as generous as the sun" (chapter 55). Laura indeed signs over a fortune of £40,000 to pay her brother's debts. But it is not because she has given up this money that she marries Kennedy, as she later tries to console herself in her wretched marriage. Laura wants to think, in retrospect, that "she would have given way to that romance . . . had she not put it out of her own power to marry a poor man by her generosity to her brother" (chapter 22), but in fact, she gets rid of her fortune *in order* to put it out of her power to marry the "almost nobody" Phineas, as well as to help Chiltern, whom she dearly loves. It is, then, the influence that Kennedy's great wealth makes possible that she chooses over love. And as the paradigm Gindin has given us suggests, Laura's decision to forgo love in favor of money stems at least in part from the masculine cultural lessons she has learned from her father, the Earl. Trollope locates the ironic source of Laura's tragedy in these lessons: while they may give Laura the self-confidence and power the narrator finds so "worthy of admiration," they also lead her to adopt a value system that encourages a disastrous marriage. In his portrait of the Earl and his examination of the Earl's influence on Laura, Trollope exposes the dehumanizing psychological ravages of patriarchy.

In *Phineas Finn,* the chief indication that something might be amiss with the Earl's paternal instincts is his quarrel with his son, Lord Chiltern—and we are more likely to attribute that "total estrangement" (chapter 11) to the son's fiery nature than to the father's obstinacy.⁶ The reader tends at first to sympathize with Lord Brentford when the narrator comments that "the son was a constant thorn in the father's side" (chapter 11). But as Chiltern's relentless truth to himself and to Violet is revealed, we begin to listen to his complaints about his father with a more sympathetic ear. Chiltern angrily insists that Lord Brentford is "blindly unreasonable" (chapter 59), and that his lack of belief in his son has contributed more than anything else to Chiltern's bad reputation, and to his outlaw status in society. As Chiltern rebukes his father, "You have told everybody that I am the devil, and now all the old women believe it" (chapter 19). His feeling is that his father has "wronged me throughout, from beginning to end" (chapter 49). When Phineas protests that the Earl is always "very civil" to him, Chiltern retorts sharply, "He is the very pink of civility when he pleases, but the most unjust man I ever met" (chapter 24). He tells Violet that Lord Brentford "has ever believed evil of me, and has believed it often when all the world knew that he was wrong. I care little for being reconciled to a father who has been so cruel to me" (chapter 19). By the end of *Phineas Finn,* we believe Chiltern's indictment of the Earl to the extent that Lord Brentford seems sadly lacking in imaginative sympathy; he seems more loyal to the rigid dictates of respectability than to his son.

Lord Brentford's deficiencies as a father come into sharper focus in *Phineas Redux.* In this work, the Earl, now living at Dresden with Laura, is nearly in his dotage. Despite the fact that he seems to exhibit positive paternal instincts in exiling himself with his daughter, there are several hints that indicate that it is money—not love—that is uppermost in the Earl's mind. Most importantly, Lord Brentford wants Laura to return to her husband—despite her abhorrence of him—for the sake both of respectability and of family finances: Kennedy's wealth, and her own inheritance, which has been handed over to her husband after the marriage, upon his demand. The Earl becomes obsessed with the loss of Laura's money to the Standish family, but as Laura tells Phineas, "I cannot, however, return to such a husband for the sake of £40,000" (*Phineas Redux (PR),* chapter 20). But Lord Brentford persists, turning to Phineas for help when he returns to England. In this scene, the Earl indicts himself unwittingly in Laura's tragedy. He first declares to Phineas that "I suppose this wretched man is really mad. . . . He never was anything else since I knew him." (And yet the Earl encouraged Laura's marriage to this man, because he was rich!) The Earl then goes on: " . . . and if she were to die to-morrow it [Laura's fortune] would be lost to the family. Something must be done, you know. I can't let her money go in that way" (*PR,* chapter 38). That the Earl's concern is for his daughter's fortune more than for her welfare is implicit, but Trollope makes it clear enough.

Trollope subtly intimates in other passages as well that the Earl is not the best of fathers. In another conversation between Phineas and Lord Brentford at Dresden, Phineas tells him that Kennedy is perhaps mad, yet the Earl suggests that Laura should return to her husband. Then Lord Brentford harps on the inadequacy of Chiltern's position as Master of Hounds. When he complains that "other men keep hounds and farm too," Phineas responds: "But Chiltern is not like other men. He gives his whole mind to it, and finds full employment. And then he is quite happy, and so is she. What more can you want for him? Everybody respects him" (*PR*, chapter 12).

Phineas's last defense of Chiltern's occupation, that "everybody respects" the Earl's son, convinces Lord Brentford far more than do the arguments about Chiltern's individuality or his happiness. When he admits that Chiltern's respectability "goes a very great way," Trollope indicates that it is this public self that counts in Lord Brentford's estimation. The damage to that public self and to the Standish respectability make him think that Laura should return to her husband, whatever the cost to her private self. In a characteristic Trollopian summary of a character's state of mind, the narrator suggests Lord Brentford's very limited conception of a parent's responsibility to his children when he ironically remarks that after this brief, chiefly critical discussion of his children's lives, the Earl "felt that now as ever he had done his duty by his family" (*PR*, chapter 12).

Finally, Lord Brentford shows that he is deficient in humanity when he fails to care about Phineas's fate when he is in prison, on trial for his life. In *Phineas Redux*, Trollope measures each character's nature in reference to his attitude toward Phineas in his extremity,[7] and Lord Brentford comes out worst of those who were supposed to be Phineas's closest friends. Laura complains to Phineas that after Kennedy's death, "her father was talking to her always of her money"; the narrator pointedly remarks that the Earl "could hardly be induced to express the slightest interest as to the fate of this friend who was to be tried for murder" (chapter 52). He deflects Laura's attempt to enlist his sympathy for Phineas with urgent talk about the Saulsby mortgages. The Earl's values—in particular, his attitude toward money and his emphasis on the primacy of the public self—have clearly had an insidious effect on Laura.

While Laura is damaged by her father's patriarchal influence, she does not recognize how dehumanizing these patriarchal standards are until she feels the full weight of their repressive force in her marriage to the coldly just Kennedy. In this marriage, Trollope examines the destructive power that a Victorian husband is able to exert over a wife because of the ingrained sexual ideals of his society and the codifying of those ideals in the law of the land. Trollope signals his concern with this issue by including the parody story of marital discord in *Phineas Redux:* that between the bogus preacher, Mr. Emilius, and Lizzie Eustace. Mr. Emilius is a parodic version of Kennedy. Emilius uses his unprincipled devotion to fashionable religion in the same way that Kennedy uses his strict adherence to rigid puritanism—as a legalistic weapon to oppress their wives. The literal imprisonment Lizzie undergoes in Portray Castle to escape the totally unscrupulous Mr. Emilius, who feels "the necessity . . . of subjecting his young wife to marital authority" (*PR*, chapter 45) shadows Kennedy's subjugation of his wife and her exile to Dresden in *Phineas Finn*. It even appears to be conscious on Trollope's part that Emilius's murder of Bonteen, who is helping to free Lizzie from her husband's

"Violet, they will murder him."
(Illustration by F. Holl)

marital power, shadows Kennedy's attempted murder of Phineas, whom he suspects of being his wife's paramour. The care with which Trollope constructs this parallel tells the reader that Kennedy's male prerogatives are a mask for domination, and puts the Kennedy marriage into an even clearer perspective.

In the Kennedy marriage, Trollope shows the dark implications of patriarchal authority unrestrained by compassion. The destructiveness of male power when it is not tempered by both a sympathetic imagination and a high sense of principle is a major Trollopian concern, centering in that complex morality embodied by the figure of the gentleman. The necessity of the civilizing influence of the gentlemanly ideal is examined from another aspect when Trollope creates the Lopez marriage in the next book of the Palliser series, *The Prime Minister,* as we shall discuss in chapter 3; Lopez exercises male authority unchecked by a sense of principle, with consequences as dire to the wife as Kennedy's lack of kindness.

That parallel is indeed instructive, for as different as the hyperscrupulous Kennedy and the unscrupulous Lopez are, they are alike in that neither is a gentleman, in the complete moral sense of that term. Both men are taken to be gentlemen by their society—but society is wrong. Phineas immediately recognizes Kennedy's deficiency, silently remarking that Kennedy (who is vying for Lady Laura's attentions at a dinner party) "hardly looked like a gentleman"; the narrator mildly comments in response to Phineas's jealous thought that Kennedy "was not unlike a gentleman in his usual demeanour" (*PF,* chapter 6), a strangely equivocal statement that still leaves the question of Kennedy's gentlemanliness open. What Kennedy's "usual demeanour" conceals is a rigid will for mastery that is untempered by the Trollopian virtue which Frank O'Connor has called "heart" (170); as Robin Gilmour points out in his fine book, *The Idea of the Gentleman in the Victorian Novel,* "no man can be a true gentleman without it" (155). The concept of "heart," as Gilmour defines it, is "kindness, the capacity for warm sympathy, an instinctive rather than coldly moral or theoretical approach to life" (155). In a conversation between Laura and Phineas shortly after her marriage to Kennedy, the difference between her two suitors—and indeed between her husband and herself—is crystallized around this concept of the "heart" necessary to a true gentleman. When Phineas fails to speak on the issue of the ballot, he goes to Laura for comfort. Phineas speaks first:

> "Your opinion is all in all to me,—only that I know you are too kind to me."
> "He would not be too kind to you. He is never too kind to anyone. He is justice itself."
> Phineas, as he heard the tones of her voice, could not but feel that there was in Lady Laura's words something of an accusation against her husband.
> "I hate justice," said Phineas. "I know justice would condemn me. But love and friendship know nothing of justice. The value of love is that it overlooks faults, and forgives even crimes."
> "I, at any rate," said Lady Laura, "will forgive the crime of your silence in the House."
> (Chapter 20)

Kennedy is, certainly, never "too kind" to his wife, as Lady Laura has already discovered. She finds that his own scrupulous sense of duty is imposed upon her in all things, and she soon feels that "certain habits of his had become rather bonds than habits to her" (*PF*, chapter 23). He not only recommends a course of reading for her, but requires that she read the books in the time allotted, an order upon which the narrator comments shortly, "This, I think, was tyranny" (*PF*, chapter 23). In the great chapter of *Phineas Finn* in which the Kennedy marriage is defined, "Sunday in Grosvenor Place" (*PF*, chapter 23), Trollope shows how Kennedy's puritanical religious convictions join with his strictly patriarchal view of marriage to imprison his wife. She is compelled to attend church twice on Sundays, and is allowed neither guests nor novels, and thus "the Sundays were very wearisome to her, and made her feel that her lord and master was—her lord and master." Instead of the great political work for which Laura has married, she finds that she is expected to help only in Kennedy's mundane business matters, which "her quick intellect discovered . . . was all form and verbiage, and pretense at business." The description of her realization about the quality of her husband's mind and work reminds the reader of another high-minded woman, Dorothea Brooke, when she discovers the meaninglessness of assisting Casaubon with his *Key to All Mythologies*. As Laura laments to herself, "She had married a rich man in order that she might be able to do something in the world;—and now that she was this rich man's wife she found that she could do nothing" (*PF*, chapter 32).

Another link between Dorothea and Laura is the sexual incompatibility with their husbands that makes both women suffer. Although Casaubon is probably impotent, and there is no hint of this in Kennedy, one cannot imagine that he would be a very passionate lover. In the chapter significantly titled "Lady Laura's Headache" (*PF*, chapter 32), Trollope dramatizes this unhappy aspect of the Kennedy marriage. As Laura realizes that "there was something in the hard, dry, unsympathizing, unchanging virtues of her husband which almost revolted her," she develops a sexual aversion to Kennedy. He, in his turn, has an intimation of the truth: "What if this headache meant simple dislike to him, and to his modes of life?" His retaliation is to coerce her into doing the account books, one of the "homely duties" he expects of her. But Laura finally refuses to live up to his ideal of woman as efficient domestic manager. She will not sublimate her sexuality in housekeeping; as she declares roundly to her husband, "I mean to tell you that I will not try to cure a headache by doing sums." Meanwhile, she begins to think more and more of Phineas, to whom she has always been strongly attracted sexually. In an explicit subversion of the woman as sexless angel ideal, Trollope explicitly emphasizes Laura's powerful sexuality when she thinks of Phineas as a "Phoebus" (*PF*, chapter 32)[8] in the very chapter in which Laura tells her husband that she has a headache for ten days in a row—with the obvious implications.[9]

Laura finds out that the emotion she has called "her fancy" is the controlling passion of her life. As she tells Phineas when they are together at Königstein, after she has fled her husband, the emotion that "had made the world a blank for me . . . was, and has been, and still will be my strong, unalterable, unquenchable love for you." Laura hastens to add to her declaration, "I ask for nothing in return.

"I will send for Dr. Macnuthrie at once."
(Illustration by J. E. Millais)

As God is my judge, if I thought it possible that your heart could be to me as mine is to you, I could have put a pistol to my ear sooner than speak as I have spoken" (*PR,* chapter 12). Laura's words reverberate forward in the Palliser novels to *The Duke's Children,* when Lady Mabel Grex, another woman who has realized too late that she cannot change her love, says to Tregear: "I think, I think, that I would go with you now anywhere, facing all misery, all judgments, all disgrace. You know, do you not, that if it were possible, I should not say so. But as I know that you would not stir a step with me, I do say so" (*The Duke's Children,* chapter 77). These declarations of hopeless passion spoken to men whom Laura and Mabel never expect to marry attest to Trollope's knowledge that women are sexual beings. And they do something further, something more radically subversive: this assertion of the powerful sexuality of women together with our memory of Laura's "sale she made of herself in her wretched marriage" (*Autobiography,* 264) and Lady Mabel's frustrated attempt to sell herself to Silverbridge, link the most reviled of Victorian women, the "fallen" woman, with these respectable aristocratic ladies who contemplate but refrain from "falling." With Laura, a married woman, and Mabel, a woman who loves an engaged man, these thoughts are expressed in words rather than in deeds. Trollope has Laura and Mabel distinguish themselves from women who do indeed "fall" in the disclaimers that accompany their protestations of love, but in his recognition of the common sexuality and exploitation of all women, he implicitly questions the strict categories of his culture's feminine roles.

It is when Laura is a widow that the most intensely emotional episode between Phineas and her occurs. He has come to Saulsby to tell her that he will soon propose to Marie Goesler, and his news precipitates a scene of sorrow and passion that is to my mind one of the most poignant in all of Trollope's works:

> He held her to his breast while she sobbed, and then relaxed his hold as she raised herself to look into his face. After a moment she took his hat from his head with one hand, and with the other swept the hair back from his brow. "Oh, Phineas," she said, "Oh, my darling! My idol that I have worshipped when I should have worshipped my God!" (*PF,* chapter 78)

Laura's lesson is a bitter one, and she pronounces sentence on herself, accepting responsibility for her fate: "When I was younger I did not understand how strong the heart can be. I should have known it, and I pay for my ignorance with the penalty of my whole life" (*PR,* chapter 78).[10] Trollope certainly appears to punish Laura for her unwomanly sacrifice of love in favor of political power and social prestige. But despite the tragic ending Trollope gives to her story, the sympathy with which he dramatizes it testifies to his disquiet with the influences upon women in his society that have made such a fate possible. In the end, Laura seems more sinned against than sinning, more a victim of male dictates for Woman than a betrayer of femininity. Trollope symbolizes the force of patriarchy in determining Laura's fate when he describes her at the end of *Phineas Redux,* the last we are to hear of her: "Of poor Lady Laura hardly a word need be said. She lives the life of a recluse, and the old Earl her father is still alive" (*PR,* chapter 80). Holl's il-

Lady Laura at the Glass
(Illustration by F. Holl)

*Then she suddenly turned upon him, throwing her Arms round his Neck
(Illustration by F. Holl)*

lustration of Laura at Saulsby, brooding over her first meeting with Phineas after he is acquitted of murdering Bonteen (chapter 68), appears to depict Laura's fate symbolically. In the illustration, a matronly Laura, who is dressed in mourning, sits crying in front of the fire. The caption reads: "And she sat weeping alone in her father's house."

Fate is much kinder to Phineas's third love, Violet Effingham, who ends up happily married to Lord Chiltern, the man she has loved since childhood. But it is not simply chance that makes Violet's fate so much happier than Laura's.[11] Violet's characterization is expressive of an important Trollopian attitude toward a woman's self-fulfillment: that a woman must live her own life, not the lives of the men around her.[12] Laura tries to live too much through men: her father, her brother, her husband—and she is left with a life in which she is "nobody" (*PF*, chapter 70). In contrast, Violet eludes the attempts of nearly everyone to make her "sacrifice" herself for some man—and she ends up with an intact identity. However, Violet too finds that self-realization is a difficult task in a society in which women are constrained on every side by conventional ideals as to their proper "nature and mission." In the witty, articulate Violet, Trollope portrays the frustrations that a high-spirited Victorian woman might feel as she tries to assert an identity that is independent of these expectations.

In Trollope's first description of Violet, he introduces one of the male expectations of her: that because she looks delicate, she should *be* delicate and easily manipulated. The narrator states that this is, however, an impression that is belied by the reality of her physical strength and force of character:

> In figure she was small, but not so small as she looked to be. Her feet and hands were delicately fine, and there was a softness about her whole person, an apparent compressibility, which seemed to indicate that she might go into very small compass. Into what compass and how compressed, there were very many men who held very different opinions. Violet Effingham was certainly no puppet. She was great at dancing,—as perhaps might be a puppet,—but she was great also at archery, great at skating,—and great, too, at hunting. (*PF*, chapter 10)

Violet's rebellion against conventional expectations of submissive womanhood is introduced immediately in her story. The first we hear of Violet, in a vignette the narrator approvingly relates, she defies her aunt, Lady Baldock, who forbids her to go to a hunting meet. The story is important because it exemplifies the toughness in Violet that allows her successfully to resist the pressures of all those who would like to "compress" her "into very small compass":

> "My dear aunt . . . I am going to the meet with George . . . and there, let there be an end of it."
> "And you will promise me that you will not go further," said the dragon.
> "I will promise nothing to-day to any man or to any woman," said Violet. What was to be said to a young lady who spoke this way, and who had become of age only a fortnight since? She rode that day the famous run from Bagnall's Gorse to Foulsham Common, and was in at the death. (*PF*, chapter 10)

And she sat weeping alone in her Father's House
(Illustration by F. Holl)

In this description of Violet, there seems to be an implicit comparison to Mary, the other physically small woman whose story is told in *Phineas Finn*. Both women are very sexually attractive to men, and men want to "devour" Mary just as they want to "compress" Violet. But while Mary encourages the lion in man, having "a look about her which seemed to ask to be devoured," Violet refuses to be sacrificed to men's imaginative constructions of her. It is no coincidence that she has the stamina to be "in at the death" in the fox hunt. Riding with the men, she refuses to be their prey.

Indeed, Violet refuses to sacrifice herself even for Chiltern, the man she loves, in an explicit subversion of the feminine ideal of self-sacrifice. As she tells Laura, "he is a dangerous wild beast. I daresay he is noble-minded, and I will call him a lion if you like it better. But even with a lion there is risk" (*PF,* chapter 10).[13] In contrast to Mary's willingness to be "devoured" by her lion, Violet wants to tame hers—at least to the point where she is no longer in danger of being eaten.[14] Unlike Glencora and Alice in *Can You Forgive Her?,* Violet has a high opinion of her worth, and Trollope shows how this self-respect undermines the ideal of self-denying Woman. When Laura "gravely" tasks Violet to "remember . . . that you might be a saviour to him [Chiltern]", Violet retorts stoutly: "I do not believe in girls being saviours to men. It is the man who should be the saviour to the girl. If I marry at all, I have the right to expect that protection shall be given to me,—not that I shall have to give it" (*PF,* chapter 19).

At the same time, Violet declares that her frankly sexual nature disqualifies her to be the pure Angel whose "mission" is to be the moral saviour to sinful man. To another of Laura's suggestions that Violet should marry Chiltern because "it would save him," Violet objects:

> "I don't know that I have any special mission for saving young men. I sometimes think that I shall have quite enough to do to save myself. It is strange what propensity I feel for the wrong side of the post. . . . I like a roué myself. . . . I prefer men who are improper, and all that sort of thing. If I were a man myself I should go in for everything I ought to leave alone. I know I should. But you see,—I'm not a man, and I must take care of myself. The wrong side of a post for a woman is so very much the wrong side. I like a fast man, but I know that I must not dare to marry the sort of man that I like." (*PF,* chapter 10)

Trollope makes it clear that Violet is sexually attracted to Chiltern, but she recognizes that his violent nature might be very dangerous to her: "It looked as though he would not hesitate to wring his wife's neck round, if ever he should be brought to threaten to do so" (*PF,* chapter 11). When she finally decides to marry Chiltern, it is because of her deep love for him, and because she has satisfied herself that his love for her is so true that he will be able to temper his violent nature—at least in relation to her. She never succumbs to the argument that she is obligated by virtue of her sex to try to save an erring man. As the astute Madame Max Goesler tells Phineas, after only a week's close acquaintance with Violet: "She seems to me to be the most independent girl I ever knew in my life. I do believe that nothing would make her marry a man unless she loved him and honoured him, and I think it is so very seldom that you can say that of a girl'' (*PF*, chapter 40).

Despite Violet's rebellion against male ideas about her nature, she is well aware of the powerful conventions that hem in Victorian womanhood. Although she may be attracted to a "roué," she realizes that she cannot be one herself, without being outlawed from respectable society forever. As she tells Laura: "When I was a child they used to be always telling me to mind myself. It seems to me that a child and a man need not mind themselves. Let them do what they may, they can be set right again. . . . But a woman has to mind herself—and very hard work it is when she has a dragon of her own driving her ever the wrong way" (*PF*, chapter 10).

However, Violet does manage to teach men a few lessons on the absurdity of those very conventions, and Phineas does not escape her sharp commentary on men's expectations of women's nature. In the chapter titled "The Mousetrap," Lady Laura has helped Phineas to get Violet alone so that he might propose to her. Violet invokes the chivalric idea of protecting women, only to mock it:

> "I am alone,—a poor unprotected female. But I fear nothing. I have strong reason for believing that Lord Brentford is somewhere about. And Pomfret the butler, who has known me since I was a baby, is a host in himself."
> "With such allies you have nothing to fear. . . ."
> "Nor even without them, Mr. Finn. We unprotected females in these days are so self-reliant that our natural protectors fall off from us, finding themselves to be no longer wanted." (*PF*, chapter 45)

Violet's aunt, Lady Baldock, is constantly descrying this very self-reliance in her niece; she is horrified, as she complains to her daughter, that Violet "seldom tells me what she means to do,—and sometimes she will walk out quite alone!" (*PF*, chapter 45). Violet, like Glencora in *Can You Forgive Her?*, also expresses her independence through her language: she delights in her aunt's horrified reaction when she describes Phineas as "A-1" (*PF*, chapter 42), much as Glencora insists to the disgruntled Palliser that "the long and short of it" is "good English" (*Can You Forgive Her,* chapter 49). Trollope shows his approval of Violet's independence in his comic portrayal of the "dragon," Lady Baldock, the voice of respectability: "Why had not the law, or the executors, or the Lord Chancellor, or some power levied for the protection of the proprieties, made Violet absolutely subject to her guardian till she should be subject to a husband?" (*PF*, chapter 45). Lady Baldock is explicitly invoking the Woman-as-Child ideal, but as a mature woman, Violet refuses to be treated as if she is a child. Her rebellion against her aunt recalls Glencora's resistance to her husband and her duennas, Mrs. Marsham and Mr. Bott, in *Can You Forgive Her?* As Violet tells Laura: "I know I am very naughty; but I can't help feeling that I cannot be good without being a fool at the same time. I must either fight my aunt, or give way to her. If I were to yield, what a life I should have;—and I should despise myself after all" (*PF*, chapter 45).

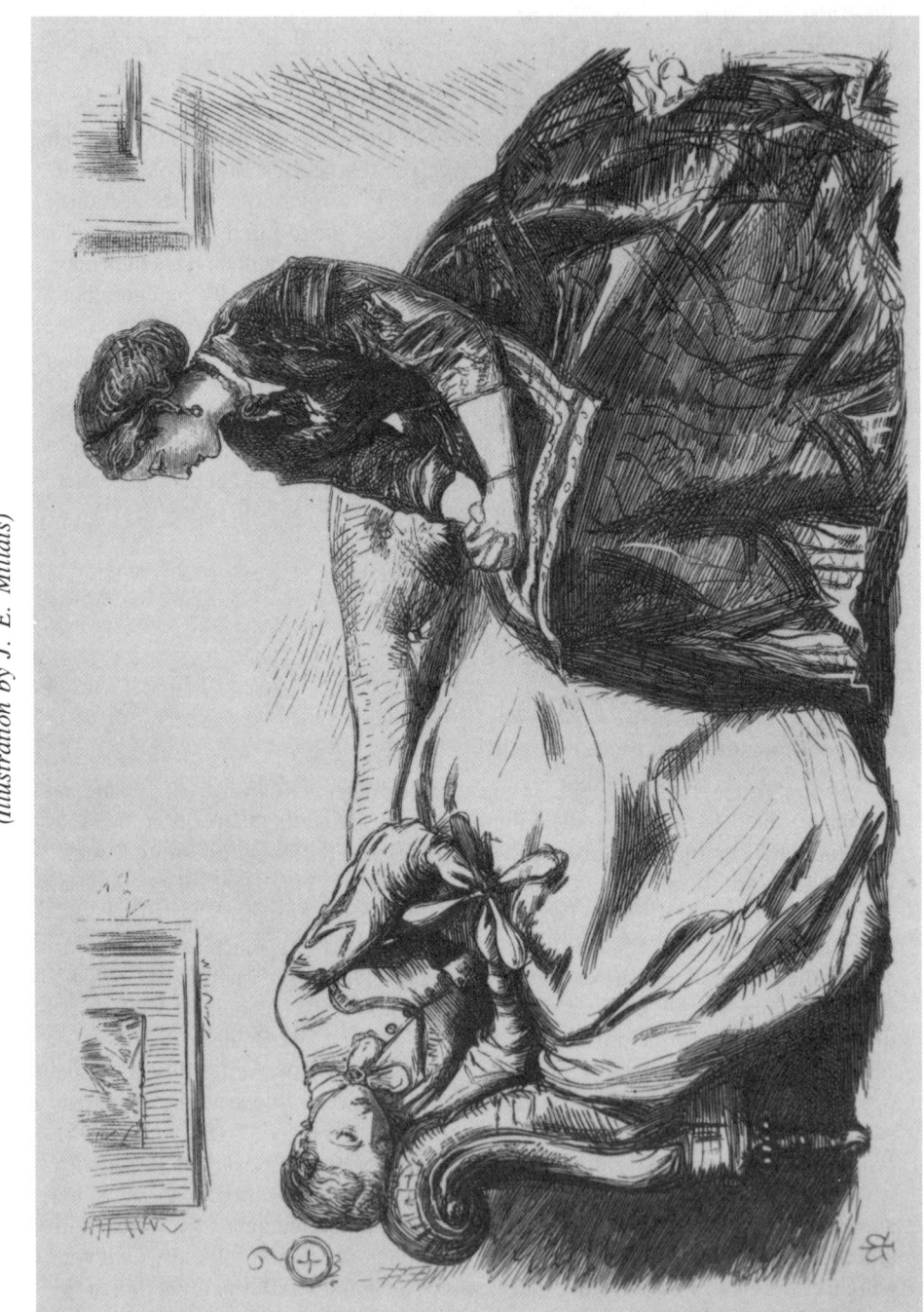

"I wish you would be in earnest with me."
(Illustration by J. E. Millais)

Violet will never "despise" herself, as Glencora did after her marriage, for submitting to others' ideas of what is good for her as if she were a child. She retains her self-respect because she acts according to her intelligence; she would rather be "naughty" than be a "fool" in order to comply with conventional expectations of what is "good" for women. And yet Violet does not fly in the face of convention. She refuses to be as submissive as a child, but she also recognizes that she cannot enjoy a child's irresponsibility. A child need not fear irreparable damage to his reputation because of his transgressions, but "a woman has to mind herself." The crux of the matter is that Violet minds herself—she will not allow anyone else to "mind" her. When Laura tries to convince Violet that it would be "right, or rather not wrong," to visit Lord Chiltern in his rooms after his hunting accident, Violet replies firmly: "I will do nothing that I should be ashamed to tell any one. . . . I know what I may do, Laura, and I know what I mayn't" (*PF*, chapter 30). She stays at her aunt's because she knows that a young woman is expected to be under the protection of her relatives until she is under the protection of her husband—however absurd that may seem to Violet. She isn't willing to outlaw herself from respectable society, and to become a Bohemian—although she dreams of this possibility. Laura suggests a cure for Violet's chafing against Lady Baldock's dominion: "Marry Oswald, and be your own mistress." But Violet is not at all sure that marriage to Chiltern would result in that outcome, so she suggests her own ideal plan:

> "I mean to be my own mistress without marrying Oswald, though I don't see my way quite clearly as yet. I think I shall set up a little house of my own, and let the world say what it pleases. I suppose they couldn't make me out to be a lunatic."
> "I shouldn't wonder if they were to try," said Lady Laura. (*PF*, chapter 22)

Despite Laura's assurances to Violet that marrying Chiltern would ensure her freedom, in the very next chapter, the chilling "Sunday in Grosvenor Place," Trollope details Laura's failure to be her "own mistress" in her miserable marriage with Kennedy. Violet's prudence seems wise in light of Laura's subjugation to her husband. But after Violet has quarrelled with Chiltern and they have broken their engagement, she herself realizes that her dream of being entirely independent of these societal expectations for Woman is unrealistic:

> she had come to find that it was almost impossible any longer to endure Lady Baldock, and quite impossible to escape from Lady Baldock. In former days she had had a dream that she might escape, and live alone if she chose to be alone; that she might be independent in her life, as a man is independent, if she chose to live after that fashion; that she might take her own fortune in her own hand, as the law certainly allowed her to do, and act with it as she might please. But latterly she had learned to understand that all this was not possible for her. Though one law allowed it, another law disallowed it, and the latter law was at least as powerful as the former. (*PF*, chapter 45)

Violet thinks of being wholly independent of authority other than her own—of not marrying—but she is aware that this is not a realistic choice for her. She knows the inevitable answer to Laura's bitter query, "And yet what can a woman become if she remains single?" (*PF,* chapter 51). Violet lives with Augusta Baldock, Lady Baldock's daughter, and she knows that the spinster daughter's thralldom is much more powerful than her own—although we find in *Phineas Redux* that "Gussie" escapes her mother by entering a nunnery. Aspasia Fitzgibbon, the other spinster in *Phineas Finn,* appears to offer a more positive image: she "lived in a small house by herself . . . and walked about sturdily by herself, and spoke her mind about everything." Trollope seems to respect Miss Fitzgibbon. He portrays her as kind to Phineas when she buys back the note he has cosigned for her brother Laurence, to whom she is devoted. But he takes care to depict the spinster's own unhappiness, expressed in "the violence of her jokes and the bitterness of her remarks." Moreover, Miss Fitzgibbon is regarded by both men and women in this society as insignificant, one of the unfortunate "redundant women" of Victorian England.[15] Phineas "cared very little what Miss Fitzgibbon said to him" (*PF,* chapter 5). Violet herself mocks the spinster when she remarks to Phineas (whom Miss Fitzgibbon has just kindly warned to avoid money entanglements with her brother), "I did not know . . . that you and the divine Aspasia were such close allies" (*PF,* chapter 22). Clearly, Violet prefers a better position than Miss Fitzgibbon's. Her realization about the inferior status of a spinster in Victorian society is echoed by Adelaide Palliser in *Phineas Redux,* when she thinks she has sent Gerard Maule away forever: "What would life be without a lover?—without the prospect of marriage?" (*PR,* chapter 69). Her question resonates through the final novel of the series, *The Duke's Children,* in which Mabel Grex's bitter experience seems to vindicate Adelaide's fears and to provide an answer to her desperate question: "A girl unless she marries becomes nothing, as I have become nothing now" (*The Duke's Children,* chapter 77).

Laura's tragic experience engenders the bitter answer to her own question: "The curse is to be a woman at all." But Violet protests that "I have always felt so proud of the privileges of my sex" (*PF,* chapter 51). However, although Violet fully enjoys those privileges, she recognizes Woman's liabilities in Victorian society. But Violet is like Laura in her rejection of a public solution to those liabilities. She jokes about her aunt's "Female Protestant Unmarried Women's Emigration Society," telling Phineas and Lord Fawn that "my aunt wants me to go out as a sort of leading Protestant unmarried female emigrant pioneer myself" (chapter 41).[16] To Violet, women's rights defined as complete legal equality with men is a myth; she views John Stuart Mill's advocacy of this important issue of the "Woman Question" debate as ludicrous. Indeed, Violet explicitly jokes about Mill several times in *Phineas Finn.* When Phineas says that "A man should try to be something," Violet jests, "And a woman must be content to be nothing,—unless Mr. Mill can pull us through!" (*PF,* chapter 59). Earlier, she tells Laura that she will not marry Chiltern, but instead "shall knock under to Mr. Mill, and go in for women's rights, and look forward to stand for some female borough'' (*PF,* chapter 51). But Violet's real decision is not between Mr. Mill and her suitors, but between Lady Baldock and her suitors—and in the very next chapter, she decides to marry Chiltern.

Trollope indicates that marrying Chiltern is the best decision that Violet can make. She has always loved him, and the question has been whether she can trust his violent nature. But Laura, who knows Chiltern better than anyone, and who loves him deeply, says to Violet, ''You never knew a man with a softer heart or with a finer spirit'' (*PF,* chapter 10). Laura is an accurate judge of Chiltern's character, despite her egregious misjudgment of Kennedy. Violet formed the same opinion of Chiltern when they were children, and she first grew to love him. She recurs several times during the narrative to her childhood outing with Chiltern in Saulsby Wood; it is clear that in Violet's mind—and in Trollope's—it is emblematic of Chiltern's true nature.[17] In this passage Violet speaks to Chiltern: ''I think it was the happiest day in my life. His pockets were crammed full of gingerbread and Everton toffy, and we had three bottles of lemonade slung on to the pony's saddle-bows. I thought it was a pity that we should ever come back. . . . You took off my shoes and dried them for me at a woodman's cottage'' (*PF,* chapter 11).

In a later passage, when Phineas is riding with Violet in Saulsby Wood, she tells him about this childhood escapade, and she asks his opinion about Chiltern. When Phineas (who does not know that Chiltern has been a suitor for Violet) declares that ''there is a savagery about him which would make him an uncomfortable companion for a woman,'' Violet defends Chiltern: ''He was so good to me in that cottage'' (*PF,* chapter 13). In another episode, when Phineas is again at Saulsby with the intention of proposing to Violet, she tries to discourage him with these words: ''I must go round by the woodman's cottage. . . . I always come here when I am at Saulsby that I may teach myself to think kindly of Lord Chiltern.'' When she and Phineas return to the other riders, she says, ''I have done my devotions now, and am ready to return to ordinary life'' (*PF,* chapter 34).

But Violet has always recognized the perilous side of Chiltern's nature too. As she tells Laura after she has accepted Chiltern, ''Your brother, Laura, is dangerous. He is like the bad ice in the parks where they stick up the poles. He has had a pole stuck upon him ever since he was a boy'' (*PF,* chapter 52).[18] Chiltern gambles, he has committed violent acts when he was drunk and when he was sober, and he likes dangerous horses. But Trollope is careful to add a disclaimer to each of Lord Chiltern's disreputable pursuits; he is never portrayed as vicious or dishonorable. In relation to his gambling, Chiltern ''had sacrificed himself on one or two memorable occasions in conformity with turf laws of honour, and men said of him, either that he was very honest or very chivalric'' (*PF,* chapter 11). Chiltern is not a drunk, or even a heavy drinker, when we come upon his story: ''When a man hunts six days a week he can afford to drink beer. I'm on an allowance,— three pints a day. That's not too much'' (*PF,* chapter 24). He is absolved from any guilt—as well as from the charge of drunkenness—in the fatal act of violence he commits, when he kills the "ruffian"(*PF,* chapter 11) at Newmarket with his fists. As for Chiltern's preference for dangerous horses, Trollope makes it clear that it is the tremendous energy and the personal bravery of the man that makes him choose a strong beast. Indeed, Chiltern treats his horses well.[19] Since Trollope often uses a man's treatment of his horse as indicative of his probable treatment of his woman—as, for instance, he does with Burgo Fitzgerald in *Can You Forgive Her?*—it is instructive to look at Chiltern's philosophy of riding horses. As he tells Phineas, "Just let him have his own way at everything . . . and if you'll only sit on his back he'll carry you through as safe as a church" (*PF,* chapter 24). Phineas successfully follows this advice; as he later explains, "The brute began in his own way, and carried on after in the same fashion all through." In contrast to Chiltern's belief that a man should ride *with* his horse, Burgo forces his horse past its limits—and kills it.

Chiltern clearly needs some way to discipline his excessive energies. Trollope makes it clear that he is capable of discipline by telling us of Chiltern's early reputation as a scholar. When he is a man, he at last finds the perfect employment for his energies and intellect in the position of Master of Hounds. Violet tells Phineas: "You can't alter a man's nature. Oswald was born to be a master of hounds" (*PR,* chapter 2). Trollope, an avid hunter himself, agrees with Violet:

> he understood hunting, not only as a huntsman understands it,—in that branch of the science which refers simply to the judicious pursuit of the fox . . . but he knew exactly what men should do, and what they should not. In regard to all those various interests with which he was brought in contact, he knew when to hold fast to his own claims, and when to make no claims at all. He was afraid of no one, but he was possessed of a sense of justice which induced him to acknowledge the rights of those around him (*PR,* chapter 7).

There is another clue in this passage that indicates why Chiltern is a good choice for Violet. He does not need to prove his authority to anyone; he commands respect because of his manly nature. Chiltern is able to "make no claims at all," and he can as easily "acknowledge the rights of those around him" as his own. Trollope makes a deliberate contrast in this passage to Kennedy, who "had that great desire to enjoy his full rights, so strong in the minds of weak, ambitious men" (*PF,* chapter 51). Trollope has pointedly compared the two men before, perhaps most clearly in the chapter entitled "The Willingford Bull," which comes immediately after the grim "Sunday at Grosvenor Place." The "Bull," where Chiltern stays when he hunts, represents a Bohemian freedom that seems very attractive when placed alongside the imprisonment Laura suffers under Kennedy. Yet Chiltern is termed the "red devil" by most of the respectable men in the hunting country around the Bull, while Kennedy is considered a respectable, godly man. Chiltern tells Phineas that Kennedy is a "log of wood. . . . It is such men as he who drive me out of the pale of decent life. If that is decency, I'd sooner be indecent" (*PF,* chapter 24). Chiltern's characterization of his proper brother-in-law as a "log of wood" exactly defines the lack of vitality and the inhuman intransigence that characterize Kennedy, against which Trollope wants us to measure Chiltern's fallible humanity.

The gentleness that Violet recognized when Chiltern was with her in Saulsby Wood in their childhood is expressed again in his proposal to her. In Trollope, proposal scenes often suggest what the nature of a marriage will be. When Violet has at last accepted him, Chiltern kneels before her again, as he did in the woodman's cottage long ago when he took off Violet's shoes to dry them for her:

> [H]e approached her, and went down on both knees close at her feet. Then he took her hands again, for the third time, and looked up into her eyes.
> "Oswald, you on your knees!" she said.
> "I would not bend to a princess," he said, "to ask for half her throne; but I will kneel here all day, if you will let me, in thanks for the gift of your love. I never kneeled to beg for it."
> "This is the man who cannot make speeches." (*PF*, chapter 52)

Chiltern's ability to "kneel" to Violet bodes well for her equality in a society in which women are expected to be in a subservient posture. The significance of his speech becomes clearer when it is compared to the proposal scenes in the love stories of *Can You Forgive Her?* In chapter 1, I discussed the proposal scene between Alice and John Grey, in which he demands that she bend to him, because she has proved herself unfit to manage her own life. Alice admits that she "had found her master" and reluctantly tells him that "You win everything—always" (*Can You Forgive Her?*, chapter 74). In the more formal proposal between Glencora and Palliser, after their matrimonial alliance has been decided upon, she tells him the story of her love for Burgo, and he commands: "You must love me now" (*Can You Forgive Her?*, chapter 24). As we shall see in the next chapter, the male authority manifest in these speeches has its counterpart in the proposal scene between Emily and Arthur Fletcher in *The Prime Minister*. Like Alice, Emily forfeits her judgment to her lover, relinquishing all authority to him. In contrast, Chiltern's graceful words of thanks connote reciprocity. Moreover, Violet's promise to love Chiltern, in contrast to Laura's "sale of herself" to Kennedy, is a "gift." Laura "handed herself over as a bale of goods to an unloved, unloving husband" (*PF*, chapter 55), but Violet refuses to consider marriage as a market in which she will sell herself. She knows that most men think of her as a lovely possession, a pretty bubble—"a dear duck of a thing," as she tells Laura (*PF*, chapter 10).

Violet ultimately contrasts this knowledge of how men typically measure her value to the absolute truth of Chiltern's love for her. Earlier in the proposal scene, Violet says to Chiltern, "But I am not the only woman," and he answers, "To me you are,—absolutely, as though there were none other on the face of God's earth" (*PF*, chapter 52). Violet's other serious suitor, Phineas, could never make that claim—and it is in part because of the ease with which he can change his love that Violet rejects him. As she tells Laura, "One doesn't know how many marks he has wiped off. They are like the inn-keeper's score which he makes in chalk. A damp cloth brings them all away, and leaves nothing behind" (*PF*, chapter 71). Violet recognizes that it is Phineas's lack of self-knowledge that somehow allows these easy changes. She turns the tables on the men who measure her when she tells Laura that after she measured Phineas, he "was just half an inch too short. He lacks something in individuality. He is a little too much a friend to everybody" (*PF*, chapter 71). At this point in Phineas's career, Violet is of course right about his precarious identity—although later in his story, he emerges from his ordeal in *Phineas Redux* with a hard-won clarity of self. In contrast to Phineas's facile adaptability, Chiltern is uncompromisingly himself, a man who is "not like anyone else in the world" (*PF*, chapter 59). His own insistence upon an unconventional identity suggests that he will not try to fit Violet into any conventional role, but will allow her to realize all her possibilities.

But even with Chiltern, Violet must fight to resist male dominion. After the break in her engagement with Chiltern, Violet tells Laura that "we are not fit to be man and wife . . . we are too much alike. Each is too violent, too headstrong, and too masterful." Despite the misery of her own experience, Laura conventionally advises, "You, as the woman, ought to give way" (*PF*, chapter 71). But it is Chiltern, not Violet, who asks for another chance. Violet, who "could not bear the idea of being tamed by anyone," resists Chiltern's "resolution to tame the thing with which he was angry," and insists upon the freedom to be herself (*PF*, chapter 73). Contrary to Alice's grateful acceptance of her "master" (*Can You Forgive Her?*) or Laura's angry rebellion against her "lord and master" (*PF*, chapter 23), between Violet and Chiltern there is to be no mastery. When we see the married couple in *Phineas Redux*, Violet is as witty and outspoken as ever, and Chiltern is joyfully ferocious in his work as Master of Hounds. The fertile sexuality of their marriage—they have several babies by the end of the Phineas saga—stands in happy contrast to the sterility of Laura's union with Kennedy; instead of begetting life, the Kennedy marriage engenders only Kennedy's madness and death, and Laura's morbid wish that "I would die if I knew how" (*PF*, chapter 55). Ironically, it is Laura, who has so disastrously managed her own life, who seems to voice Trollope's own high opinion of Violet's conduct when she tells Phineas, "With all her seeming frolic, Violet Effingham is very wise" (*PR*, chapter 17).

However, despite Trollope's obvious appreciation of Violet in both novels of the Phineas saga, the lingering ambivalence he feels about the kind of powerful womanhood Violet represents is still evident toward the end of *Phineas Finn*. Phineas compares Violet to Mary Flood Jones, whom he has finally decided to marry: "Dear Violet! But, after all, Violet lacked that sweet, clinging, feminine softness which made Mary Flood Jones so preeminently the most charming of her sex" (*PF*, chapter 68). When he thinks of betraying Mary by marrying Madame Max, he fortifies himself against treachery with a talisman—Mary's first love letter:

Violet, with all her skill, and all her strength, and all her grace, could never have written such a letter as that which he still held in his pocket. The best charm of a woman is that she should be soft, and trusting, and generous; and who ever had been more soft, more trusting, and more generous than his Mary? (*PF*, chapter 69)

Thus, in Violet's story, Trollope expresses his ambivalence toward Victorian ideals of femininity through the tension between his obvious admiration of Violet throughout *Phineas Finn* and the effort he makes to downplay this admiration at the end of the book. He tries to make the reader feel that in Mary Flood Jones, Phineas has won the finer woman. His attempt to portray Mary as superior is too weak to win over even a Victorian audience indoctrinated in conventional feminine ideology; modern readers generally remember only that Mary dies before the opening of *Phineas Redux,* while the witty, Shakespearean Violet is a favorite Trollopian heroine. Trollope's inability to portray Mary as attractively as Violet suggests his own wavering belief in the conventional ideal of Victorian womanhood that Mary embodies—and that Violet so delightfully subverts.

Trollope's questioning of the ideals for Victorian womanhood in Violet's story is carried further in the story of Madame Max Goesler, whose strength, integrity and wisdom define a new model of femininity. Indeed, Madame Max comes to embody an ideal of intelligent, principled behavior for both sexes. As Shirley Letwin has stated, "The most perfect gentleman in Trollope's novels is Madame Max Goesler" (74).[21] But although Madame Max is the exemplar of the complex morality of the gentleman, she is certainly *not* that moral paragon, the Angel-in-the-House. Instead of guarding Man from the moral dangers of the world beyond the home, she actually spends a good deal of time working in that outer male sphere, tending to her business in Vienna. As she tells Phineas, "I rather like it. It makes me feel that I do something in the world" (*PF*, chapter 64). Madame Max is a worldly woman who is "highly ambitious" (*PF*, chapter 57) to succeed in the social counterpart of the high political realm—although she dreams of being much more than an ornament of society. As she tells Phineas, "For myself, I would prefer to be of use somewhere,—to some one, if it were possible. I strive sometimes" (*PF*, chapter 64).

As Letwin has cogently argued, Madame Max combines the cardinal gentlemanly qualities of discrimination, diffidence, courage and honesty to produce integrity. She demonstrates these male qualities rather than the traditionally female virtues of purity, modesty, softness and delicacy. She is a politic statesman rather than an angel, a model of how intelligence and imagination can unite to create the delicate understanding necessary in human affairs, rather than a figure embodying virtue beyond human capacity. Unlike a conventional angelic heroine, Madame Max is sorely tempted by the Duke's coronet, even though she doesn't love him. Like a true gentleman, she acts with as much courage in her "duel" (*PF*, chapter 61) with Glencora over the Duke as Phineas does in his duel with Chiltern over

Violet. When she refuses the Duke's legacy, it is evidence of self-respect, not of unworldliness. She doesn't despise the jewels, but she cares more for the high opinion of the Duke's family, of Society—and of herself. Glencora objects: "Nobody ever repudiates legacies. The Queen would take the jewels if they were left to her." Madame Max's response is: "I am not the Queen. I have to be more careful what I do than any queen" (*PR,* chapter 26). As we will see in chapter 4, when I discuss *The Duke's Children,* Madame Max's integrity is exemplified in her relations with the new Duke (Palliser), who blames her unjustly for his daughter Mary's secret engagement with the commoner Tregear. Phineas is right when he praises Madame Max's conduct: "Whatever is best to be done, you will do it;—I know that." Her response again differentiates the difficult and complex morality of the gentleman from the simple virtue of the conventional novel heroine: "Your praise goes beyond the mark, my friend. I can be both generous and discreet;—but the difficulty is to be true" (*PR,* chapter 30).

But although Trollope always admires Madame Max, he doesn't yet seem to prefer her novel brand of femininity in *Phineas Finn.* Phineas, although strongly attracted to her, extols Mary's traditional virtues as superior to hers, and he rejects the German widow in favor of his lovely Irish sweetheart. But Madame Max dramatically emerges in *Phineas Redux* as the heroine of the Phineas saga—a heroine who is, however, more along the lines of Lancelot than of Guinevere. She is the knight in shining armor who rescues her damsel in distress, Phineas, from the dungeon in which he has been imprisoned, and she gets the knight's fabled reward: marriage to the one she loves. In this sexual role reversal Trollope seems to question the very premise of separate ideals for the sexes: that men and women have inherently different natures, which define their respective "missions," and limit their possibilities.

Madame Max's possibilities seem to be chiefly curtailed not by her sex, but by her un-English background. As a Jewess, the rich widow of an Austrian banker, she is an outsider as well as an exotic. She is very ambitious, and has won her place in the highest circles of society through her beauty, charm and intellect. In order to succeed with the English upper class, she has been compelled to the strictest observance of convention; nevertheless, even with all her careful attention to propriety of conduct, her foreign origins beget ill-natured gossip about her sexual relations. During the scenes in which Madame Max is introduced into the narrative, both Lord Fawn and Lady Laura allude to her reputed second husband; later, after the Duke's homage to her becomes public knowledge, she is alleged to be the Duke's mistress. She repudiates the Duke's legacy in part because "there are people who will say that—I was his mistress" (*PR,* chapter 30). When Phineas remarks to her that "you are free as air," Madame Max exclaims: "The most cabined, cribbed, and confined creature in the world! I have been fighting my way up for the last four years, and have not allowed myself the liberty of one flirtation;—not often even the recreation of a natural laugh" (*PF,* chapter 72).

Although Madame Max may not have "one flirtation," she does have three suitors during the course of the Phineas novels. As with Phineas's other loves—Laura, Violet and Mary—we learn a good deal about male perceptions of ideal womanhood from Madame Max's relationships with men. We also discover that Madame Max, despite her public observation of feminine conventions of propriety, is highly unconventional in her ideal conception of male-female relations. She is offered two unequal relationships, both of which she refuses: the first, in *Phineas Finn*, with the old Duke of Omnium, whose social prominence is rivalled only by royalty; the second, in *Phineas Redux*, with the unscrupulous dandy, Maurice Maule. At the end of *Phineas Finn*, she offers herself to Phineas, whom she perceives as her equal, but he reluctantly refuses her. It is not until the conclusion of *Phineas Redux* that her dream of self-fulfillment in a relation between equals is realized.[22]

Her first suitor is the Duke of Omnium, the nobleman of highest rank in the kingdom. Their relationship begins when the haughty Duke snubs Madame Max, but the "triumphantly successful operations of that lady" (*PF*, chapter 48) have soon enthralled him during the very same dinner party. Thereafter, the Duke pursues Madame Goesler, whom he perceives as the last pleasure remaining in a life that has been a succession of sated desires. At first, he thinks he can sustain a covert relation with Madame Max—but he doesn't know his woman. Like other admirable Trollopian heroines—Violet, for example, or Isabel Boncassen in *The Duke's Children*—Madame Max insists upon openness in her relations with men. She compels the Duke to publicly acknowledge his friendship with her by dining at her home in Park Lane; when he invites her to be his mistress, she flatly declines. The language of the Duke's request and of Madame Max's refusal is significant. He reminds her that "a man at my age does not like to be denied," but Madame Max's response demonstrates her knowledge of the destructive possibilities of Man's expectations of Woman's sacrifice: "What man likes to be denied anything by a woman at any age? A woman who denies anything is called cruel at once,—even though it be her very soul" (*PF*, chapter 60). Moreover, like Violet when she refuses to visit Lord Chiltern in his rooms, Madame Max's sense of self-respect impels her to avoid even the appearance of doing wrong. Like another foreigner, the American Isabel Boncassen in *The Duke's Children*, she recognizes that as an outsider to English ways she must attend very closely to society's rules to be accepted within its upper ranks;[23] an open flouting of decorum, no matter how innocent, would be disastrous to her hard-won position. While the unmarried maiden Violet cannot live in her own house without incurring censure, the widowed Madame Max tells the Duke that "it behoves me to live in houses of my own. Women of whom more is known can afford to be your guests" (*PF*, chapter 57).

But Madame Max's refusal only whets the Duke's appetite for her. He wants her in part because she is exotic; for him, her foreignness and the mystery of her background are not an obstacle to intimacy (as they might be to a man of lesser rank), but an enticement:

> She had a beauty which he had learned to think more alluring than other beauty. He was sick of fair faces, and fat arms, and free necks. Madame Goesler's eyes sparkled as other eyes did not sparkle, and there was something of the vagueness of mystery in the very blackness and gloss and abundance of her hair,—as though her beauty was the beauty of some world which he had not yet known. And there was a quickness and yet a grace of motion about her which was quite new to him . . . In his early youth he remembered to have seen, somewhere in Greece, such a houri as was this Madame Goesler. The houri in that case had run off with the captain of a Russian vessel engaged in the tallow trade; but none the less was there left on his Grace's mind some dreamy memory of charms which had impressed him very strongly when he was simply a young Mr. Palliser, and had had at his command not so convenient a mode of sudden abduction as the Russian captain's tallow ship. (*PF*, chapter 60)

This passage points up one aspect of the inequality of this relation. The narrator makes fun of the Duke's attempt to recapture the romance of his youth in wooing this later version of his Greek houri. Much as the Russian captain performed his "sudden abduction," his Grace dreams of carrying Madame Max off to his villa at Como. Their union would be the traditionally precarious—and amusing—mating of May to January. Madame Max is young (thirty-two) and full of life: her sparkling eyes and her energetic movements express her great vitality. The Duke is seventy. He "moved slowly, and turned his limbs, when he did turn them, as though the joints were stiff in their sockets" (*PF*, chapter 57). Madame Max has to curb her energies when she and the Duke ride together on the very morning after they meet, suggesting the constricting quality of a marriage with the old Duke. She "was known as a perfect horsewoman,—one indeed who was rather fond of going a little fast on horseback, and who rode well to hounds," but he "seldom moved out of a walk, and on this occasion Madame Max was as steady in her seat and almost as slow as the mounted ghost in Don Juan" (*PF*, chapter 48). In the course of this same ride, the Duke and Madame Max have a conversation about flirting that symbolizes the difference between the intense vitality of the German widow and the weary lassitude of the Duke:

> "What do you say to a mountain-top at dawn on a summer day?" asked Madame Max Goesler.
> "You make me shiver," said the Duke.
> "Or a boat on a lake on a summer evening, or a good lead after hounds with nobody else within three fields, or the bottom of a salt-mine, or the deck of an ocean steamer, or a military hospital in time of war, or a railway journey from Paris to Marseilles?"
> "Madame Max Goesler, you have the most uncomfortable ideas."
> "I have no doubt your Grace has tried each of them,—successfully. But perhaps, after all, a comfortable chair over a good fire, in a pretty room, beats everything."
> "I think it does—certainly," said the Duke. (*PF*, chapter 48)

Although one might make an argument that in Madame Max's catalogue of dramatic scenarios for flirtation, Trollope is poking fun at the typical novelistic setting for romantic encounters, the important point for our purposes is that she envisions these scenes as appropriate for passion, while the Duke perceives them as simply "uncomfortable." His scenario for illicit dalliance is his Italian villa beside a lake at Como, a setting which in Trollope is redolent of decadence—the corrupt Lord Brotherton in *Is He Popenjoy?* lives in Italy, as does the dissolute Wharton heir who precedes Everett in *The Prime Minister,* and the unprincipled Stanhope family in *Barchester Towers* has lived in Italy for many years before their return to England. The respective settings for romance that Madame Max and the Duke choose symbolize their characters and desires: she longs for the drama of love, while he wants titillation.

It is no wonder that the Duke disagrees with Madame Max's energetic ideas of romance, because he is characterized by quiescence. He is ornamental, a grand "snowy peak" (*PF,* chapter 64), as Madame Max describes him to Phineas. For a long time, she sees this grandeur as necessary because it is symbolic. At the end of *Phineas Finn,* when Phineas criticizes the Duke as "all buckram," Madame Max defends his Grace: "He has to maintain the prestige of the highest aristocracy in Europe." Because he carries himself like a duke, Madame Max sees his life as having some merit and purpose. As she tells Phineas, "I own that to me there is something glorious in the dignity of a man too high to do anything,—if only he knows how to carry that dignity with a proper grace. I think that there should be breasts made to carry stars" (*PF,* chapter 64). But three years later, when the Duke is about to die, she has learned another lesson from his life, although "she told him he had ever lived as a great nobleman ought to live. . . . Nevertheless, her nature was much nobler than his; and she knew that no man should dare to live idly as the Duke had lived" (*PR,* chapter 25).

Indeed, in Madame Max's relation with the Duke, Trollope explores the ideal of Woman as ornament of society in three ways. First, he explores this feminine ideal in part by making the "ornament" a man—the formidable Duke—rather than a woman. Second, although he initially presents the Duke as a glittering ornament of society, he then proceeds to undermine that grand image through his characterization of the Duke and of those—especially of Mr. Maule, Sr.—who admire him. Third, he subverts the ornamental ideal through Madame Max's probing thoughts about the purpose of her life, which end in her rejection of the Duke's proposal of marriage.

When we are first introduced to the Duke, he is gracing Glencora's dinner party at Matching, and nearly everyone considers his mere presence to be a great honor. But Trollope penetrates the Duke's mystique right from the beginning of his Grace's story. He does this initially by comparing the unworthy Duke of Omnium to that other worthy Duke, the Duke of St. Bungay, in order to show just how unmerited the Duke's glamour is:

> I hardly know why it should have been so, but the Duke of Omnium was certainly a greater man in public estimation than the other duke then present,—the Duke of St. Bungay. The Duke of St. Bungay was a useful man, and had been so all his life. . . . But the Duke of Omnium had never yet done a day's work on behalf of his country. . . . The one was a moral, good man, a good husband, a good father, and a good friend. The other,—did not bear quite so high a reputation. But men and women thought but little of the Duke of St. Bungay, while the other duke was regard-

ed with an almost reverential awe. I think the secret lay in the simple fact that the Duke of Omnium had not been common in the eyes of the people. He had contrived to envelope himself in something of the ancient mystery of wealth and rank. (*PF*, chapter 48)

Trollope immediately undercuts the Duke's aura of magnificence when he makes the petty Mrs. Bonteen the first admirer to comment upon the Duke. Mrs. Bonteen, an obsequious gossip, tries to impress Phineas with her knowledge of the Duke, of Glencora's former entanglement with Burgo Fitzgerald, and of the Palliser family generally, and it is to Phineas's credit that he "was not very fond of the lady [Mrs. Bonteen]" (*PF*, chapter 48). Another great admirer of the Duke is the unprincipled aesthete, Maurice Maule (Gerard's father), the only character other than Mr. Emilius in the entire Phineas saga who is absolutely unredeemed by any virtues. (Mr. Bonteen is at least hard-working!) In the following scene, Mr. Maule has been eulogizing the Duke, who has just died; he compares the old Duke favorably to the new Duke of Omnium, Plantagenet Palliser, whom he criticizes because his hard work makes him common. The scene is ironic for two reasons: Madame Max has just been meditating on the emptiness of her friendship with the Duke, and Mr. Maule, the eulogist of a useless but graceful life, is himself a grotesque, more insidious version of the Duke. Maule, who styles himself a "man of taste" (*PF*, chapter 21), lacks even the excuse of rank to justify his sole occupation—the gratification of his own desires:

> "I dare say that Mr. Palliser, as Mr. Palliser, has been a useful man. But so is a coal-heaver a useful man. The grace and beauty of life will be clean gone when we all become useful men."
> "I don't think we are near that yet."
> "Upon my word, Madame Goesler, I am not so sure about it. Here are sons of noblemen going into trade on every side of us. We have earls dealing in butter, and marquises sending their peaches to market. There was nothing of that kind about the Duke. A great fortune had been entrusted to him, and he knew that it was his duty to spend it. He did spend it, and all the world looked up to him. It must have been a great pleasure to you to know him so well." (*PR*, chapter 30)

But contrary to Maule's final statement in this passage, Madame Max confesses to herself after the Duke's death that it hasn't been a "great pleasure" to know the Duke so well. Knowing him intimately has meant realizing that behind his grand façade is a selfish, childish old man who has been caught in this state of arrested development because his interpretation of his rank's obligations—unlike that of his nephew Palliser—includes only the responsibility to indulge his own appetites. As he tells Madame Max when he proposes to her, and she asks him how his friends might react: "My dear, I may venture to please myself in this,—as in everything" (*PF*, chapter 60). Trollope subverts the "woman as child" ideal when he portrays the old Duke, not Madame Max, as a child who wants the "top brick of the chimney" (*PF*, chapter 57). She is aware that for him she is a toy; if she married him, she knows that "he would be tired of his new plaything after a month" (*PF*, chapter 62). When Mr. Maule comments on the Duke's "special dignity," the image that comes to Madame Max's mind is of his Grace throwing a tantrum like a two-year-old when he is refused a glass of curaçoa (*PR*, chapter 30).

Finally, Trollope shows that the Duke himself is a victim of expectations that he be grandly decorative. He is forced, as Glencora shrewdly guesses, to seem "so hard; but I suppose he was only acting his part" (*PR*, chapter 26). He is not allowed to be merely human, and after a while he loses much of his humanity. The last words we hear him say are a wish that he could have been more intimate with someone. On his deathbed, he poignantly tells Madame Max: "I could have talked to you about things which I never did talk of to any one. I wonder why I should have been a duke, and another man a servant. . . . I'm afraid I have not done it well" (*PR*, chapter 25).

If the Duke has doubts that he was worthy of being worshipped, Madame Max has regrets about the object she has chosen for her devotion. After the Duke's death, she admits to herself that "she had tried to believe in the Duke of Omnium, but she had failed" (*PR*, chapter 30). Finally, she thinks of the relationship in these unsentimental terms:

> The last three years of her life had been sacrificed to an old man with whom she had not in truth possessed aught in common. She had persuaded herself that there had existed a warm friendship between them;—but of what nature could have been a friendship with one whom she had not known till he had been in his dotage? What words of the Duke's speaking had she ever heard with pleasure, except certain terms of affection which had been half mawkish and half senile? (*PR*, chapter 30)[24]

If there is some value in Madame Max's relation with the Duke, Trollope shows that it lies in the profound questioning of her life's meaning that the Duke's death forces upon her. The three years of her life that she has sacrificed as the Duke's nursemaid are not wholly wasted; she has learned firsthand from him about the emptiness of a life that is devoted only to oneself. She now recognizes that her great efforts to shine in society are unsatisfying because they are unaccompanied by some purpose higher than simply ornamenting social and political gatherings:

> And yet what had all this done for her? Dukes and duchesses, dinner-parties and drawing-rooms,—what did they all amount to? What was it that she wanted?
> She was ashamed to tell herself that it was love. But she knew this,—that it was necessary for her happiness that she should devote herself to some one. All the elegancies and outward charms of life were delightful, if only they could be used as the means to some end. As an end in themselves they were nothing. (*PR*, chapter 30)[25]

If Madame Max ultimately perceives the Duke's life as less than noble, she finds nothing at all to admire in her next suitor, Maurice Maule. In Maule, Trollope portrays a man who is not a gentleman in the moral sense of that term, but who is accepted by society as a gentleman: "That Mr. Maurice Maule was a real gentleman no judge in such matters had ever doubted" (*PR*, chapter 21).[26] When Phineas

"I would—I would."
(Illustration by F. Holl)

asks who he is, Madame Max identifies him precisely: "A battered old beau about London, selfish and civil, pleasant and penniless, and I should think utterly without a principle" (*PR*, chapter 30). Maule is one of a small band of corrupt old roués who are depicted throughout Trollope's novels. His cohorts include Colonel Marrable in *The Vicar of Bullhampton*, Lionel Bertram in *The Bertrams* and Colonel Osborne in *He Knew He Was Right*. Through the characterization of Maule and his kind, Trollope reveals a good deal about how women were perceived and used by men in Victorian society, and about the parasitic quality of male conceptions of female nature. In all his relationships with women, Maule relies on womanly self-sacrifice; he considers only how women—his wife, his mistress, Madame Max—can serve him.

The history of Maule's marriage illustrates just how accurately Madame Max has divined his character: "He had ill-used his wife, and had continued a long-continued liaison with a complaisant friend" (*PR*, chapter 21). His mistreated wife soon dies, but the mistress lives on. As Mr. Maule enters the narrative, he is trying to discard her in favor of a rich second wife, whom he hopes "might be of service to him;—for that idea of blazing once more out into the world on a wife's fortune was always present to him" (*PR*, chapter 21). He is currently on the trail of wealthy Madame Max.

Maule is as poor a parent as he was a husband, and "of his children he now took but little notice. . . . His younger son had disappeared, and the father was perhaps thankful that he was thus saved from trouble" (*PR*, chapter 21). Indeed, when the elder son, Gerard, is evaluated in the light of his father's dark character, the son's lackadaisical pose looks almost like a virtue—if he doesn't do anything, at least he doesn't do anything bad. Trollope creates sympathy for Gerard when the reader discovers that the father's indifference to his son has engendered the son's attitude of indifference. Gerard doesn't like work, but his father's view of work as "employing his good looks, conversational powers and his excellent manners on a second marriage which might be lucrative" (*PR*, chapter 21) puts the son's laziness in a better light. Maule looks on his son's plan to marry the penniless Adelaide because he loves her as "simple madness" (*PR*, chapter 21); the father calculates his chances for a splendid marriage not on love, but on his observation that "there are women always in the market to buy for themselves the right to hang on the arm of a real gentleman" (*PR*, chapter 21). So he proposes to Madame Max. Like the Duke when he assumes "Marie" will be his mistress, Maurice Maule mistakes his woman. Her sense of self-respect justifies her in refusing the fortune-hunting Maule "almost indignantly" (*PR*, chapter 69).

If Madame Max scornfully recognizes Maule as her inferior, as she has earlier reluctantly confessed that the Duke's nature was less noble than her own, she perceives Phineas as her equal. Indeed, one way in which Trollope examines the different conventions for men and women in his society in the Phineas novels is to parallel Madame Max and Phineas, the two major characters in these works who must create their places in Society.[27] Even a cursory glance at the careers of

Phineas and Madame Max illustrates that women are more confined than men are by ideas of what is thought proper for them. In contrast to the necessity for Madame Max to restrict natural expression within the bounds of decorum, to deny herself even "the recreation of a natural laugh" (*PF,* chapter 72), Phineas leads a volatile existence: by the end of *Phineas Finn,* he has been romantically involved with three women (four, if one counts Madame Max), has befriended Chiltern—a man most respectable people think of as a "red devil"—and has fought a notorious duel. Yet none of his adventures slows his social rise. (Only in *Phineas Redux,* when he is publicly accused of being the paramour of Lady Laura Kennedy, a Cabinet Minister's wife, does he find that his reputation is clouded.)

Trollope parallels the careers of Phineas and Madame Max, but he by no means suggests that she emulate Phineas's attempt to succeed in politics. However, the first words that Madame Max ever speaks to Phineas imply that she might be seeking public equality with men: "[W]hat would I not give to be a member of the British Parliament at such a moment as this! . . . The one great drawback to the life of women is that they cannot act in politics" (*PF,* chapter 40). But Trollope soon makes it clear that it is not public but private equality—a marriage between equals—that Madame Max desires. Trollope's idea of women's rights is expressed much later in Madame Max's story, when she is happily married to Phineas. In *The Prime Minister,* when Barrington Erle remarks to her, "I don't suppose you will go in for your 'rights,'" she responds: "Not by Act of Parliament, or by platform meeting. I have a great idea of a woman's rights. But that is the way, I think, to throw them away" (*The Prime Minister,* chapter 11). Like Violet, who states to Laura that "I have always been so proud of the privileges of my sex" (*PF,* chapter 51), Madame Max tells Mr. Erle that "I think upon the whole we women have the best of it" (*The Prime Minister,* chapter 11).

Trollope's ambivalence toward Victorian ideals of femininity is apparent in the tension between the character of Madame Goesler and her aspirations. She is the perfect statesman, perhaps the wisest and most politic character in the entire Phineas saga (The Duke of St. Bungay and Mr. Monk are the only competitiors), but Trollope makes her thoroughly content to find equality in the private relation of marriage, rather than in the public realm of politics. In contrast, in *The Prime Minister,* the book following *Phineas Redux* in the Palliser series, Trollope tells the story of another woman, Glencora, who does try to expand her sphere into the political arena, although she is compelled by her sex to operate by indirection. Glencora is not the statesman that Madame Max is, and the contribution to her failure that her personality makes undercuts the role that feminine ideals have played in her defeat. If Trollope had portrayed Madame Max seeking to enter the political lists, *The Prime Minister* might have told a much clearer tale of Woman's subjection in Victorian society. But that is a story Trollope never tells.

The story that Trollope does tell is quite subversive in its own right. The first unconventional aspect of the relation between Madame Max and Phineas is that she is the one who first feels sexual desire for him; conventionally, the woman does not discover her love for a man until he tells her of his love for her. When the Duke asks her to go with him to Como, she thinks not of the Duke but of Phineas, "with whom it might be pleasant to look at the colour of Italian skies and feel the softness of Italian breezes" (*PF,* chapter 60). Her love for Phineas (who is still a suitor for Violet) is the real reason that she will not marry the Duke. As she consoles herself when she has sent her refusal to his Grace:

> "She would still be free,—Marie Max Goesler,—unless in abandoning her freedom she would obtain something she might in truth prefer to it . . . but of what avail was it to love a man who, when he came to her, would speak to her of nothing but of the charms which he found in another woman!" (*PF,* chapter 62).

Despite her belief that Phineas probably still loves Violet (actually he's engaged to Mary by now, but it's difficult to keep up with his romantic adventures), Madame Max obliquely offers herself to him. When Phineas laughs about the necessity of a "poor fellow" serving the Government, Madame Max responds, "A poor fellow need not be a poor fellow unless he likes" (*PF,* chapter 67). When that doesn't suffice, she proposes to him directly in the chapter significantly titled "Madame Goesler's Generosity" (*PF,* chapter 72), indicating Trollope's approval of Madame Max's unconventional gesture. It is important that her proposal is couched in terms of friendship because the intimacy between these two—the easy camaraderie that is found elsewhere in the Phineas novels only in Violet's and Chiltern's love—is evidence of their equality. Phineas, who respects this assumption of equality in Madame Max, realizes that "she was so earnest in her friendship that he owed it to her to tell her everything" (*PF,* chapter 72). Just before she proposes to him, Phineas notices that "there was a strength about her of which he had not been aware. She was stronger, larger, more robust physically than he had hitherto conceived" (*PF,* chapter 72). Madame Max is on the verge of enacting her equality with men by assuming the masculine role in a traditional sexual ritual; instead of manifesting the soft graces of a conventional heroine, she looks—strong. Trollope suggests that Madame Max's "robust" physique images a tough moral fiber. According to her sense of equality with men, she acts not like a perfect lady—i.e., with delicate modesty—but according to the gentlemanly code of conduct, which stresses courage and generosity:

> "It is because you are a woman, and young, and beautiful, that no man may take wealth from your hands. . . ."
> "If I were a man you might take it, though I were young and beautiful as the morning?"
> "No; presents of money are always bad. They stain and load the spirit, and break the heart."
> "And specially when given by a woman's hand?"
> "It seems so to me. But I cannot argue of it . . ."
> "Nor can I argue. I cannot argue, but I can be generous,—very generous. I can deny myself for my friend,—can even lower myself in my own esteem for my friend. I can do more than a man can do for a friend. You will not take money from my hand?"
> "No, Madame Goesler;—I cannot do that."

"What is the Use of sticking to a Man who doesn't want You?"
(Illustration by F. Holl)

> "Take the hand then first. When it and all that it holds are your own, you can help yourself as you list." (*PF,* chapter 72)

After Phineas reluctantly declines Madame Max's generous offer because of his engagement to Mary, he compares the German widow—and all his London women—to his Irish sweetheart. Phineas's effort to console himself indicates once again that Laura, Violet and Madame Max possess superior attributes of their own, while Mary's chief virtue is her love for Phineas:

> A thousand times he had told himself that she [Mary] had not the spirit of Lady Laura, or the bright wit of Violet Effingham, or the beauty of Madame Goesler. But Mary had charms of her own that were more valuable than them all. Was there one among the three who had trusted him as she trusted him,—or loved him with the same satisfied devotion? (*PF,* chapter 74)

Although Phineas refuses Madame Max, they remain friends. Madame Max again takes the initiative when she writes to Phineas before he leaves for Ireland, assuring him of her friendship, and he responds in kind. Two years later, when they resume their friendship in Broughton Spinnies (*PR,* chapters 16, 17), they fall easily into their old intimacy.

In this resumption of their relation, two conventions of romance are broken, indicating the untraditional nature of this love between man and woman. First, it is Phineas who is in distress when his horse throws him, and it is Madame Max who succors him. Second, although in a conventional romance, the man tells the woman of his adventures, it is Madame Max, not Phineas, who tells the tale about her friendship with the Duke of Omnium. As she says, "Is it not odd that I should have told you all this history?" (*PR,* chapter 17). This sexual role reversal is even more clear in Madame Max's heroic journey to Bohemia, undertaken to save Phineas's life when he is on trial for the murder of Mr. Bonteen. When she returns from her search for the key, her quest has already become myth:

> It was of course known to everybody that Madame Goesler had undertaken a journey to Bohemia,—and, as many supposed, a roving tour through all the wilder parts of unknown Europe, Poland, Hungary, and the Principalities for instance,—with the object of looking for evidence to save the life of Phineas Finn; and grandly romantic tales were told of her wit, her wealth, and her beauty. (*PR,* chapter 64)

It is not only in her journey that Madame Max reverses sexual roles. Both she and Glencora undermine conventional assumptions about the male's superior logical mind when they calculate how Emilius might have committed the murder. That supremely logical man, Mr. Low, disregards the women's plan to search for the key, bludgeon and gray coat—but it is this quest that saves Phineas. Madame Max's demurring words to Mr. Low, "of course we are very ignorant" (*PR,* chapter 54) prove to be highly ironic.

"I suppose I shall shake it off."
(Illustration by F. Holl)

If Madame Max usurps male hegemony on the logical mind, Phineas can act with the intuitive certainty usually attributed to women. In one of the most memorable scenes in *Phineas Redux,* Phineas greets Madame Max for the first time since before his imprisonment:

> "Yes, there she is," said the Duchess, laughing. . . ."If ever one friend was grateful to another, you should be grateful to her, Mr. Finn."
> He did not speak, but walking across the room to the window by which Marie Goesler stood, took her right hand in his, and passing his left arm round her waist, kissed her first on one cheek and then the other. . . . As for him, he had no thought of it at all. He had made no plan. (*PR,* chapter 74)²⁸

The kiss is both a gesture of gratitude and an emblem of the changed nature of their future relation, which will include romantic, sexual love as well as friendship. Like Lord Chiltern in *Phineas Finn,* Madame Max at last proves the absolute truth of her love—with a good deal more trouble than Chiltern's duel over Violet! She has long *felt* as true to Phineas as any wife. When she first hears about the accusation against Phineas, she has this exchange with Glencora:

> "Nothing shall make me believe it. If I did, I could never again believe in any one. If they told you that your husband had murdered a man, what would you say?"
> "But he isn't your husband, Madame Max."
> "No;—certainly not. I cannot fly at them, when they say so, as you would do. But I can be just as sure." (*PR,* chapter 48)

The scene in which Phineas at last proposes to Madame Max clearly symbolizes the equality of their relation. As Madame Max tells Phineas, "It must be an even partnership" (*PR,* chapter 79). In this insistence on equality, Madame Max is echoed later on in the Palliser novels by another Trollopian heroine, Isabel Boncassen, when she says to Silverbridge that "I have no idea of going on such a journey except on terms of equality" (*The Duke's Children,* chapter 53). Perhaps Madame Max's assertion is even more unconventional than Isabel's, because Madame Max is referring specifically to the business responsibilities that she and Phineas must share as well as to their marriage as a whole. In this "partnership," both husband and wife will work in the male sphere of business. As with Isabel and with Violet, Madame Max's demand for equality is born of a profound self-respect. As she tells Phineas when he asks her whether she thinks he is marrying her for her money: "Have you ever known me to have a low opinion of myself? Is it probable that I shall account myself to be so mean and of so little value as to imagine that you cannot love me? I know that you love me" (*PR,* chapter 79).

As is usual in Trollope, the posture of the lovers in a proposal scene is significant because it indicates the nature of the marriage that will follow. After Phineas has told Madame Max that he loves her and they embrace, "he found himself seated beside her, holding her hand." Rather than Phineas assuming all authority in the marriage, "it seemed to him that from that moment all the explanations, and all the statements, and most of the assurances were made by her and not by him" (*PR,* chapter 79). There is an immense difference between this proposal scene and central proposal scenes in other Palliser novels: for example, Alice is thoroughly mastered at last by John Grey, and Palliser orders Glencora to love him in *Can You Forgive Her?;* Emily guiltily cedes her authority to Arthur Fletcher at the end of *The Prime Minister.*

Within the Phineas novels themselves, this marriage must be compared to that of Laura and Kennedy, and that of Violet and Chiltern. In contrast to Kennedy's attempt to enslave Laura, the promise in this union—as in the marriage of Violet and Chiltern—is that there will be no mastering, but a reciprocity born of mutual respect. These are, finally, the only "terms" upon which Trollope feels a woman's rights can be secured.

3

The Prime Minister:
The Cost of Civilization

In *The Prime Minister,* the fifth book of the Palliser series, one of the novel's two plots once again focuses on Glencora. In *Can You Forgive Her?* Glencora's yearning for self-realization centered on a romantic passion for Burgo Fitzgerald. In *The Prime Minister* her overt interest is in enhancing her husband's position, but she is actually trying to establish a career for herself. The book's other plot concentrates on the fate of Emily Wharton, the daughter of a rich judge of old gentry stock, who marries an unscrupulous adventurer, Ferdinand Lopez. Both stories are about a woman's attempt to gain some sense of herself, to create a distinctive identity. The rebellion of Glencora and Emily against their husbands' marital authority comes to represent a revolt against the Victorian cultural ideals of femininity upon which that male authority depends. Both stories exemplify Victorian male perception of women, and the manner in which inculcated feminine deals manifest themselves in the expectations and behavior of the sexes. Neither Glencora nor Emily gains authority in her own right, and the resolution of each plot is conventional: Glencora is returned to the domestic sphere, and Emily marries her worthy lover, Arthur Fletcher. However, the struggles of both women are sympathetically chronicled, with the result that the subversive implications of the narrative conflict with the novel's conclusion. This tension seems to reflect Trollope's ambivalence about the cultural ideals of femininity that the book indirectly questions, but eventually upholds.

The very structure of the book expresses an ambivalence about the narrative conventions that reflect traditional ideas about what constitutes a woman's fulfillment—i.e., marriage to the right man. The severe disruptions of the traditional courtship plot seem to indicate its inability to encompass the imperfection of Victorian sexual relations. The first alteration of traditional structure is that both Glencora's and Emily's stories concentrate not upon the prelude to marriage, but on marital relations themselves. This emphasis does two unconventional things. First, it focuses attention on the dynamics within the marital relation rather than on the courtship. Since both wives are discontented in their marriages, the idea of marriage as sufficient for feminine fulfillment is questioned. Second, because Emily and Glencora are married and thus sexually experienced, it implicitly argues against the convention that the pure, sexually uninitiated woman is the most interesting heroine.

Another way in which the structure of both plots is unconventional is in its alterations of the "convention of the two suitors" (Kennard, 10–11), which we discussed in chapter 1 in connection with the structure of both Glencora's and Alice's stories in *Can You Forgive Her?* Emily's narrative, in which two suitors vie for her love, clearly draws upon the convention, but it is subverted in several crucial ways. First, Emily chooses the unworthy suitor, Ferdinand Lopez, instead of the worthy suitor, Arthur Fletcher. Second, it is through marriage, rather than through courtship, that she learns who her proper suitor should be. Finally, she is freed only by her husband's suicide, and it is as a widow, not a maid, that she at last marries the worthy man. Glencora's story, unlike that in *Can You Forgive Her?*, doesn't seem to concentrate on a courtship plot at all. Yet there are two suitors for Glencora. The competition is not between two men but between her husband and her career—therefore, between her husband and herself. She herself stands in the place of one of the suitors. Thus, in Glencora's story, there is an even more drastic distortion of the courtship plot than in Emily's. By opposing Glencora to Palliser rather than making her the apex of a lovers' triangle, as in *Can You Forgive Her?*, Trollope focuses the primacy of her attention on the question of whether she is really working for her husband or for herself. The ideal of feminine self-sacrifice versus Woman's self-realization thus becomes a crucial issue.

Trollope sets up this unconventional structure in *The Prime Minister* by telling the story of two parallel careers: that of Palliser, now Duke of Omnium and Prime Minister of England, and that of Glencora, who tries, in the "career" of political hostess, to find an occupation that will satisfy her ambition. The competition of these marital partners in their careers is one of the main tools Trollope uses for illustrating his ambivalence about feminine ideals. The very fact that Trollope is structuring Glencora's plot as the story of two parallel careers suggests that he is comparing a man and woman of equal social stature to see what their respective possibilities are. While both Glencora and her husband ultimately fail, Trollope suggests that the woman is frustrated by social convention much more than by her indiscretions, while the man is limited only by his own rigid nature. Even the most intelligent, spirited, highly-positioned woman cannot overleap society's expectations for Victorian womanhood. Trollope wants to examine those dissatisfactions rather than submerge them. He has an articulate spokeswoman for voicing those frustrations, and he so clearly admires Glencora that the reader is unable to dismiss her arguments, even when the resolution of the novel suggests that her arguments were untenable.

But despite Trollope's sympathy with Glencora's frustration, there are limits to his own enlightened thinking on the subject of women's rights. Trollope's rejection of a public extension of those rights ironically gives overt approval to that very state of women's possibilities that is so confining for Glencora. Indeed, organized feminism—the vision of women's rights as complete political, legal, economic and sexual equality in both domestic and professional matters that was espoused by J. S. Mill, Harriet Taylor, Barbara Leigh Smith Bodichon, Millicent Garrett Fawcett, and a militant, vocal minority—is treated as a joke in this novel. Glencora herself teases her husband when he is angry with her over her interference in the Silverbridge election: "Really, you are becoming so autocratic that I shall have to go in for women's rights" (chapter 33). As Juliet McMaster has noted, Trollope's beliefs on this subject seem to be voiced early on in the novel in the politic wisdom of Mrs. Finn, as she converses with that pragmatic Liberal, Barrington Earle:[1]

> "I think upon the whole, Mr. Erle, we women have the best of it."
> "I don't suppose you will go in for your 'rights.'"
> "Not by Act of Parliament, or by platform meeting. I have a great idea of a woman's rights; but that is the way, I think, to throw them away." (Chapter 11)

Both the wit at the expense of women's rights and this definition of "a woman's rights" as a private concern are in tension with Glencora's story, which tells of a woman's thwarted need to find significant work in a male-dominated society. For Glencora, self-realization means establishing a public identity—one that has substance and worth comparable to her husband's. As the narrator comments, Glencora already had more identity and influence than most women could hope to enjoy:

> She already possessed all that rank and wealth could give her, and together with those good things a peculiar position of her own of which she was proud, and which she had made her own not by her wealth or rank, but by a certain fearless energy and power of raillery which never deserted her. . . . One would have been inclined to say that politics were altogether unnecessary to her, and that as Duchess of Omnium, lately known as Lady Glencora Palliser, she had a wider and a pleasanter influence than could belong to any woman as wife of a Prime Minister. And she was essentially one of those women who are not contented to be known simply as the wives of their husbands. She had a celebrity of her own, quite independent of his position, and which could not be enhanced by any glory or any power added to him. (Chapter 6)

But for Glencora, this role as essentially an "ornament of society" is insufficient. She longs for involvement in the world of work, which for her is Parliament, the center of the political arena. As she states to Mrs. Finn, "I'd sit up all night every night of my life,—I'd listen to every debate in the house myself,—to have Plantagenet Prime Minister. I like to be busy" (chapter 6). The very phrasing Glencora uses suggests that it is her new employment of which she is thinking; her husband is almost an afterthought in her declaration. Her speech recalls that of other strong, ambitious women in the Palliser novels: Alice's pronouncement about political life in London— "Were I a man, no earthly consideration should induce me to live elsewhere" (*Can You Forgive Her?*, chapter 3); Lady Laura's poignant statement about Parliament, spoken to Phineas Finn when she is exiled at Dresden, that "you and I understand equally well that no other life is worth having after it" (*Phineas Redux,* chapter 12). The importance with which Glencora views her new position is indicated in her only half-jesting assertion to Mrs. Finn that "I mean to have a cabinet of my own, and I mean that you shall do the foreign affairs" (chapter 6).

The theme of parallel careers further expresses Trollope's ambivalence because it is subversive of the Victorian doctrine of the two spheres, articulated at the beginning of Victoria's reign by Sarah Lewis in her book, *Woman's Mission* (1839), and given its most famous High Victorian expression in Ruskin's "Of Queens' Gardens" (1865). The essence of this idea is that women and men are ordained by God and nature to reign in different "spheres" of life; Woman's "mission" is to rule the domestic sphere through the "influence" of her moral purity, and Man rules the public sphere because of his superior intellect and physical strength.[2] Glencora's story unfolds in a series of skirmishes with her husband in which her ambition to expand beyond the boundaries of her domestic province is frustrated. The first disagreement arises when she wants to be made Mistress of the Robes. Palliser gives as his first objection the restrictions of court life on her free spirit. However, he then gives an answer that clarifies his ideas about her proper role as a married woman:[3] "I may say that in no condition should I wish my wife to be subject to other restraint than that which is common to all married women. I should not choose that she should have any duties unconnected with our joint family and home" (chapter 7). This conventional declaration, informed by the doctrine of the two spheres, introduces a tension crucial to an understanding of the ambivalence about cultural ideals of femininity that Trollope manifests in this novel. On one hand, Trollope endorses Palliser, identifying him in the *Autobiography* as the "perfect gentleman" (300), the embodiment of a complex moral tradition necessary to the stability of England's social structure.[4] However, there is a conflict between Trollope's view of Palliser as the human incarnation of the ideal of civilization, and his recognition that this perfect gentleman limits the aspirations of an intelligent, spirited woman. Despite his admiration for Palliser, Trollope has the honesty to show that there is a cost to the coherence which this ethic provides.

The problem arises in the code of chivalry, which is central to the gentlemanly ideal. Mrs. Finn, always a moral touchstone for Trollope, praises Palliser's character, hailing him as Don Quixote, and even Glencora speaks of his gallantry with admiration: "there is a dash of chivalry about him worthy of the old poets. To him a woman, particularly his own woman, is a thing so fine and so precious that the winds of heaven should hardly be allowed to blow upon her" (chapter 56). Despite these encomia, Trollope criticizes the chivalrous code Palliser stands for through his characterization of Glencora. This code may be appropriate for the Victorian ideal of delicate womanhood in need of male protection, but it is woefully inadequate to cope with Glencora's real personality. In truth, she is tough and audacious enough not only to endure but to enjoy sitting in the gallery when the notorious Lopez payment is discussed and her name may be mentioned. Her husband forbids this indiscretion because it violates the image of modest, delicate womanhood which the gentlemanly view of women posits:

> There never had been, in the memory of them all, a matter that was so interesting to them, for it was the only matter they remembered in which a woman's conduct might probably be called in question in the House of Commons. . . . Had the welfare of the Indian Empire occupied the House, the House would have been empty. But the hope that a certain woman's name would have to be mentioned, crammed it from the floor to the ceiling. (Chapter 57)

In this passage, Trollope emphasizes that the ideal of feminine delicacy is double-edged. Implicit in the comments of the narrator that Parliament would be packed because "a woman's conduct might probably be called in question," and that those attending were buoyed by "the hope that a certain woman's name would have to be mentioned," is the underlying titillation provided by the ideal of modest, chaste womanhood. In her book, *The Proper Lady and the Woman Writer,* Mary Poovey describes the "paradox of chastity/sexuality," as it developed in the eighteenth and nineteenth centuries, in which modesty is construed by men to be "a woman's most effective lure . . . even as modesty was proclaimed to be the most reliable guardian of a woman's chastity—and hence the external sign of her internal integrity—it was also declared to be an advertisement for—and hence an attraction to—her sexuality" (21).[5] The episode of the Lopez payment controversy highlights Trollope's unresolved tensions in relation to his culture's feminine ideals. Trollope approves the Duke's protection of his wife's name, indicating his endorsement of chivalrous conduct. However, his exposure of another, less elevated aspect of the ideal of Woman's purity and the concomitant critique of male perception of this ideal undermine this code. Finally, Trollope shows that as admirable as chivalry is as an ideal, it nevertheless is not only irrelevant but debilitating to a strong woman like Glencora.

In Trollope, at least implicitly, there is a "gentleman question" that is a corollary to the "Woman Question." Necessarily, they are two sides of the same coin, since the feminine ideals of Victorian culture are dependent upon certain assumptions of the gentlemanly ideal. The darker side of chivalry is its dangerous limitation of the power of the weaker sex it is sworn to protect. One can better understand the form Trollope's ambivalence took when one recognizes that Trollope perceived this danger at the same time that he believed that the gentlemanly ideal, implying a certain social structure, was absolutely necessary to civilization.

Another scene which illustrates the tensions in Trollope's attitude toward femininity, particularly in his belief in the doctrine of the two spheres, is the marital argument that follows Glencora's attempts to influence the Silverbridge election, in direct opposition to the Duke's wishes. Palliser voices conventional ideas about the distinct line separating the realms of influence proper for Man and Woman, but the scene's comedy is subversive of those ideas.⁶ Glencora is the victor in this confrontation because her feisty nature refuses to acquiesce in his patronizing authority. The vitality expressed in her jaunty slang serves to ridicule the formal Latin motto in which he justifies his male ascendancy in "public matters"; Trollope ironically suggests the limits to the Duke's grand idea of justice, the gap between it and his idea of fairness with regard to his wife:

> "You know how anxious I am," he began, "that you should share everything with me, even in politics. But in all things there must be one voice that shall be the ruling voice."
> "And that is to be yours,—of course."
> "In such a matter as this it must be."
> "And therefore, I like to do a little business of my own behind your back. It's human nature, and you've got to put up with it. . . . You had better make the best you can of your bargain and not expect too much from her. And don't ride over her with a very high horse. And let her have her own way a little if you really believe that she has your interest at heart."
> ". . . Ruat caelum, fiat—proper subordination from his wife in regard to public matters! No wife had a fuller allowance of privilege, or more complete power in her hands, as to things fit for women's management. But it was intolerable to him that she should seek to interfere with him in matters of a public nature. And she was constantly doing so. . . . Ruat caelum, fiat justitia. Now 'justitia' to him was not compatible with feminine interference in his own special work."
> (Chapter 32)

An even more trenchant critique of the doctrine of the two spheres lies in Trollope's portrayal of Glencora's wholly unconventional nature, a nature at variance with the feminine ideals of Victorian culture. Trollope depicts the tough, pragmatic Glencora as better fitted than her highly scrupulous, hypersensitive husband to endure comfortably in the male sphere of politics, that arena in which men do the "rough work in the open world" of which Ruskin writes in "Of Queens' Gardens." A clue to the unconventionality of Glencora's characterization as a Victorian woman lies in her several bantering comparisons of herself to Lady Macbeth:⁷ "He's Prime Minister, which is a great thing, and I begin to find myself filled to the full with political ambition. I feel myself to be a Lady MacBeth [sic], prepared for the murder of any Duncan or any Daubeny who may stand in my lord's way" (chapter 11). Although the allusion is characteristically extravagant, there are certain traits the two women have in common, as Glencora recognizes. Both wives have "unwomanly" ambitions to be great themselves, which must be channelled into exertion on their husband's behalf. Moreover, Glencora is aware that, like her Shakespearean counterpart, she is less scrupulous than her husband. As she exclaims to Mrs. Finn:

> "They should have made me Prime Minister, and have let him be Chancellor of the Exchequer. I begin to see the ways of Government now. I could have done all the dirty work. I could have given away garters and ribbons, and made my bargains while giving them. I could select sleek, easy bishops who wouldn't be troublesome. I could give pensions or withhold them, and

make the stupid men peers. . . . I could brazen out a job and let the "People's Banners" and the Slides make their worst of it . . . I could do a Mansion House dinner to a marvel. . . . Oh, I do so wish I had the opportunity!" (Chapter 56)

This portrait of the worldly, politic Glencora is very far indeed from the idealized moral figure required by the doctrine of the two spheres. Glencora longs to be immersed in the world's sordid concerns, not to redeem man from them. Her characterization not only points to a limitation in the idea of the two spheres, but it also undermines the ideals that Palliser expects her to uphold. Indeed, there is a subversive element in the characterizations of this husband and wife, because the moral influence is Palliser, far more principled than Glencora, "honour complete from head to foot" (chapter 56), as she ruefully praises him to Mrs. Finn. The ideal of woman as moral teacher is turned upside down in this book. Glencora, in the accents of Lady Macbeth, tries to give lessons to her scrupulous husband on the need to be not quite so upright: "Why blench if your conscience accuses you of no fault? I would not blench if it did" (chapter 51).

The related inversion of the "delicacy" ideal for women is pointed up by the Prime Minister's acute sensitivity to Quintus Slide's attacks in *The People's Banner*. Glencora is the tougher partner, while Palliser is prostrated by the newspaper's assault. In the chapter significantly titled "Coddling the Prime Minister," Glencora complains of her husband to Mrs. Finn: "Men shouldn't be made of Sèvres china, but of good stone earthenware" (chapter 51). That women should be made of the same sturdy material is implicit in Glencora's pronouncement, and overt in her behavior. She certainly shows herself to be "good stone earthenware"; her words to Mrs. Finn might have been spoken by a brave emigrant gentlewoman: "Let me bear it. My back is broad enough" (chapter 51). As Glencora exclaims to her husband in exasperation:

> "I sometimes think, Plantagenet, that I should have been the man, my skin is so thick; and that you should have been the woman, yours is so tender."
> "You say that I am thin-skinned."
> "Certainly you are. What people call a delicate organization,—whereas I am rough and thick and monstrously commonplace."
> "Then should you too be thin-skinned for my sake."
> "I wish I could make you thick-skinned for your own. It's the only way to be decently comfortable in such a coarse, rough-and-tumble world as this is." (Chapter 42)

The irony of this situation is clear. In an explicit reversal of the idea of the two spheres, Glencora is portrayed as the marital partner better adapted to the "coarse, rough-and-tumble" world, the sphere of business and politics, although her husband is constantly trying to confine her energies to the home sphere, the Ruskinian Queens' Gardens. The irony created by the implicit comparison of reality versus doctrine is deepened by another reversal of an ideal for Victorian womanhood, that of woman as child. Palliser is acting like a child, as his moping and his need for "coddling" (pointed up in the title Trollope gives this chapter) explicitly demonstrate, but he insists upon treating Glencora as if *she* were the child. He both chastises and indulges her. With the ideal of woman as irresponsible child in mind, he condescendingly explains to Glencora that wives "may do foolish things, dear; and yet . . . not interfere in politics" (chapter 51).

Trollope's irony continues as he portrays the husband's uneasy reaction to the wife's success in the public sphere. Palliser begins to suspect that "Lady Glencora, of whose wild impulses and general impracticability he had always been in dread . . . was Prime Minister rather than he himself" (chapter 18), so he simply divests her of her public role, asserting his marital authority as a parent orders a child, in order to return her to the domestic sphere. When Trollope underscores the husband's sense of being threatened by his realization that "in such a state of things he of course, as her husband, must be nominal Prime Minister" (chapter 18), he makes the subversive inference that the doctrine of the two spheres and the ideal of Woman as Child are motivated by male fear of women. He suggests that they are at bottom self-serving, keeping women dependent rather than competitive. When Glencora does act with the impulsiveness of a child, as in the Lopez entanglement, Trollope indicates that her capricious behavior stems from her lack of real power to influence that outer sphere. She rebels against Palliser's patriarchal authority because, as an adult, she refuses to be as powerless as a child.

Yet, while Trollope indicates that the ideal of woman as child is used as an excuse for denying women power, his fond portrayal of the charm of the childlike aspect of Glencora's personality suggests his own ambivalent attitude toward the Child-Woman ideal. He perceives Glencora's childishness as a double-edged quality: on one hand, it is a source of her energy, spontaneity, charm and sense of fun; on the other hand, it is a source of the impulsive gestures that get her into some of her more notable scrapes. She is, after all, wrong about interfering for Lopez in the Silverbridge election, both in principle and in her judgment of the man himself. Trollope doesn't seem to find childishness charming in mature gentlemen. There is no prominent example of a mature ideal man in all of Trollope who is capricious—certainly not Palliser, nor his counterpart in the Emily plot of the novel, Arthur Fletcher, nor John Grey, the hero of *Can You Forgive Her?*. Although in earlier novels, heroes such as the "hobbledehoy" Johnny Eames (*The Small House at Allington*) and young Frank Gresham (*Doctor Thorne*) are beloved by Trollope in their boyhood, in the Palliser novels, only Phineas and Silverbridge (*The Duke's Children*) are looked upon with fondness in their wild, impetuous days.[8] Moreover, their wayward behavior is seen as immaturity, and they outgrow it when they become ideal gentlemen. Perhaps Glencora is created with the conventional feminine flaws of impetuosity and willfulness, so that her ambitions to rule the state are undercut by our question as to her fitness to realize them. If Trollope had placed the wise, politic Madame Max in Glencora's position, one can see how much less equivocal his criticism of social prohibitions for Woman would have been. However, as I discussed in the last chapter, Trollope created the perfect statesman in Madame Max, but he made her content to find fulfillment in the equality of her marriage to Phineas.

If Trollope's ambivalence toward the idea of separate spheres for men and women is evident in his undermining of the Woman-as-Child ideal, it is more obvious still in his treatment of the ideal of feminine self-denial, the ideal which is at the heart of the doctrine of the two spheres. While Sarah Lewis and John Ruskin view Christlike self-renunciation as the source of "Woman's influence," Glencora is interested in exerting political, not moral influence. Ruskin proclaims that the moral influence a self-sacrificing woman radiates from her domestic province constitutes "the woman's true place and power," but it is clear that Glencora desires not this "queenly power," but the political power reserved for men. As she declares to Mrs. Finn: "They should have made me Prime Minister. . . . Oh, I do so wish I had the opportunity!" (chapter 56). However, because Glencora is prohibited by her sex from seeking direct authority, she must work through indirection, through politic, coercive feminine influence rather than by means of the pure moral radiance that Lewis and Ruskin had in mind. Glencora's unprincipled machinations illustrate J. S. Mill's dictum in *The Subjection of Women* (1869) that "where there is least liberty, the passion for power is the most ardent and unscrupulous" (Mill, 167).

One of the most unconventional elements of Glencora's story is that it concerns a woman's ambition to be great herself, not just to shine with reflected glory from her husband. As Glencora expresses it to Mrs. Finn when she advises Glencora to cease her endeavors because of the Duke's vexation: "She, too, wished to be written of in memoirs, and to make a niche for herself in history. And now she was told that she was to let it 'die out!'" (chapter 18). The greatest conflict Glencora faces is that she needs to create and sustain a public identity separate from her husband's, but neither marital partner can identify this yearning as what it is: self-aggrandizing ambition, rather than an impulse to further her husband's career. It is clear that Palliser's generous but rather inaccurate construction of his wife's motives in opening up Gatherum is colored not by knowledge of Glencora's nature, but by an ideal of woman as self-sacrificing minister to others' needs. This conversation points up how different the husband's idyllic view of domesticity is from the wife's perception of the home as undesirable confinement:

> "And I should wish you to go with me, when we do go to Matching."
> "Oh, Plantagenet," said the wife, "what a Darby and Joan kind of thing you like to have it!"
> "Yes, I do. The Darby and Joan kind of thing is what I like."
> "Only Darby is to be in an office all day, and in Parliament all night,—and Joan is to stay at home."
> "Would you wish me not to be in an office, and not to be in Parliament? But don't let us misunderstand each other. You are doing the best you can to further what you think to be my interests."
> "I am," said the Duchess.

"I love you the better for it, day by day." This is so surprised her, that as she took him by the arm, her eyes were filled with tears. "I know that you are working for me quite as hard as I work myself, and that you are doing so with the pure ambition of seeing your husband a great man."
"And myself a great man's wife."
"It is the same thing." (Chapter 18)

However, despite the affection the couple feel for one another, it's not, of course, "the same thing."[9] Although Glencora insists here on her own ambition, at times she finds she can defend her actions, both to herself and to others, only by wrapping herself in the mantle of self-sacrificing womanhood. As she pleads to the Duke of St. Bungay, after her husband's outraged reaction to Major Pountney's impudence has given him cause to shut down the festivities at Gatherum: "I have endeavoured to make his home pleasant to people, in order that they might look upon him with grace and favour. Is that wrong? Is that unbecoming a wife?" (chapter 28). But her real motives, as Trollope makes clear, are very different. In a telling passage in which Glencora mentally rehearses her wrongs, although she begins by defending herself as servitor of her husband, in the very next sentence she questions the necessity of that premier wifely duty; in the following sentence she asks why she should be judged by special feminine standards at all, rather than in the same way men are valued out in the world—by success or failure: "All that she did,—was it not for his sake? And why should she not have her ambition in life as well as he his? And had she not succeeded in all that she had done?" (chapter 32).

Indeed, when she is compelled by her husband to relinquish her role as political hostess, when "his domestic authority sufficed to shut up Gatherum for the time," she feels that he has stripped her of identity, because she has come to measure herself by the male standard of public achievement: "He, at any rate, was Prime Minister, and it seemed to her that she was to be reduced to nothing" (chapter 42). In Glencora's thoughts, we hear echoings of Violet Effingham's bantering response to Phineas Finn's remark that "a man should try to be something": "And a woman can be content to be nothing . . . unless Mr. Mill can pull us through!" (*Phineas Finn,* chapter 59). Although this jest of Violet's has always been taken to indicate Trollope's opposition to political, organized feminism,[10] it seems to me that it is consciously echoed throughout the Palliser series. Within *Phineas Finn* itself, it can be heard in Lady Laura's bitter comment after her separation from her husband that "I am nobody,—or worse than nobody" (chapter 75), a realization that deepens when she is compelled to exile herself in Dresden to avoid her husband's legal right to claim her body as his property (*Phineas Redux*). In the other novels of the series, Violet's words ramify from Kate's exclamation to Alice in *Can You Forgive Her?* that when George marries, "I should have literally nothing to do in the world; literally nothing—nothing—nothing!" (*Can You Forgive Her?,* chapter 6) to Glencora's thoughts in the passage quoted, to Lady Mabel's remarks at the end of *The Duke's Children,* first to Silverbridge when he refuses to marry her ("And I am nothing" [chapter 59]) and then to Tregear, when she asserts that she has "no other affairs" than her isolation and her dispossession (chapter 77). The fact that a woman's identity can be conferred or taken away by a man—husband, brother, suitor, father—causes Violet's joke to resound differently in the reader's memory by the conclusion of the Palliser series. A wife is disgraced, and reduced to living in exile in order to escape her husband's tyranny; a sister lives for her brother, who sees her only as a pawn in his machinations; a Prime Minister can divest his wife of her public role with a word; the heir to a dukedom can deny title and position to his former love (for now we leave aside the question of his justification); a degraded earl and his brutish son can disinherit the family's highly gifted daughter. Perhaps Mr. Mill *is* the man to turn to.

This resonance of Glencora's thoughts throughout the Palliser novels exemplifies an important aspect of Trollope's fictional method. In his fine article on the thematic structure of Trollope's novels, Jerome Thale describes Trollope's method of organization as dependent upon "parallels, contrasts, repetitions with slight variations" (149). Thale's definition of Trollope's structural principles within a single novel can be expanded to explain the method of organization within groups of novels that are meant to be read as one work: first, the novels of the Barsetshire series, and second, the novels of the Palliser series. Thale defines this compositional technique as "panoramic" (155). He quotes Aldous Huxley's famous passage on the "musicalization of fiction" (*Point Counter Point,* chapter 22) to explain how this technique embodies what Thale calls the "comprehensive vision." Thale states that in Trollope's work, this vision "had its function in reminding us of the complexity of human affairs, of urging tolerance, of making us wary of simple views and monisms" (157).[11] This broadening of the reader's vision is precisely what occurs with the statements about being "nothing" that Trollope's women make during the course of the Palliser novels. Their accretive effect is to question the lack of public roles and public power for women, and to darken the ironical tone of Violet's jest.[12]

In a poignant, contradictory speech, Glencora tries to explain to Mrs. Finn why she needs a public role. It is worthwhile to look closely at this apologia, because the guilty confusion exemplified in Glencora's explanation points up the psychological damage wrought by the expectation placed upon Victorian womanhood that their "nature and mission" is to serve others at their own expense. In its denial of ambition to go beyond prescribed roles for women, and its concomitant vindication of her individual identity, Glencora reveals both her desire to fulfill Victorian cultural ideals of femininity, and the impossibility of self-realization if she does fulfill these ideals:

> "I can't live with him, because he shuts himself up reading blue books, and is always at his office or at the House; but I would if I could. Am I not doing it all for him? . . . Think of your life and of mine. You have had lovers. . . . I am Duchess of Omnium, and I am the wife of the Prime Minister, and I had a larger property of my own than any other young woman that ever was born; and I am myself, too,—Glencora M'Cluskie that was, and I've made for myself a

character that I'm not ashamed of. But I'd be the curate's wife tomorrow, and make puddings, if I could only have my own husband and my own children with me. What's the use of it all?'' (Chapter 37)

The centerpiece of this speech is Glencora's declaration of her identity. She carefully names her public roles—Duchess of Omnium, wife of the Prime Minister—titles acquired through her marriage, and dependent upon her husband's position. Going back into the past, she concludes with a definition of Glencora as a private, separate self, ''Glencora M'Cluskie that was,'' who has created a public character quite apart from her husband's titles.[13] But this assertion of an independent self is in conflict with all the feminine ideals of her culture. The rest of the speech tries to defend Glencora's acts of self-realization as acts of womanly self-sacrifice.

The first statement Glencora makes indicates that her need for a public role stems partly from a feeling that she has failed in her private role of wife. She feels dissatisfied with her marriage, and she feels guilty because she feels dissatisfied. She makes a candid admission, given Victorian standards of censorship, that she and her husband are incompatible in more than temperament; ''I can't live with him'' seems to connote sexual distance as well.[14] The lack of romance and sexuality in her marriage to the dry Duke is implicit in her demand to Mrs. Finn: ''Think of your life and of mine. You have had lovers.'' One of the reasons that Glencora so strongly desires success in her worldly endeavors is that they are, for her, a substitute for passion, and a public means to be devoted to her husband in a way that she cannot be in private. As the Duke of St. Bungay has shrewdly noted, ''It now seemed to him that though she had failed to love the man, she had given her entire heart to the Prime Minister'' (chapter 66).

Because she feels guilty about her failure to be the loving wife required by the ideals of her culture, Glencora justifies her public role by appealing to the feminine ideal of self-sacrifice: ''Am I not doing it all for him?'' This question echoes her defense to the Duke of St. Bungay—''Is that unbecoming a wife?'' (chapter 28)—and to herself—'''All that she did—was it not for his sake?'' (chapter 32). She insists that *she* wants simple domesticity, to be ''the curate's wife tomorrow, and make puddings, if I could only have my own husband and my own children with me.'' In the creation of an illusory vision of domesticity as retreat, the terms she uses—''make puddings,'' ''my own husband,'' ''my own children''—lapse defensively into other ideals central to the doctrine of the two spheres, that of domestic manager and wife-mother. Her pronouncement that she prefers domesticity to public affairs is belied when the Duke later defines *his* domestic idyll to her, declaring that ''I am dreaming always of some day when we may go away together with the children, and rest in some pretty spot, and live as other people live.'' Her response discloses her true feelings: ''It would be very stupid'' (chapter 51).

The irony that Trollope emphasizes is that *neither* the Duke nor the Duchess is satisfied with the domestic sphere, although both romanticize it. He suggests that its power is that of cultural myth, and that it is in fact just that—a myth. He shows that only Glencora, as a woman, wife and mother, must feel guilty for her dissatisfaction, because only she is failing to live up to the cultural ideals for her sex. The duke's ideal of private domesticity is not what he really wants, either. When he is no longer Prime Minister, and his dream of a life centered around hearth and home can become a reality, he laments to himself that "there could be nothing for him now until the insipidity of life should gradually fade away into the grave" (chapter 72). However, he has already recognized by this time that the Duchess is not suited to a life of dull domesticity. He reproachfully comments to her that "whatever may be my feelings, I hardly think that you are fitted for that kind of thing" (chapter 42).

The domestic retreat may be illusory, yet in Glencora's mind, it is comforting proof that she has not abandoned her proper sphere by choice—especially now that the public sphere has also proven unsatisfying. Her final plaintive "What's the use of it all?" reveals her disappointment with public efforts. These words reverberate until the end of the novel, when Glencora informally renounces her public function, in the final words we hear her say: "I shall never again think that I can help to rule England by coaxing unpleasant men. It is done and gone, and can never come back again" (chapter 80).

Trollope's ambivalence is expressed in a tension between this final retreat back into the domestic sphere, and his exploration of Glencora's frustration not only with the ideal of feminine self-sacrifice, but with the limits upon self-realization that are set by all cultural ideals for Victorian womanhood. In an earlier conversation, Mrs. Finn pronounces upon a related feminine ideal, that of Woman as Redeemer, as moral savior to sinful Man. The two women are discussing the Duke; Mrs. Finn speaks first:

> "You ought to love him."
> "I do—but what's the use of it? He is a god, but I am not a goddess; and then, though he is a god, he is a dry, silent, uncongenial and uncomfortable god. It would have suited me much better to have married a sinner. But then the sinner that I would have married was so irredeemable a scapegrace."
> "I do not believe in a woman marrying a bad man in the hope of making him good."
> (Chapter 56)

In the last chapter I quoted Violet Effingham saying much the same thing— "I do not believe in girls being saviours to men" (*Phineas Finn,* chapter 19)— and her accents can be heard in Mrs. Finn's words. Violet's voice, proclaiming to Lady Laura that she has "a dragon of her own driving her ever the wrong way," (*Phineas Finn,* chapter 10) can also be heard in Glencora's declaration of her unangelic nature, of her closer affinity to the "sinner" than to the "god." These statements throughout the Palliser novels, spoken by the women Trollope most admires, undermine all those fictional Victorian heroines who sacrifice themselves in order to be the salvation of some erring man, from Dickens's Louisa Gradgrind in *Hard Times,* who marries the despised Mr. Bounderby in order to serve her delinquent brother Tom, to Helen in Anne Brontë's *The Tenant of Wildfell Hall,* who learns to rue the day she married the dissolute Huntingdon.

Trollope also has some acute perceptions about the fictional embodiments of another feminine ideal, the efficient domestic manager.[15] This ideal informs all those asexual housekeepers in Victorian fiction, from Nelly Dean, with her shining, well-ordered kitchen (opposed to the dark, chaotic mysteries of the bedroom associated with Catherine), to Esther Summerson, cheerfully clinking her enormous ring of keys. In his characterization of Glencora, Trollope subverts this admirable model by making it pretty obvious that the imprisoned source of energy motivating her—and all those busy women—is sexual frustration. Glencora is unable to love the "dry, silent, uncongenial and uncomfortable" Duke passionately, although "she revered, admired, and almost loved him" (chapter 18). In the public role of political hostess, Glencora sublimates what is obviously sexual energy, as she unconsciously assumes the role of superior domestic manager, looking after the sheets and towels at Gatherum in a life "of incessant work" (chapter 19).

Not only Glencora's political aspirations, but her desire to influence others' love affairs can be attributed to the lack of passion in her own life. She needs the vicarious experience of passion, seeming to recreate her own lost possibilities in the experiences of others. Throughout the Palliser series, Glencora has intrigued in others' love affairs. In *Can You Forgive Her?* she suggests that Alice encourage the attentions of Plantagenet's cousin, Jeffrey Palliser, and later gives support to John Grey when he follows Alice to Lucerne, promising to "give him her most cordial co-operation" (chapter 70). In *The Eustace Diamonds,* Glencora (and everyone else, it's true) avidly follows Lizzie Eustace's romantic ventures. In *Phineas Redux,* Glencora acts as *dea ex machina* to an impoverished cousin, Adelaide Palliser, and her lackadaisical lover, Gerard Maule, diverting the old Duke's legacy to Madame Max into a dowry for Adelaide, and she also delights in the love between Madame Max (now her closest friend) and Phineas. In *The Prime Minister,* Glencora interests herself first in Lopez and his love for Emily Wharton, and then in Arthur Fletcher's love for Emily. Finally, in *The Duke's Children,* after Glencora has died, we discover that she has encouraged the engagement between her daughter, Mary, and the Burgo-like Tregear, the discovery of which finally compels the Duke to confront the dissatisfactions Glencora felt during their marriage.

Despite her former blithe success, on both occasions in *The Prime Minister* when Glencora tries to influence others' love affairs, her efforts are unfulfilling for her, reflecting all her undertakings in this book. Glencora's first romantic intervention, her countenancing of Lopez, helps him to overcome the opposition of Abel Wharton to his marriage with Emily. Glencora's ironic reward occurs twice: first when Lopez, the Duchess's "new swan" (chapter 21) is offensive at her garden party at the Horns, metamorphosing into a very ugly duckling indeed, as he berates his wife publicly for her friendliness toward Arthur Fletcher; again when he commits suicide at Tenway Junction, about which Glencora says: "I have a feeling, you know, that among us we made the train run over him" (chapter 76). Moreover, the influence she tries to give Lopez for the Silverbridge election precipitates the major marital crisis of the book between Palliser and Glencora.

Glencora's other vicarious romantic involvement is a result of this entanglement with Lopez. Motivated partly by a longing to make restitution for any fault in that affair, she attempts to persuade Emily to marry Arthur Fletcher. Glencora embarks upon her "mission" to Manchester Square, "intent on performing good offices on behalf of the widow" (chapter 77). Trollope explicitly uses the terms of the "two spheres" doctrine when describing Glencora's visit to Emily. Glencora is the Angel-out-of-the-House, whose "mission" is philanthropy.[16] According to Victorian doctrine, she should be particularly well-suited to these errands of mercy because of the sympathetic qualities of her feminine nature. However, Glencora fails to influence that intransigent widow Emily, who is determined upon enacting a course of expiation of her own:

> The Duchess when she went away suffered under a sense of failure. . . . She had intended to bring about some crisis of female tenderness in which she might have rushed into future hopes and joyous anticipations, and with the freedom which will come from ebullitions of feeling have told the widow that the peculiar circumstances of her position would not only justify her in marrying this other man but absolutely called upon her to do it. (Chapter 77)

The intensely emotional, almost amorous language with which Glencora's intentions are defined ("crisis of female tenderness," "rushed into future hopes and joyous anticipations") strongly suggests that for Glencora, these involvements are also directly romantic, opening up her constricted emotional life to "the freedom which will come from ebullitions of feeling." In this way, Trollope suggests that Glencora's vicarious romances are a serious attempt at self-realization rather than philanthropic efforts issuing from peculiarly feminine sympathy and self-sacrifice, and he thus subverts the conventional view of woman's "mission."

In his exploration of the possibilities from which Glencora may choose according to the ideals of Victorian womanhood, Trollope undermines another ideal in his ironic comparison of Glencora to the epitome of the ornament of society ideal of femininity, the Marchioness of Hartletop, née Griselda Grantly. When Glencora's role of political hostess is attacked by her husband, who accuses her of vulgarity in her grand entertainments at Gatherum, she is driven to consider a retreat into a merely ornamental role: "Would it not be better to give it all up, and be a great woman, une grande dame, of another kind,—difficult of access, sparing of her favors, aristocratic to the backbone,—a very Duchess of duchesses?" (chapter 19).

We know what Trollope thought of this feminine ideal from his portrait of that very "grande dame," Griselda, whose impassive mien and emotional vacuity he pillories in at least four novels.[17] In this characterization, he subverts all those fictional grand ladies of the previous era's "silver fork" novels as well as the later heroines of the novelist "Ouida" (Marie Louise de la Ramée) who are exemplars of the ideal of decorative womanhood. At the same time, Trollope leagues himself with socially concerned Victorian novelists writing since the forties in his rejection of this ideal. The creation of Griselda, although in the comic mode, is motivated by the same impulse to undermine the Victorian Lady as "ornament of society" that is given serious expression in very different forms in Charlotte Brontë's Blanche Ingram, Dickens' Estella and Lady Dedlock (or in the satiric portrait of Mrs. Merdle), or Thackeray's Beatrix Esmond and Ethel Newcome, or George Eliot's Rosamond Vincy or Gwendolen Harleth.

In his questioning of the various ideals proposed for Victorian womanhood, Trollope perceives another alternative to the conflict between woman's self-realization and the feminine self-sacrifice required by the doctrine of the two spheres. He suggests the possibility of mutuality in marriage, a kind of give-and-take in which there is no mastering. The mutual affection in the Pallisers' union is another thread interwoven in the fabric of this marriage, which crosses those of Glencora's struggle for self-rule and her husband's insistence on dominance as his male birthright. In several tableaux throughout the Palliser series, Trollope sets up a juxtaposition between a marital scene in which the husband is exercising his institutionalized male prerogative of superior authority, and a second scene, into which the first dissolves, and which is a resolution of the first, in which authority is replaced by mutuality. The very structure of these scenes suggests that Trollope is more sympathetic to marital equality than has been recognized by critics who take the statements he makes in private letters or public forums to represent his deepest convictions.[18] This critical stance disregards the implications of the fiction, and it does not take into account the likelihood that Trollope would create a conventional persona when expounding on the issue of sexual relations to an audience of Victorian gentlemen, whether it be one or many.

In *Can You Forgive Her?* the first of these passages occurs in the chapter, "The Pallisers at Breakfast" (chapter 58), the morning after Lady Monk's ball. At the end of that evening, Glencora has declared "with more of defiance in her tone than Mr. Palliser had ever hitherto heard," that she will never again see her despised guardians, Mrs. Marsham and Mr. Bott, "in her own house." In response, Palliser makes an appointment with his wife for breakfast, announcing that "I have work still to do tonight, and I will not disturb you by coming to your room," characteristically choosing to make their encounter verbal rather than sexual. Glencora spends the night alone, crouched before the fire, brooding upon whether she should leave her husband.[19]

Palliser has set himself the task of scolding his recalcitrant wife because "she had defied him,—defied him by saying she would see his friends no more; and it was the remembrance of this . . . that made him feel that he could not pass in silence over what had been done." However, the scene of conjugal authority ends in an embrace between the couple, after Glencora has declared her love for Burgo and her willingness to sacrifice—even destroy—herself, so that Palliser might marry again and have an heir.[20] The change from authority to mutuality is imaged in the altered stance of the couple and in his quiet declaration of love in answer to her passionate exclamations of despair:

> He was a tall man and she was short of stature, so that he stood over her and looked upon her, and now she was looking up into his face with all her eyes. "I would," she said. "I would—I would! What is there left for me that I should wish to live?"
> Softly, slowly, very gradually, as though he were afraid of what he was doing, he put his arm round her waist. "You are wrong in one thing," he said. "I do love you." (*Can You Forgive Her?*, chapter 58)

The scene ends in the first mutual sacrifice the couple makes, as Palliser gives up his long-cherished hope to be Chancellor of the Exchequer in exchange for Glencora's tacit promise that she will try to love him, or at least try to keep the marriage together. Their trip abroad, beginning as an escape from Burgo, marks a turning point in their relations which results in Glencora's pregnancy.

A tableau with much more marked implications of patriarchal authority manifested in both stance and gesture occurs in *The Prime Minister*.[21] This scene takes place after the Duke receives the grievance letter from Lopez:

> When he came in she had been seated on a sofa, which she constantly used herself, and he had stood over her, masterful, imperious, and almost tyrannical. She felt his tyranny, but resented it less than usual,—or rather had been less determined in holding her own against him and asserting herself as his equal,—because she confessed to herself she had injured him. She had, she thought, done but little, but that which she had done had produced this injury. So she had sat and endured the oppression of his standing posture. (Chapter 42)

However, the husband's reprimand ends in a very different posture: "But now he sat down by her, very close to her, and put his hand upon her shoulder, almost round her waist." And that change in his physical position obviously reflects his altered mental attitude, from a demand for obedience to a request for understanding:

> "I wish you would think that in all that you do you are dealing with my feelings, with my heartstrings, with my reputation. You cannot divide yourself from me; nor, for the value of it all, would I wish that such division were possible. . . . Let us both do our best," he said, now putting his arm round her and kissing her. (Chapter 42)

The Duke's words, as well as the embrace and kiss, indicate a kind of recognition of equality in the relationship of husband and wife. He does not treat her like a child, but instead appeals to Glencora's reason when he says, "I wish you would think." The concluding words, "let us both do our best," acknowledge mutual responsibility for marital concord, rather than expecting emotional peace to depend on the sacrifices of the wife. A similar change in their relation from confrontation to rapprochement is evident in the scene of mutual comforting that occurs when the Duke's ministry is at an end, and both their ambitions have been thwarted:

Lady Glencora
(Illustration by E. Taylor)

"Before God, my first wish is to free you from the misfortune I have brought on you."
(Illustration by E. Taylor)

> "Yes;—Othello's occupation will be gone, for awhile; for awhile." Then she came up to him and put both her hands on his breast. "But Othello, I shall not be all unhappy."
> "Where will be your contentment?"
> "In you. It was making you ill. Rough people, whom the tenderness of your nature could not well endure, tread upon you, and worried you with their teeth and wounded you everywhere. I could have turned at them again with my teeth, and given them worry for worry; but you could not. Now you will be saved from them, and so I shall not be discontented...."
> "Then I will be contented too," he said as he kissed her. (Chapter 72)

But of course neither of them *is* contented. The narrator comments with more than a touch of irony that the Duke "feared that it was all over with him, and that for the rest of his days he must simply be the Duke of Omnium" (chapter 73). The Duchess laments, only half in jest, that she is "almost as much divorced as Catherine, and have had my head cut off as completely as Anne Bullen" (chapter 73). As usual, Glencora's joking analogy is pointed, as it was when she compared herself to Lady Macbeth. First, she was able to love the Prime Minister more than she ever could love the private man, Plantagenet Palliser; when he no longer plays that public role, she does feel, if not "divorced," certainly less passionately committed to him. But the irony of Glencora's statement is that her "divorce" is not from her husband at all, but from her public career. She realizes that her reign is over for good, that "it is done and gone, and can never come back again" (chapter 80). That unconventional avenue to self-realization is now closed to her forever. This loss of the public role that has become an important part of her identity makes her feel that she has "had my head cut off as completely as Anne Bullen." In contrast, the ending is hopeful for the Duke, whose last words in the novel are in direct contrast to Glencora's: "But I will endeavor to look forward to a time when I may again perhaps be of some humble use" (chapter 80).

In an overtly conventional resolution, Glencora will remain in the domestic sphere now, while it is clear that the Duke will eventually return to the public sphere. Glencora's rebellious attempt to achieve power and identity in a male world has failed. But in the very telling of her story, Trollope has questioned all those patriarchal assumptions that have caused her defeat.

Moreover, the tale of her quest for self-realization does not end here. Toward the end of the novel, Glencora says to Mrs. Finn: "I'm almost sick of schemes. Oh, dear, I wish I knew something that was really pleasant to do. I never really enjoyed anything since I was in love, and I only liked that because it was wicked" (chapter 72). But Glencora, with characteristic energy, does find something else that is "really pleasant to do," when, unknown to the Duke, she encourages the love between her daughter, Mary, and Mary's Burgo-like lover, Francis Tregear (*The Duke's Children*). This is her last act of rebellion, overtly "wicked" because she knows her husband would disapprove of the poor commoner, Tregear, as a lover for Mary, but much more subtly "wicked" because her imaginative absorption in the passion of these lovers allows her to relive her own intense desire for Burgo. Glencora's fulfillment exists, in the end, only in her own mind—and in Trollope's—and this is the subject of the next chapter.

The sympathy with which Trollope portrays Glencora's attempt to oppose cultural ideals of femininity is reinforced in the story of Emily Wharton, the novel's other heroine. Emily, unlike Glencora, conventionally wants only to be a wife and mother; when she questions the conventional assumptions that underlie her husband's tyranny, Glencora's heterodox ambition is given increased credence. Emily's marriage to Lopez offers a double-edged perspective on Glencora's union with Palliser, and this ambivalent attitude exemplifies Trollope's divided mind on the subject of the feminine ideals which were at the foundation of Victorian marriage.

On one hand, Trollope's sympathy with Glencora is deepened by comparing her marital rebellion to Emily's fight against Lopez' crude oppression, because both husbands rely on patriarchal institutions for their power. Trollope shadows Palliser's gentlemanly attitudes about the proper role for women with their ungentlemanlike extreme in Lopez to show just what the implications can be. In the marriage of Lopez and Emily, Trollope examines a husband's power over his wife when it is not restrained by the code of the gentleman. This display of violent power in the Lopez marriage illuminates the identical power and potential for violence in the Palliser marriage, forces which are controlled by the gentlemanly ethic.

On the other hand, this comparison paradoxically places Glencora's final acquiescence in a more favorable light. The Lopez marriage clarifies what civilization would become without the ideal of the gentleman, the ideal that Palliser embodies. Ultimately, Trollope decides that, understandable as it may be, society cannot afford women's rebellion, so Glencora is returned to the domestic sphere, and Emily is matched the second time around with Arthur Fletcher, a true gentleman. Trollope concludes that the price of limited self-realization that both Glencora and Emily pay for a stable society is worth it, arbitrary and unfortunate as it may be. Ultimately, for Trollope, the cost of civilization is Woman's sacrifice.

While Glencora's marriage begins as an act of submission to patriarchal authority, Emily rebels against her father and her people in choosing her husband. She is a member of an ancient, clannish gentry family. Her father, Abel Wharton, is a wealthy and successful barrister who has risen to be a judge. As defined by the tribe's oldest woman, Mrs. Fletcher, the duties of the Wharton and Fletcher womenfolk are clear: "among these duties the chiefest of them incumbent on females was that of so restraining their affections that they should never damage the good cause by leaving it. They might marry within the pale,—or remain single, as might be their lot" (chapter 26).

Emily does neither of these things. Instead, she marries Ferdinand Lopez, a Portuguese "adventurer," as her father terms him (chapter 5). In the decision that most determines a woman's life, Emily chooses to assert an identity separate from her clan's. The narrator acknowledges the importance of this decision for a woman, as the choice determining the quality of her marital career:

> Like other girls she had been taught to presume that it was her destiny to be married, and like other girls she had thought much about her destiny. A young man generally regards it as his destiny either to succeed or to fail in the world, and he thinks about that. To him marriage, when it comes,

is an accident to which he has hardly as yet given a thought. But to the girl the matrimony which is or is not to be her destiny contains within itself the only success or failure which she anticipates. (Chapter 5)

Trollope's ambivalence toward cultural ideals of femininity is reflected in the tension between the narrator's statement, which seems to accept the status quo with regard to the respective position of the sexes, and the implications of Emily's story. One of the narrative structures by which Trollope demonstrates the inequity of the sexes' possibilities is a comparison of Emily's career to that of her brother, Everett, whose "destiny" is comfortably taken care of by the end of the novel. Much as he did in Glencora's story, when he compared the parallel careers of the Prime Minister and his wife, in Emily's story, Trollope compares the careers of a man and a woman of equal social stature, this time siblings rather than marital partners. In contrast to the debacle of Emily's marriage to Lopez, Everett becomes the heir to Sir Alured Wharton and the husband of his daughter, Mary. Trollope makes it clear that this difference in the siblings' fates is arbitrary, based entirely on gender rather than on merit; although Everett is condescending toward Emily, the narrator states flatly that "the sister . . . was endowed with infinitely finer gifts than his" (chapter 2). While Emily, as a daughter, must rebel in order to exert power and define her identity, Everett, as an eldest son, simply inherits traditional male prerogatives with his role as squire.

This disparity between the experiences of sister and brother contributes to a tension between the narrator's apparently reasonable explanation of Victorian gender expectations, and the fate of not only Emily and Everett, but also of all the men and women of the novel. While Glencora and Emily are frustrated in their attempts to rebel against conventional expectations for women, the Trollopian gentlemen in the book either triumph resoundingly or are given hope of success. Arthur Fletcher gets the girl and a seat in Parliament, with far more justification than there is for Everett's success in both the public and private spheres, but with a good deal more struggle. The Duke will most likely go back into office. Abel Wharton's world is finally coherent again, with his son married to the proper Wharton and heir to the squire, and his daughter married to "the very pearl of the Fletcher tribe."

Why does Emily marry Lopez in the first place? Several passages in the story suggest that she is trying to rebel against the traditional expectations of her clan, as pronounced in old Mrs. Fletcher's statement. First, Emily has formed her attachment without the knowledge of her father, although she must know that he will be displeased by her choice of Lopez as a suitor. She goes to the Zoological Gardens with him, but as Abel Wharton says, "I heard about the Gardens. But I heard nothing of the man" (chapter 4). Second, the long description of Arthur Fletcher as "the very pearl of the Fletcher tribe" (chapter 15) clearly identifies him as not just a part of the Wharton-Fletcher clan, but its embodiment. Emily rejects him repeatedly, although it is evident that she is at least subliminally aware of his superiority to Lopez: "For a moment the idea of a comparison between the two men forced itself upon her,—but she drove it from her as she hurried back to the house" (chapter 17). This passage recalls Alice's pointed rejoinder when Kate praises George at the expense of John Grey; to Kate's scornful pronouncement that "It is Hyperion to a Satyr," Alice questions, "And which is the Satyr?" (*Can You Forgive Her?*, chapter 6). Alice's irony indicates that she also recognizes which of her lovers is the finer man. Emily, like Alice, makes an unwise choice because she needs to establish her identity. She wants to be more than a piece of property necessary to the continuance of the Whartons and Fletchers, the role defined for the clan's "womenfolk" by old Mrs. Fletcher.[22]

Emily is attracted to Lopez largely because he *is* an outsider, a foreigner. She equates marriage to Lopez, the unworthy suitor, with expansion of her possibilities beyond what is familiar to her, much as James's later heroine, Isabel Archer, does when she chooses the insidious Gilbert Osmond. And at first, her experiences seem to her to justify her marital choice. Emily is initiated into the realm of sexuality by Lopez, and her affectionate manner to him suggests that that experience is satisfying. The newly married couple tour Europe together, study Italian, and "everything had been as yet delightful to Emily" (chapter 25).

But Emily soon discovers that she has made a bad bargain. She has exchanged the benevolent mastery of her social enclave's dictates for women for the tyranny of marriage with the unprincipled Lopez. Trollope's ambivalence toward the cultural ideals of womanhood that underlie both sets of rules lies in the tension between his subversion of these ideals as they operate in the Lopez marriage, and his acceptance of essentially those same ideals when they are proposed in the civilized realm of the Fletcher-Wharton clan, the world of the Gentleman. Within the Lopez union, Trollope sympathetically chronicles Emily's gradual realizations about Lopez' character, and the necessity that she establish her own identity, guided by her own intelligence. However, the first resolution that Lopez makes is that her perceptions must be altered, that she must "look at the world with his eyes," and his vision of life assumes that "the most important pursuit in the world was the acquiring of money" (chapter 25). Instead of broadening her life, marriage with Lopez brings a narrowing of focus to only mercenary concerns. While the Palliser marriage is ultimately based on a mutual respect for the separateness of the partners' personalities, and moves toward a gradual if uneasy accommodation of two very different natures, the Lopez marriage, as defined by the husband, is conceived as the subsuming of the wife's personality into his own.

The lesson is begun on the couple's honeymoon, where initiation into sexual intimacy is intertwined with an introduction to the world of money matters. This is Lopez' reaction when he receives a promise of three thousand pounds from Abel Wharton: "Then he chucked the letter, lightly, in among the tea-cups, and coming to her took her closely in his arms and almost hurt her by the violence of his repeated kisses" (chapter 26). He rewards her with violent passion for her obedience in learning his financial lessons much as he will later threaten her with passionate violence when she refuses to submit to his mercenary plans. Indeed, Lopez is associated with a whip, surely a symbol of male sexual dominance. In the contest at Silverbridge, Lopez carries a "cutting whip" in his hand, and is only prevented by a constable from trying to use it on Arthur Fletcher, whom he accuses of writing an insulting letter to Emily. (Fletcher is forced to carry a stick in self-defense, and the result is an encounter that is primitively male, two men wielding phallic symbols, poised to fight for the territory of Silverbridge and sexual rights to a woman.) After Lopez receives Mr. Wharton's letter, he tells Emily that her father has "answered to the whip, and the money is there" (chapter 26). In a more general sense, the symbol of the whip is connected in the male imagination with patriarchal authority, specifically financial power. In another scene, Everett tells Lopez that his father "has the whiphand of me, because he has money and I have none" (chapter 35). A whip comes to symbolize the potential violence of male power in this society, violence that Lopez unleashes, and that is kept in check only by the gentlemanly ideal.

In the Lopez marriage, an expression of that violence is his conception of marital discourse as male dictatorship. At the conclusion of what Lopez refers to as their first "real domestic talk," in which he tells Emily about the importance of money, he explains his immediate need for her aid in getting funds from Abel Wharton. Emily agrees to write to her father, and a telling exchange between the husband and wife follows:

> "Would it not be better from you? I only ask, Ferdinand. I never have even spoken to him about money, and of course he would know that you had dictated what I said."
> "No doubt he would. It is natural that I should do so." (Chapter 25)

The ideal of Woman as Child, as both an innocent, and a passive, yielding creature, clearly informs Lopez' conception of Emily. He expects her to submit automatically to his authority, as a child would. Emily soon learns that the husband's prerogative to "dictate" to his wife extends to a desire to control her very thoughts. In the episode in which Lopez accuses Arthur Fletcher of telling a lie in his letter to Emily explaining his candidacy for Silverbridge, the husband tells the wife, "You are a child, my dear, and must allow me to dictate to you what you ought to think in such a matter as this" (chapter 30). For Lopez, Emily is a tabula rasa upon which he can engrave his personality.[23] But Emily decides that she is not a child, but an adult capable of making moral judgments on her own. As she ponders her husband's words, Emily resolves on her first step of rebellion—to think for herself:

> "Could it be that marriage meant as much as that,—that a husband was to claim to dictate to his wife what opinions she was to form about this and that person,—about a person she had known so well, whom he had never known? Surely she could think in accordance with her own experience and her own intelligence! She was certain that Arthur Fletcher was no liar. Not even her own husband could make her think that." (Chapter 30)

In this comparison of the ruffian Lopez to the true gentleman Arthur, Trollope indicates that Emily's first rebellion against her family was a mistake, while her second rebellion against her husband is justified. The tyranny of Lopez casts a benign perspective on the subtle coercions of the Fletchers and Whartons.[24] Emily's sturdy conviction that "Arthur Fletcher was no liar" makes her reflect upon the ideal of the gentleman, which she had once thought was "but a weak, spiritless quality" (chapter 31). In a deeper sense than she at first realizes, she has "divided herself from her own people" (chapter 30). In comparing the two men, having now known both of them familiarly, she is compelled to judge them by the ingrained lessons of this ethic, which has ruled the lives of her kin, because its pervasive influence has formed her morality. Emily therefore begins, subtly at first, to revolt against her unethical husband, as she discovers the falsity of his gentlemanly demeanor.

As Shirley Letwin points out in her book, *The Gentleman in Trollope,* honesty is one of the cardinal attributes of a gentleman.[25] Like Arthur, Emily "could not lie" (chapter 31). The narrator tells us that Lopez, in contrast, "did not know that there was such a quality as honesty, nor did he understand what the word meant" (chapter 60). Lopez' ludicrous construction of Fletcher's letter is the first strong indication to Emily that, as the narrator later explains, Lopez "had not the faintest notion of the feelings of a gentleman" (chapter 58); she finally acknowledges to herself that "he was a lie from head to foot" (chapter 71). Emily soon recognizes the crucial difference between Fletcher and Lopez, the difference that Trollope finds essential to civilized existence: "there was some peculiar gift, or grace, or acquirement belonging without dispute to the one, and which the other lacked. . . . But now,—ay, from the very hour of her marriage,—she had commenced to learn which it was that her father had meant when he spoke of living with gentlemen. Arthur Fletcher certainly was a gentleman" (chapter 31).

If we consider Letwin's definition of gentlemanly love as characterized by "a profound appreciation of another human being—the apotheosis of regard for individuality" (139), we can more readily see how Lopez' desire to change Emily's very nature is the antithesis of the gentlemanly ideal of love. We can also compare Lopez' attitude to that of Plantagenet Palliser, Duke of Omnium, Trollope's perfect gentleman. The Duke is often angry and frustrated by his wife's ebullient subversions of male authority, but he does acknowledge that she has a personality which is separate from his; as he admits to her, "You are what you have made yourself" (chapter 8).

Another instance of patriarchal oppression is the ignorance in which Lopez keeps Emily about money matters. While he pretends to be confidential with her, even tutorial, in actual fact he carefully hides the true state of his financial affairs and even lies about the payment of their rent. Although Emily's refrain, "I know nothing about money," is irritating to the modern reader, it is important to recognize that no one has thought it necessary that she be taught about finances prior to her marriage, any more than they have thought it proper that she be introduced to the mysteries of sexuality. The ideals of woman as innocent child and pure, sexless angel have informed the vision of Emily that shelters her before her marriage. Thereafter, although Lopez gestures at informing Emily about his affairs, in truth he speaks only in generalities about his speculations, and never gives her any concrete information. Ironically, Emily learns more about her husband's affairs from another woman, the lower-class, kindly Mrs. Parker, whose husband is ruined by Lopez, than she does from the secretive Lopez himself. What Lopez really wants is Emily's unquestioning help in getting Abel Wharton's money.

Juliet McMaster has condemned Emily for being willfully ignorant of her husband's financial dealings. In fact, she blames Emily for Mrs. Parker's fate, stating that the destitute Mrs. Parker is "a lasting reproach on wifely withdrawal from men's affairs" (*Palliser Novels,* 115). As the following passage makes clear, however, Emily is willing to get involved in unravelling her husband's affairs; the problem is that as a married woman in a patriarchal society, she is powerless to influence them except through her father, who has both money and authority that he can put in force on her behalf. Abel Wharton is discussing Lopez; he speaks first:

> "I wish he would be open with me, and tell me everything."
> "Shall I let him know that you say so?"
> "If you think that he will not be annoyed with you, you may do so."
> ". . . I am not afraid to say anything to him." (Chapter 63)

In truth, Emily wants to understand her husband's concerns. The implicit emphasis of Trollope's criticism is not on Emily, but upon the men who exclude her—and all women—from genuine involvement in the business sphere. Trollope subtly indicts the doctrine of the two spheres itself, with the premise that the morally pure domestic "queen" will guard the male's morality out in the unscrupulous world. The experiences of Mrs. Parker and of Emily seem to invalidate that ideal, and to expose the "queen's" true impotence in the face of men ravening for money—"thirsting for blood," as Mrs. Parker describes them (chapter 47).

The submerged violence in the Lopez marriage erupts at Glencora's garden party. In Lopez' public display of aggression, Trollope depicts society without the civilizing force of the gentlemanly ethic:

> "You will wilfully disobey me."
> "In that I must." He glared at her, as though he were going to strike her, but she bore his look without flinching. . . . He was most desirous to make her subject to his will in all things, and was quite prepared to exercise tyranny over her to any extent, so that her father should know nothing of it. (Chapter 37)

Lopez tries not only "to make her subject to his will in all things," but to negate her separate will. Announcing a trip to Dovercourt, he states that "I think we have made up our mind," implying that the decision was made by marital conclave. Emily immediately divorces her own mind from his by objecting to the falsehood implicit in his phrasing: "'I did not understand that you had made up your mind to go to Dovecourt.'. . . She quite understood that he meant to have his own way in such things. But it seemed to her that he wanted to be a tyrant without having the courage necessary for tyranny" (chapter 43).

Emily realizes that Lopez has absorbed her personality, and that since he is only doing that which the law codifies—subsuming the wife's identity in the husband's—there is "no escape" (chapter 48). When Lopez writes invitations, clandestinely sending them in her name, she reacts with both anger and resignation: "Well! She was the man's wife, and she supposed that he was entitled to put any words that he pleased into her mouth" (chapter 47).

Trollope implicitly compares old Mrs. Fletcher's conception of Emily as the property of the Whartons and Fletchers to Lopez' eventual perception of her as a marketable commodity. This comparison again serves to underplay her first rebellion, because her family seems benevolent when placed alongside her tyrannical husband, in whom the power that a husband has over a wife is shown in naked relief. Lopez first makes it clear to both Emily and her father that by law he "owns" Emily: "She belongs to me,—not to you or to herself" (chapter 52). However, in his desperation, Lopez finally agrees to abandon Emily to her father, although he has hoped to get a higher price for her: "£5,000 would be a low price at which to sell his wife, and all that he might get from his connection with her" (chapter 52).

After Lopez' bloody suicide at Tenway Junction ends her thralldom, Emily perversely creates a new prison for herself in the role of bereaved widow. As enacted by Emily, widowhood entails strict seclusion, the deepest weeds of mourning, and constant self-castigation. As Arthur complains to Mr. Wharton with angry impatience: "She is immolating herself like an Indian widow" (chapter 65). Glencora, too, drolly describes Emily as a "Niobe." As she tells Mrs. Finn, "her gown, and her cap, and her strings were weeping. Her voice wept, and her hair, and her nose, and her mouth" (chapter 77). The narrator's comments on Emily's demeanour shed light on Trollope's own view of the feminine ideal of delicacy:

> Undoubtedly, she was succumbing to the wretchedness of her position in a manner that was repugnant to humanity generally. There is no power so useful to man as that capacity of recovering himself after a fall, which belongs especially to those who possess a healthy mind in a healthy body. It is not rare to see one,—generally a woman,—whom a sorrow gradually kills; and there are those among us, who hardly perhaps envy, but certainly admire, a spirit so delicate as to be snuffed out by a woe. But it is the weakness of the heart rather than the strength of the feeling which has in such cases most often produced the destruction. Some endurance of fibre has been wanting, which power of endurance is a noble attribute. (Chapter 70)

Debunking the ideal of delicacy in women, Trollope asserts instead that physical and spiritual strength are admirable in both men and women. His attack is directed at the Romantic idea that links a delicate constitution to a more sensitive, superior nature. He pragmatically attributes the mourner's demise to "weakness of the heart" rather than to "strength of the feeling."

The critics generally interpret Emily's apparently masochistic behavior as self-flagellation; they say that she is punishing herself for her egregious error in judgment.[26] The text, of course, supports this view. As Arthur explains to his mother, "she has not yet brought herself to think that her life should be anything but one long period of mourning, not for him, but for her own mistake" (chapter 71). As Emily herself thinks, while Lopez is still alive, "Ah,—that she could have been so blind, she who had given herself credit for seeing so much better than her elders!" (chapter 39). After her husband's suicide, when she is visiting Wharton for the first time, and Everett has lectured her on the inappropriateness of her display of mourning, Emily thinks:

> It was not only that her love had been misbestowed,—not only that she had made so grievous an error in the one great act of her life which she had chosen to perform on her own judgment! Perhaps the most crushing memory of all was that which told her that she, who had through all her youth been regarded as a bright star in the family, had been the one person to bring a reproach upon the name of all these people who were so good to her. (Chapter 70)

Emily's severe widowhood is in part a statement of penance for Lopez' malfeasance. Despite her private dissociation from Lopez' literally dirty schemes (kauri gum, guano) while he is living, she publicly assumes a portion of Lopez' guilt at his death, by dramatizing her role as his widow. She feels irrevocably sullied by her marriage to a man who lived unscrupulously and died in spectacular sordidness. The language with which she describes her feelings about herself to Arthur indicates that she condemns herself for more than her bad judgment. She feels so besmirched in part because she thinks she has violated the canons of ideal Victorian womanhood:

> "I have lain among the pots until I am foul and blackened. . . . [Y]ou, the chosen one, the bright star among us all, you, whose wife should be the fairest, the purest, the tenderest of us all, a flower that has yet been hardly breathed on! While I—Arthur," she said, "I know my duty better than that. You have my word as a woman that it shall not be so." (Chapter 74)

Clearly, Emily subscribes to a belief in the purity of womanhood. She feels that she has fallen from that angelic height and will tarnish Arthur, the "bright star," if she marries him. Her duty "as a woman," as she perceives it, is to protect the code of womanly purity even if she is not herself its most shining exemplar. As she thinks to herself in an earlier passage, "she could not endure to think that that other man [Arthur] should even touch her. It was forbidden to her, she believed, by all the canons of womanhood even to think of love again" (chapter 67). Unexpectedly, it is Arthur himself who views Emily's misconceptions clearly:

> She was so warped from herself by the conviction of her great mistake, so prone to take shame to herself for her own error, so keenly alive to the degradation to which she had been submit-

ted, that it might yet be impossible to teach her that, though her husband had been vile and she mistaken, yet she had not been soiled by his baseness. (Chapter 74)

Perhaps it is not too far-fetched to view this scene, with its opposing views about Emily's feminine purity, as indicative of Trollope's own conflicting feelings about the ideal of pure womanhood. As a Victorian gentleman, Trollope was undoubtedly influenced by the conventions of his culture even as he questioned them. On one hand, Trollope allows Emily's scene of vehement self-abasement to continue for a very long time. This dramatizing suggests not only her own belief in her spritual downfall, but also, perhaps, that Trollope too thinks that this judgment should be forcefully presented. The very power of her words, and the fact that Arthur, who represents the opposing view, is left "speechless," tend to undercut the rational explanation of Emily's mind that Arthur later provides. On the other hand, Arthur does sound awfully sensible when he insists that Emily has not been "soiled" by her contact with Lopez. The two viewpoints, Emily's and Arthur's, seem to embody Trollope's own divided mind on the subject of his culture's feminine ideals.

Because Emily believes that she is no longer worthy of a gentleman's love, her ugly mourning attire expresses a refusal to be sexually attractive. She recognizes, however, that she is still quite capable of passion. Therefore, she deliberately obscures her feminine beauty, creating a "monument of bereaved woe" (chapter 70) in its place. She resists taking off her widow's weeds at Everett's wedding, and immediately resumes them after the celebration, in part because she feels uncomfortable at this joyful celebration that she feels is forbidden to her now because of her marriage to Lopez:[27]

> She had made herself unfit to have any dealings of that nature. It was not that she could not love. Oh, no! She knew well enough that she did love, love with all her heart. If it were not that she were so torn to rags that she was not fit to be worn again, she could now have thrown herself into his arms with a whole heaven of joy before her. A woman, she told herself, had no right to a second chance in life, after having made such shipwreck of herself in the first. But the danger of being seduced from her judgment by Arthur Fletcher was all over. (Chapter 71)

In a peculiar sense, Emily's attempt at self-realization is both affirmed and denied in the novel's conventional resolution: she becomes engaged to marry Arthur, the man she passionately loves, but she is compelled to renounce her independence, which she clings to up until the moment she capitulates to Arthur. She refutes Arthur's argument that she should recognize her father's authority to judge for her, asserting the greater authority of "personal feelings":

> The time has gone by, Arthur, in which I might well have been guided by my father. There comes a time when personal feelings must be stronger than a father's authority. Papa cannot see me with my own eyes; he cannot understand what I feel. It is simply this,—that he would have me to be other than I am. But I am what I have made myself. (Chapter 74)

However, it is by invoking patriarchal authority finally that Arthur quells Emily's resistance. He declares to her that after the disastrous decision to marry Lopez: "You have no right to set yourself up to judge what may be best for my happiness. They who know how to judge are all united" (chapter 79). The form that Emily's assent takes is also significant; her murmured words, "I should disgrace you," suggest that she, like Alice in *Can You Forgive Her?*, will enter the marriage as a penitent.

This conclusion recalls the final interview between Alice Vavasor and John Grey in *Can You Forgive Her?* The validity that has been given throughout the texts to the heroines' need to break free of patriarchal control to discover their own identities is overtly repudiated by the conventional closure of both novels. Further, both Fletcher and Grey vanquish the women they love by assuming all authority to make decisions, relegating Emily and Alice to the position of woman-child. As Alice surrenders to Grey, she whispers: "You win everything,—always" (*Can You Forgive Her?*, chapter 74). As is so often the case in Trollope, the reader hears in Fletcher's appeal to authority the echoes not only of Grey's conquest of Alice, but of another proposal spoken in the same novel: Glencora's tale of her love for Burgo, and Palliser's command: "You must love me now" (chapter 24). Although the circumstances are obviously very different—Emily and Alice are acquiescing to the men they love—all three stories connect in Trollope's overt approval of a woman's obligation to patriarchal authority.

However, Emily is united with the man she passionately loves in the novel's conclusion, and in that sense, she realizes herself more fully than Glencora ever does. Trollope carefully documents Emily's desire first for Lopez and then for Arthur Fletcher, in direct contradiction of the ideal of woman as sexless angel. When Emily is finally given her father's permission to marry Lopez, she passionately embraces him, declaring, "I am yours, my love, forever and ever": "Whether it was his doing or hers he hardly knew; but she was in his arms, and her lips were pressed to his, and his arm was tight round her waist, holding her close to his breast" (chapter 23). Later, when she is unhappily married to Lopez, she allows Arthur's illicit kiss as willingly as Glencora does Burgo's (*Can You Forgive Her?*, chapter 67). When she is a widow, Emily's protestations of "hot, passionate love" strengthen Arthur in his resolve to pursue her: "I have trembled when I have heard your voice. My heart has beat at the sound of your footstep as though it would burst!" (chapter 74).

Yet there are tensions that strain against a sense of Emily's self-fulfillment. Because of Trollope's stress upon her love for Arthur, I think that she is more fully satisfied than does Kincaid, but there is surely some truth in his statement that Emily "must abandon her search for freedom and settle for protection" (220). She marries a Trollopian gentleman, but as with John Grey, there are hints in Arthur's characterization, especially in his view of Emily, that define the conventional gentlemanly assumptions about women as a part of the limitations against which Emily is rebelling. For instance, here are Arthur's thoughts about Emily immediately after he hears of her engagement to Lopez:

> There had been a holy of holies, which he guarded within himself, keeping it free from all outer contamination for his own use. He had cherished the idea of a clear fountain of ever-running water which would at last be his, always ready for the comfort of his own lips. . . . He would never allow himself to think of it with lessened reverence, or with changed ideas as to her nature. (Chapter 17)

It is clear that Arthur regards Emily as a kind of sacred fount—and the same disturbing associations of vampirism evident in James's novel, *The Sacred Fount*, implicit in Arthur's conception of Emily. She is his "holy of holies," "a clear fountain of ever-running water." In this woman-worship, Arthur has surely been influenced by the Angel-in-the-House ideal; Emily is pure, "free from all outer contamination." On the overt level, this perception seems admirable, and certainly appears to be the view approved by the narrator, but a close analysis of the passage's language makes Arthur's conception seem more ambiguous. The reader senses the self-serving side of Arthur's idea of Emily, and, by extension, the selfishness of the idealization of women by all men. Significantly, it is the "idea" of Emily he cherishes, referred to twice as "it"; moreover, it is "for his own use," "for the comfort of his own lips." Clearly, Arthur wants Emily to fill the role of pure domestic goddess to his male need for succor from the outside world.

A second strain against the comic resolution of Emily's painful story is the tale of Everett's easy accession to power, although the novel's structure makes both endings seem harmonious, part of a general comic closure. Everett succeeds simply because he is a privileged male in a patriarchal society. In his ambiguous portrait of the conventional, amiable, but wholly mediocre Everett, Trollope embodies another aspect of his disquiet with the gentlemanly ideal—and with patriarchy itself.

In his ironic comparison of Everett and Emily, Trollope undermines the conventional Victorian gentleman's prejudices about women. The narrator makes no bones about who is the worthier sibling: "But here, in speaking of the brother, it may suffice to say that the sister, who was endowed with infinitely finer gifts than his, did give credit to the somewhat pretentious claims of her less noble brother" (chapter 2). Emily is possessed of a "clearness of intellect joined with that feminine sweetness which has its most frequent foundation in self-denial," while Everett is rather muddleheaded and self-indulgent, having "simply shown himself to be inefficient to earn his own bread" (chapter 2). Yet, those very lessons in feminine "self-denial" cause Emily to give unwarranted "credit" to her brother's inherent male capacity to conquer the world. Everett is much less flattering to Emily and to all women in his assessment of the female sex. When Lopez exclaims, during a discussion of his prospects with Emily, "God forbid that I should think anything about your sister was amiss," Everett responds casually: "I don't think there is much myself. Women are generally superficial,—but some are honestly superficial and some dishonestly. Emily is at any rate honest" (chapter 2). Moreover, Everett believes that "there isn't a man in London has a higher respect for his sister than I have for mine" (chapter 4). Everett clearly considers women to be the inferior sex; the only essential difference among them is whether they are pure ("honestly superficial") or impure ("dishonestly"). And yet, Everett "was very popular with women, to whom he was always courteous" (chapter 2). Through his portrait of Everett Wharton, Trollope suggests the latent disrespect which underlies the "courteous" manner of the Victorian gentleman, much as, in *Can You Forgive Her?* he reveals the will to master that underlies the chivalry of John Grey.

Yet despite his revelation of Everett's shortcomings, the narrator seems to be in two minds about his success: he rejoices both in the continuance of Old England and the landed gentry's way of life, and remarks rather caustically upon the arbitrariness of male inheritance. On one hand, there is a good deal of cheering when Everett becomes the heir. For instance, the narrator approvingly notes Everett's alacrity in accepting his new responsibilities: "Sir Alured had said that on such an occasion he, the heir, ought to be on the property with the shortest possible delay. His father smiled;—but with an approving smile" (chapter 67). Likewise, the old squire's tour of the estate is lovingly described. In characteristic fashion, Trollope pokes gentle fun at Sir Alured, while obviously expressing his approbation of the squire's belief in the lasting importance of land:

> Everett was taken round to every tenant and introduced as the heir. Mr. Wharton had already declared his purpose of abdicating any possible possession of the property. Should he outlive Sir Alured he must be the baronet; but when that sad event should take place, whether Mr. Wharton should then be alive or no, Everett should at once be the possessor of Wharton Hall. Sir Alured, under these circumstances, discussed his own death with extreme satisfaction, and insisted on having it discussed by the others. That he should have gone and left everything at the mercy of the spendthrift had been terrible to his old heart;—but now, the man coming to the property would have £60,000 with which to support and foster Wharton, with which to mend, as it were, the crevices, and stop up the holes of the estate. He must surely have thought that he would return to Wharton as a spirit, and take a ghostly share in the prosperity of the farms. (Chapter 70)

That Trollope sympathized with the landed gentry is a commonplace of Trollope criticism. Paul Elmer More wrote half a century ago about Trollope's respect for the ancestral estate as a "sacred responsibility to the past and the future" (123). In a recent essay, "Trollope's Country Estates," Juliet McMaster examines the ways in which Trollope shows that he "is imbued with a deep respect for the values that are rooted in the land" (70). Although McMaster does not discuss the Wharton estate, the passage just cited (and others like it in *The Prime Minister*) certainly exemplify Trollope's feelings about "the sacred institution of landowning" (81). Trollope's sense of the privileges and obligations of the landed gentry are expressed in Sir Alured's statement that "I do like the farms to go from father to son, Everett. It's the way that everything should go. Of course there's no right" (chapter 70).

However, despite Trollope's obvious belief in the patriarchal traditions of the landed gentry, the narrator distances himself from the general celebratory atmosphere at Wharton Hall. His acerbic comments extend beyond the arbitrariness of Everett's success to a probing of the institution of primogeniture itself. The ironic tone of the following passage recalls some of the narrator's comments in *Is He Popenjoy?,* a novel in which, as Robert Tracy states, "Trollope lets us speculate about the worth of that social system which possesses unquestioned value elsewhere in his work" (207). If Trollope does not question the "worth" of the patriarchal system of inheritance in *The Prime Minister,* he certainly presents its inequities, the price paid—especially by women—for the stability it provides:

> There was very much room for triumph in regard to Everett. It had already been ascertained that the Wharton who was dead had had a child,—but that the child was a daughter. Oh,—what salvation or destruction there may be to an English gentleman in the sex of an infant! This poor baby was now little better than a beggar brat, unless the relatives who were utterly disregardful of its fate, should choose, in their charity, to make some small allowance for its maintenance. Had it by chance been a boy, Everett Wharton would have been nobody; and the child, rescued from the iniquities of his parents, would have been nursed in the best bedroom of Wharton Hall, and cherished with the warmest kisses, and would have been the centre of all the hopes of all the Whartons. But the Wharton lawyer by use of reckless telegrams had certified himself that the infant was a girl, and Everett was the hero of the day. (Chapter 70)

And yet, as is so often the case in Trollope, Everett does become a kind of "hero," maturing to his newly acquired role. The common sense with which he speaks to Emily about the "luxury" of her grief, for instance, consciously echoes John Fletcher, squire of Longbarns (perhaps the most clear-sighted character in the novel), as he lectures Arthur on his unmanly "howling" (chapter 33) about his loss of Emily to Lopez. Trollope's profound belief in the "mysterious forces by which estates enforce themselves almost independently of human agents" (McMaster, "Country Estates," 84) no doubt helps to effect Everett's transformation.

At the end of the novel, Lopez and Everett's predecessor, the dissolute former heir, are both dead, and true gentlemen are victorious. The moral and social way of life that the gentlemanly ideal represents, imaged in the country estate at Wharton Hall, is once again secure. But the reader cannot help but remember that female "beggar brat," also a Wharton. For her, the cost of civilization is very high indeed. In a deeper sense than Glencora ever imagines when she speaks of her loss of identity, this female child is—nothing.

4

Glencora's Legacy: Mary, Mabel, and Isabel as Spiritual Daughters in *The Duke's Children*

In *The Duke's Children,* Glencora's struggle for self-realization is symbolically continued even after her death. Her spirit seems so powerful that, as John Hagan notes in his insightful essay on this novel, although "Lady Glencora is dead in the flesh, she pervades the action in spirit" (13). My discussion of *The Duke's Children* will focus in particular on the young women in the novel—Lady Mary Palliser, Lady Mabel Grex and Isabel Boncassen—whom I view as in one sense Glencora's alter egos, as women attempting to realize themselves within the constraints of Victorian ideals for women. These young women, Glencora's daughter and the two women whom her son loves, enact the possibilities of Glencora's life, resolved with more dramatically conclusive endings: the loves of her daughter and of her son's wife promising greater fulfillment than her own marriage, and that of Lady Mabel Grex, both her son Lord Silverbridge's and her son-in-law Tregear's first love, proving to be a much more tragic variation of her own coerced decision to put prudence over passion.

Glencora's continued rebellion is introduced as a subject in the second chapter of the novel, entitled "Lady Mary Palliser," in which the history of the Duchess's encouragement of the love between her daughter and Francis Tregear is given. The terms of Glencora's own marriage in later years are also suggested: "The Duchess too had loved him dearly,—more dearly in late years than in her early life. But her husband to her had always been an outside power which had in many cases to be evaded" (chapter 2).

That the Duchess is in part attracted to Tregear because he reminds her of Burgo Fitzgerald, Trollope does not leave us in doubt; but Trollope also makes it clear that although Glencora sees Tregear as reminiscent of Burgo, she also perceives him as a kind of idealized reincarnation, a Burgo who would have been an acceptable lover:[1]

> And then he was beautiful to look at,—putting her almost in mind of another man on whom her eyes had once loved to dwell. . . . For though she now and then would catch a glimpse

of the outer man, which would remind her of that other beautiful one whom she had known in her youth, and though, as these glimpses came, she would remember how poor in spirit and how unmanly that other had been, though she would confess to herself how terrible had been the heart shipwreck which that other one had brought upon herself; still, she was able completely to assure herself that this man, though not superior in external grace, was altogether different in mind and character. She was old enough now to see all this and to appreciate it. (Chapter 2)

After Lady Mary and Tregear fall in love, Glencora is their confidante in the love affair. It is significant that Glencora keeps her knowledge of the engagement from the Duke, that—as Mrs. Finn views it—she "assented to this imprudent concealment" (chapter 2). In part, the near certainty that the Duke will disapprove of his daughter marrying a penniless commoner has precipitated the secret. Not only Tregear and Lady Mary but also Glencora expect the Duke's displeasure, and everyone agrees "the Duchess should be the one to bell the cat" (chapter 3). However, Glencora's comparisons of Tregear with Burgo indicate other, perhaps unconscious, reasons for her unwillingness to tell the Duke immediately of her daughter's lover. The Duchess wants time to savor the romance of this reblossoming of her hopes of passion, and she feels guilty about encouraging a lover who will be to her daughter what Burgo—not her husband—was for her: a great passion.

It is for this latter reason that Glencora is not able to broach the subject of Mary's love for Tregear to her husband even when she is on her deathbed. All she is able to say to him is that "she hoped that Mary might be so circumstanced, that if her happiness depended on marrying a poor man, want of money need not prevent it" (chapter 2). Glencora herself had been the greatest heiress in England at the time of her wedding. Therefore, at least theoretically, she should have been able to marry a poor man herself, if she loved him—even the aristocratic but penniless wastrel Burgo. Tregear is not an impoverished scapegrace, but a poor and honorable gentleman of a very old Cornish gentry family, and Mary the heiress—unlike her mother—should be entitled to her choice of a husband, to Glencora's way of thinking. As far as we know from the novel, this request for Mary is Glencora's last wish, and therefore must be given a good deal of weight as an indication of her hopes for vicarious fulfillment of her own unsatisfied dreams.

In her aspirations for Mary (and through her daughter, for herself), Glencora is aided by Mary's firm nature—a nature very much more sturdy than was her own at the age of nineteen. (Another circumstance serving to identify Glencora with her daughter is that Mary is the exact age Glencora was when her own romantic episode with Burgo Fitzgerald and the coercion which led to her marriage with Palliser took place.)[2] Mary has also inherited her mother's sharp wit. Although she is more somber than Glencora (but then, we view her mostly in the year or so after her beloved mother's death, when she is mourning both Glencora and her lover, Tregear, from whom she is forcibly separated, Mary too has learned how to use her wit as a defense against those who want to entrap her. In this scene, she wards off the clumsy approaches of Lord Popplecourt, her father's favored suitor, who reveals his own dull, mercenary nature with every word he utters:

> The should-be lover immediately reverted to the Austrian tour, expressing a hope that his neighbour had enjoyed herself. "There's nothing I like so much myself," said he, remembering some of the Duke's words, "as mountains, cities, salt-mines, and all that kind of thing. There's such a lot of interest about it."
> "Did you ever see a salt-mine?"
> "Well,—not exactly a salt-mine; but I have coalmines on my property in Staffordshire. I'm very fond of coal. I hope you like coal."
> "I like salt a great deal better—to look at."
> "But which do you think pays best? I don't mind telling you,—though it's a kind of thing I never talk about to strangers,—the royalties from the Blogownie and Toodlem mines go up regularly two thousand pounds every year."
> "I thought we were talking about what was pretty to look at."
> "So we were. I'm as fond of pretty things as anybody. Do you know Reginald Dobbes?"
> "No, I don't. Is he pretty?" (Chapter 46)

Mary is passionate in her love for Tregear, as was Glencora in her love for Burgo; Mary's open avowal of her love by embracing Tregear at Lady Mabel's is perhaps the most overt evidence of this trait. She is, however, unlike Glencora in both the depth of her passion, and the fearless tenacity with which she is capable of adhering to it. In comparing Glencora's capacity for passionate love with her daughter's, it is instructive to look again at Trollope's description in *Can You Forgive Her?* of the now 21-year-old, married Glencora's love for Burgo, as it is compared to the more serious love of Alice Vavasor for John Grey:

> With all the fuss that Lady Glencora made to herself,—with all the tears that she had shed about her lost lover, and was so often shedding,—with all her continual thinking of the matter, she had never loved Burgo Fitzgerald as Alice Vavasor had loved Mr. Grey. . . . She knew Burgo Fitzgerald to be a scapegrace, and she liked him the better on that account. She despised her husband because he had no vices. She would have given everything she had to Burgo,—pouring her wealth upon him with a total disregard of herself, had she been allowed to do so. She would have forgiven him sin after sin, and might perhaps have brought him round, at last, to some life not absolutely reckless and wretched. But in all that she might have done there would have been no thoughtfulness—no true care either for him or for herself. And now that she was married there was no thoughtfulness, or care either for herself or for her husband. She was ready to sacrifice herself for him, if any sacrifice might be required of her. She believed herself to be unfit for him, and would have submitted to be divorced or smothered out of the way, for the matter of that,—if the laws of the land would have permitted it. But she had never for a moment given to herself the task of thinking what conduct on her part might be the best for his welfare. (*Can You Forgive Her?*, chapter 19)

The outstanding features of this passage are Glencora's melodramatic conception of her love and her flair for dramatization; her traditional acceptance of the role of ministering angel and moral guide to the profligate Burgo; and her concomitant willingness to "sacrifice" herself for both Burgo and her husband. Her romantic conceptions contrast sharply with the doggedness of Lady Mary, and her commonsensical ideas of what is due to her:

> She had a strong idea that she would ultimately prevail,—an idea also that that 'ultimately' should not be postponed to some undefined middle-aged period of her life. As she intended to belong to Frank Tregear, she thought it expedient that he should have the best of her days as well as what might be supposed to be the worst; and she therefore resolved that it would be her duty to make her father understand that though she would certainly obey him, she would look to be treated humanely by him, and not to be made miserable for an indefinite term of years. (Chapter 11)

Both Mary's parents are intent upon resolving their unresolved marriage, on recreating their experience in a more satisfactory manner, through Mary's love for Tregear. In part Mary senses the importance of her own romance to Glencora when she thinks of the secret of her engagement as "a legacy from her mother" (chapter 11). It seems, however, that she doesn't know the history of her mother's thwarted love for Burgo and her subsequent marriage to the Duke, and therefore Mary cannot know the deep springs of memory from which her father's resistance flows. The critical response to *The Duke's Children* has traditionally (since Hagan's article) focussed on the Duke's psychology. Hagan emphasizes the Duke's painful resolution of his marriage through his opposition to Mary's engagement with Tregear. McMaster, too, in her excellent chapter on this novel in *Trollope's Palliser Novels,* emphasizes the Duke's attempt to justify his own marriage through his opposition to Tregear, and his abysmal effort to recreate himself as an acceptable suitor in the person of that mediocre but very respectable aristocrat, Lord Popplecourt (132). I would add that upon closer inspection, the Duke discovers that Lord Popplecourt is a man very different from himself, a bland, mercenary, unidealistic man, whom the Duke—along with his daughter—eventually despises. Conversely, the Duke finally accepts Tregear as being very different from Burgo Fitzgerald, as signified by his remarks to Silverbridge after Mary's wedding, the last words of the novel: "But now I will accept as courage what I before regarded as arrogance" (chapter 80). These closing words of the Duke's—his final words in the entire Palliser series—surely must indicate a kind of thematic closure to the novel, and perhaps to the entire Palliser series.[3] The words connote a change of perception, and perhaps a change of heart.[4]

One of the most significant aspects of the Duke's opposition to Mary's love is his feeling that she is somehow less "pure" because she has experienced a passion for a man whom the Duke considers to be beneath her. He has fixed ideas about propriety for women, and these notions center, uncomfortably for the modern reader, around ownership. His ideas about what is proper for his daughter differ from those of Glencora. Part of what the Duke must learn all over again is that his daughter is her own self, as his wife was her own self—and Mary, much more than the youthful Glencora, can be as rigidly true to her nature as can be the Duke himself. The most obvious manifestation of the Duke's concept of his daughter as property is his attempt to arrange her marriage with Lord Popplecourt, an idea upon which the narrator remarks, in an early chapter significantly titled "She Must Be Made to Obey": "The idea when picked to pieces is not a nice idea" (chapter 22).

The Duke expects his girl to be pliable in part because submissiveness is a part of the Victorian womanly ideal, and in part because his own Glencora was pliable—to her own advantage, as he desperately wants to believe. The autocratic set of the Duke's mind in this respect becomes clear in his discussion of the matter with Lady Cantrip, whom he has himself chosen as temporary guardian for his daughter, and who views his obstinacy with regard to Mary's lover with alarm, as she tries to reason with him:

> "I mean to say that it is the nature of her character to be obstinate. Most girls are prone to yield. They have not character enough to stand against opposition. I am not speaking now only of affairs like this. It would be the same with her in anything. Have you not always found it so?"
> Then he had to acknowledge to himself that he had never found out anything in reference to his daughter's character. She had been properly educated; at least he hoped so. He had seen her grow up, pretty, sweet, affectionate, always obedient to him;—the most charming plaything in the world on the few occasions in which he had allowed himself to play. But as to her actual disposition, he had never taken any trouble to inform himself. . . . "She must be made to obey—like others," he said at last, speaking through his teeth.
> There was something in this which almost frightened Lady Cantrip. She could not bear to hear him say that the girl must be made to yield, with that spirit of despotic power under which women were restrained in years now passed. . . .
> "What can you do, Duke? If she be as firm as you, can you bear to see her pine away in her misery?"
> "Girls do not do like that," he said.
> "Girls, like men, are very different." (Chapter 24)

The lesson which Lady Cantrip tries unsuccessfully to teach the Duke, he is finally able to learn much later from the supremely tactful Mrs. Finn. Juliet McMaster has scrupulously analyzed the delicacy of Mrs. Finn's argument in this scene (*Palliser Novels*, 133–36); therefore, I will only touch upon her repetition of Lady Cantrip's insistence on Mary's individuality and strength of character, and on the depth of her feelings:

> "Girls are so different! There are many who though they be genuinely in love, though their natures are sweet and affectionate, are not strong enough to support their feelings in resistance to the will of those who have authority over them." Had it been so with his wife? At this moment all the former history passed through his mind. "They yield to that which seems inevitable and allow themselves to be fashioned by the purposes of others. It is well for them often that they are so plastic. Whether it would be better for her that she should be so I will not say."
> "It would be better," said the Duke doggedly.
> "But such is not her nature. She is as determined as ever." (Chapter 66)

When he accepts Lady Cantrip's and Mrs. Finn's analyses of Mary's character, the Duke must acknowledge that his daughter is a much more complex creature than he had heretofore believed her to be. And he must also assume for himself a yielding posture inimical to him, as the narrator wryly remarks: "Young people and women have to yield,—but for such a man as this, to yield is in itself a misery" (chapter 50).

The Duke's emphasis on his daughter's purity betrays a concern with convention—and the violence of the language in which the Duke thinks of what he considers to be the besmirching of his daughter's purity by her passion for Tregear indicates his very Victorian concern with his daughter's purity as a possession:

> He hardly doubted but that he could stamp it out. Though he should have to take her away into some further corner of the world, he would stamp it out. But she, when this foolish passion of hers should have been thus stamped out, could never be the pure, the bright, the unsullied, unspoiled thing, the possession of which he had thought so much. (Chapter 7)

The most striking element of this passage is the juxtaposition of the violent, thrice-repeated phrase "stamp it out" with the Duke's ethereal wording as he laments Mary's loss of that ideal state of purity he so prizes.

Moreover, because Mary seems to love a reincarnation of Burgo Fitzgerald, she seems to be replicating Glencora's gift of "her early spring of love," given to Burgo, not to the Duke: "Dear as she had been, she had not been quite what she should have been but for that. And now this girl of his, who was so much dearer to him than anything else left to him, was doing exactly as her mother had done" (chapter 7).

The Duke thinks of a "cure" for the sullying of his daughter's purity in these terms: "Could he have modelled her future course according to his own wishes, he would have had her live a gentle life for the next three years, with a pencil perhaps in her hand or a musicbook before her; and then come forth, cleansed as it were by such quarantine from the impurity to which she had been subjected" (chapter 11).

The Duke's definition of his daughter's "quarantine," designed to reinstate her purity (as if passion were an exotic, contagious illness!), is so closely aligned to the traditional recommended course of study for Victorian ladies ("a gentle life . . . with a pencil perhaps in her hand or a musicbook before her") that it must have been intended by Trollope (who descried this kind of mock education)[5] to be read ironically, as a commentary on the Duke's conventional image of what is proper for women, and how that shapes his attitude toward and constraint on his daughter.

In connection with the story of Lady Mary, the role of Mrs. Finn, Glencora's most intimate friend, rewards analysis. In several senses, Mrs. Finn can be viewed as an alter ego to Glencora. Primarily, as discussed in particular by

Hagan, Mrs. Finn is Glencora's scapegoat in the Duke's mind in reference to the affair of Lady Mary and Tregear; "in abusing that lady he can disguise from himself the true extent of his anger against Lady Glen herself" (chapter 15). In another sense, Mrs. Finn, with her "fastidiousness, sensitivity, strength and integrity . . . is the perfect female counterpart of the Duke himself" (chapter 14) and is able so to conduct herself as to demand respect (and ultimately an apology) from the Duke. As Shirley Letwin states, "The most perfect gentleman in Trollope's novels is Madame Max Goesler" (chapter 74). And it is finally Mrs. Finn, who—acting in Glencora's place—convinces the Duke of his true duty in relation to his daughter. In this sense, Glencora is vicariously successful, and her romantic hopes for her daughter—and thus imaginatively for herself—are fulfilled. Finally, Mrs. Finn's story, which we discussed in chapter 3, is part of the background of *The Duke's Children:* she has refused what Glencora accepted—marriage to a Duke of Omnium whom she does not love—and she has ultimately been united with the man whom she does fervently love, Phineas Finn. As Glencora's closest friend, her romantic story of passionate fulfillment counterpoints Glencora's unsatisfying marriage: Mrs. Finn's love for Phineas has been, moreover, one of the chief vicarious romances (others include Adelaide Spooner and Gerard Maule in *Phineas Redux,* Emily Wharton and first Lopez and then Arthur Fletcher in *The Prime Minister*), in which Glencora has interested herself, restlessly trying to bring passion into her own rather dry marriage.

Lady Mabel Grex, the woman who loves Frank Tregear, and whom both Tregear and Lord Silverbridge initially love, ultimately emerges in *The Duke's Children* as a tragic figure. If we look at Mabel symbolically, as one of the female characters of the next generation who embodies what could have been Glencora's possibilities, she can be viewed as a tragic incarnation of Glencora's fate, another Victorian aristocratic woman whose only choice seems to be between passionate love and a sensible marriage. While Glencora was compelled into her marriage, and certainly suffered from her abandonment of Burgo, her story is one neither of joy and contentment nor of tragedy, but of an ultimately unresolved struggle to realize herself within an only partially satisfying marriage. Mabel Grex, however, must abandon her great love for Frank Tregear to make what she thinks is necessary to her happiness: a brilliant marriage. She finds, tragically, that her heart cannot change to align itself with the practicality of her decision. Too late, Mabel realizes that, as she finally tells Silverbridge, "to the end of time I shall love Frank Tregear" (chapter 70). But Tregear is now out of her reach, and she is unable to accept any of her more "eligible" suitors. To Miss Casseway, she describes the thought of marrying one of them as "to be mixed somehow with an idea of suicide" (chapter 20). This startling statement powerfully describes Mabel's equation of a loveless marriage with the very opposite of self-realization: the absolute self-negation of death.

Mabel's story is a study of a passionate, intelligent woman who is trying to follow the ambivalent dictates of her culture's ideals for women. As Mabel thinks of it, "the life that was before her,—which it was necessary that she should lead,—seemed to her to be so difficult. She could not clearly see her way to be pure and good and feminine, and at the same time wise" (chapter 10).

Mabel is caught between her society's romantic ideals of love and feminine purity, and society's practical dictums about marrying wisely—that is, marrying a man with an income adequate to maintain the luxurious living to which both she and Frank had become accustomed:

> It is so much easier to think of the past than of the future,—to remember what has been then to resolve what shall be! She had reminded him of the offer which he had made and repeated to her more than once,—to share with her all his chances in life. There would have been almost no income for them. All the world would have been against her. She would have caused his ruin. Her light on the matter had been so clear that it had not taken her very long to decide that such a thing must not be thought of. She had at last been quite stern in her decision.
> Now she was broken-hearted because she found he had left her in very truth. (Chapter 37)

Mabel's lament to Miss Casseway echoes Glencora's ruminations about her loveless marriage as "this total want of sympathy, as this deadness in life" (*Can You Forgive Her?*, chapter 63). But while Glencora and Palliser are able to transform their marriage into one that includes affection and tolerance, if not passion, Mabel rejects the one marriage which for her would have included passionate love and is equally unable to accept any other suitor, even Lord Silverbridge, of whom she is at least fond. As Juliet McMaster astutely comments: "She can summon up the energy to try for him only when he is already out of her reach" (*Palliser Novels*, 143).

Tragically, Mabel does not yet know the strength of her own love for Tregear when she thinks that with Silverbridge, at least "she would not be turned from her duties by disgust, by dislike, or dismay" (chapter 59). (So much for the sexual innocence of Victorian girls; Mabel is 22.) At first, early in the novel, when Mabel is comparing Silverbridge to her other suitors, she muses: "Many of those who were buzzing around her from day to day, were distasteful to her. From among them she knew that she could not take a husband let their rank and wealth be what it might. She was too fastidious, too proud, too prone to think that things should be with her as she liked them! This last was in all things pleasant to her" (chapter 16). In her final interviews with Silverbridge and Tregear, Mabel admits her inability to be sexually attracted to any man other than Tregear—except perhaps Silverbridge. To him she asserts: "But I have liked you so well,—so much better than all the others! A dozen men have asked me to marry them. And though they might be nothing until they made that request, then they became things of horror to me. But you were not a thing of horror" (chapter 70). To Tregear she laments that all men are "abhorrent" to her because of the "virulence of the malady" of her love for him (chapter 77).

Mabel's scarifying words are not an isolated phenomenon in the novel. In the stories of all three of the novel's young women, Trollope is dramatizing something that extends beyond what may at first glance seem only to be Mabel's particular psychology. Not Mabel only, but also Mary and Isabel comment scathingly on the inferiority of the young men who approach them sexually, and Trollope comically dramatizes the inadequacies of their respective unwanted suitors, Lord Popplecourt and Dolly Longstaffe. Mary's disgust for the bland, money-grubbing Popplecourt, who "is not fast only because he did not like to risk his money" (chapter 31) is stated baldly to Lady Cantrip: 'Lord Popplecourt! He cares for nothing but his coal-mines. . . . I despise him, and if he troubles me I shall hate him. As for marrying him, I would sooner die this minute'" (chapter 48).

Avid readers of Trollope know a good deal about Dolly Longstaffe, Isabel's unwanted suitor, from the descriptions of his apathetic languor in *The Way We Live Now* (1874), and we are in on the joke from the moment he dares to approach the glorious, quicksilver Isabel. But Trollope dramatizes Dolly's foolishness fully in the scenes in which he proposes to Isabel, especially in the wonderfully comic scene in which he romances her at her river party. After his proposal, Isabel exclaims in disgust to her parents:

> Young men are pretty much the same everywhere, I guess. They never have their wits about them. They never mean what they say, because they don't understand the use of words . . . indeed, there is no such thing as a young man, for a man is not really a man till he is middle-aged. But take them at their worst they are a deal too good for us, for they become men some day, whereas we must only be women to the end. (Chapter 33)

The angry irony of Isabel's critique seems justified by a survey of the novel's young men. Only Tregear is a mature young man at the novel's outset; Silverbridge always has promise (which is eventually fulfilled by the end of the novel), and his story is that of a young man whose experience is "giving him by degrees age and flavour" (chapter 42). Gerald's admiration for his father, and the wit and loyalty he shows with his brother bode well for him—but Trollope's world of young men seems more likely to be inhabited by idle and self-indulgent men such as Dolly Longstaffe, cautious and mercenary men such as Lord Popplecourt, brutes such as Lord Percival—or just plain misogynists such as Reginald Dobbes.

Isabel's comments take on a darker cast, echoing both Mary's and Mabel's hostile statements, even as her wit and sense of irony manifest themselves in the concluding words of her tirade: "I got to be thinking if any one of them should ask me to marry him, and if moved by some evil destiny I were to take him, whether I should murder him, or myself, or run away with one of the others" (chapter 33). Mabel equates marriage with most young men in her society with suicide; Mary with death; Isabel with murder, suicide or adultery. The violence of the declarations Trollope chooses for each young woman, the uncharacteristic vehemence of feeling expressed, is intentional and significant. Surely Trollope intends a critique of patriarchal culture here. The women of the novel are on the whole so infinitely superior to the men, and yet the men as a matter of course possess the power in this society. As Isabel caustically remarks, "they become men some day, whereas we must only be women to the end" (chapter 33).

It is the dispossessed Mabel, however, who embodies the tragic side of this fact; although she is much superior in intellect, charm and breeding to most of her suitors, yet, as she bitterly exclaims to Silverbridge: "Though I have so hated those men as to be unable to endure them, still I want some man's house, and his name,—some man's bread and wine,—some man's jewels and titles and woods and parks and gardens,—if I can get them" (chapter 73).

The patriarchal oppression Mabel is forced to contend with is not only cultural but also specifically familial. Her father and brother rob her of her rightful patrimony; as she tells Frank after her father's death, "there will be scrapings . . . unless Percival refuses to agree" (chapter 57). Both her father and her brother are gamblers. When the Duke discusses the prospect of Mabel's marriage to Silverbridge, he tells his son openly that "her father is not a man I esteem" (chapter 27). Indeed, he is an only slightly more civilized version of the vicious Lord de Courcy in *The Small House at Allington*. Percival shows in his one place of prominence in the book, in which he wins a great deal of money from the inexperienced Lord Gerald and then behaves very badly about it, that he is, as Silverbridge writes to Gerald, "a beast" (chapter 40). Yet the Earl still exerts patriarchal authority: "there had been objections raised to any intimacy with Frank Tregear" (chapter 10). At the same time, Lord Grex is surly about Mabel's refusal to marry someone suitable (that is, with money) at the very same time that he demands that she surrender her monetary rights. The paragraph Trollope writes about Mabel's evening out with her father, when the Earl is "very disagreeable indeed" because she has just discouraged Silverbridge's first attempt to propose to her, is emblematic of Mabel's predicament. In the following passage, we view her most clearly in her role as "ornament of society":

> They dined out together,—of course with all the luxury that wealth can give. There was a well-appointed carriage to take them backwards and forwards to the next square, such as an Earl should have. She was splendidly dressed, as became an Earl's daughter, and he was brilliant with some star which had been accorded to him by his sovereign's grateful minister in return for staunch parliamentary support. No one looking at them could have imagined that such a father could have told such a daughter that she must marry herself out of the way because as an unmarried girl she was a burden. (Chapter 20)

Again, it seems to me that the most insightful comments about Mabel's familial life have been written by Gindin (although he introduces them as "incidental") whom I quoted in chapter 2 in relation to Laura:

> All these women, incidentally, those who deliberately and frankly choose (or even almost choose) money over love, are the products of cold, unfeeling fathers and absentee mothers or dissipated fathers who squander their wealth, or relatives entirely indifferent to them. In other words,

they have all, despite beauty and brains and birth, suffered from an inhumane environment. In contrast, most of Trollope's sweet, triumphant heroines have always been coddled in warmth and family affection. (38)

Despite the tyranny the Duke exerts over Mary, his household is one in which a "sweet triumphant heroine" might be bred; similarly, the Boncassens treat Isabel with both love and respect. Glencora's relatives, though not dissipated as Mabel's are, exercise a different cruelty—ironically, a cruelty perpetrated to preserve her wealth (or rather, the family's wealth) rather than to squander it, as Lord Grex and Percival squander Mabel's money. Yet Mabel is as much a victim of the patriarchal culture as is Glencora. Both are dispossessed of their authentic lovers, and thus of the possibility of complete self-realization. Glencora, with her vibrant resiliency, characteristically manages to salvage a relatively satisfying marriage; Mabel, who is more "prone to memories, prone to melancholy, prone at times almost to seek the gratification of sorrow" (chapter 38), and who is, as Juliet McMaster has noted, continually characterized by stasis (*Palliser Novels,* 144), cannot transform her experience, but remains locked in the past.

Barickman, MacDonald, and Stark mistake the point when they state that Mabel "misses her chance to marry Silverbridge partly because of her conventional image of masculinity" (38). Wijesinha, too, accepts Mabel's assertions that she wants to marry Silverbridge. Juliet McMaster is much nearer the mark when she states that "she can summon up the energy to try for him only when he is out of her reach" (*Palliser Novels,* 143). Butte may be more insightful yet; mindful of Trollope's statement that Mabel is prone to "the self-gratification of sorrow" (chapter 37), he suggests that "because of her paralysis Mabel loses both her lovers, as she may in the recesses of her heart have desired" (717).

It is through Mabel more fully than through the other two young heroines of *The Duke's Children* that we explore the conventions for Victorian womanhood, both because Mabel explicitly articulates those conventions, and because she feels constrained to defy them.

One of the comments continually made about Mabel throughout the novel is that she seems old. Both Mabel and Silverbridge recognize that she seems more mature than he, and both attribute this to her "peculiar circumstances,"—that is, her familial situation. Lady Mabel has always had to fend for herself, and her premature "wisdom" (as Silverbridge initially perceives it) is due to this. However, the psychological abuse she has endured from the male members of her family, and the lack of a mother (other than her paid companion, Miss Cassewary, who is more like a fond maiden aunt), have caused Mabel to develop protective psychological weapons—her irony, her caution, the artifice Silverbridge finally comes to view with dismay, when comparing Mabel to Isabel:

> Lady Mabel with all her grace, with all her beauty, with all her talent, was a creature of efforts, or, as it might he called, a manufactured article. She strove to be graceful, to be lovely, to be agreeable and clever. Isabel was all this and infinitely more without any struggle. When

> he was most fond of Mabel, most anxious to make her his wife, there had always been present to him a feeling that she was old. Though he knew her age to a day, and knew her to be younger than himself, yet she was old. Something had gone of her native bloom, something had been scratched and chipped from the first fair surface, and this had been repaired with varnish and veneering. Though he had loved her he had never been altogether satisfied with her. But Isabel was as young as Hebe. (Chapter 48)

Mabel has become a creature of artifice in part because she has felt compelled to reject the longings of her real self, in part as a protection against her unfeeling father and brother. That she is "a creature of efforts" is due to her dislocation from her authentic self.[6]

In her discussion with Tregear and with Silverbridge, Mabel rails against "how women are trammelled":

> "Only think how a girl such as I am is placed; or indeed any girl. You, if you see a woman that you fancy, can pursue her, can win and triumph, or lose her and gnaw your heart;—at any rate you can do something. . . . What can a girl do?"
> "Girls work hard too sometimes."
> "Of course they do;—but everybody feels that they are sinning against their sex. Of love, such as a man's is, a woman ought to know nothing. How can she love with passion when she should never give her love till it has been asked, and not then unless her friends tell her that the thing is suitable? Love such as that to me is out of the question." (Chapter 10)

But of course the irony in Mabel's statements *is* that she even yet loves Tregear with a passion "such as that." Through Mabel, Trollope unmasks the basic untruth about this feminine convention of passivity of both feeling and action. Similarly, Trollope shows sympathy for Mabel's decision to have her "revenge" on Silverbridge (even though he doesn't deserve her rebukes for changing his mind, since Mabel repulsed him and practically thrust him into Isabel's arms) rather than to refrain from confronting him. Tregear addresses her first:

> "I would have said nothing."
> "You would have recommended—delicacy! No doubt you think that women should be delicate, let them suffer what they may. A woman should not let it be known that she has any human nature in her. I had him on the hip, and for a moment I used my power!" (Chapter 57)

Glencora's accents can be heard in the scene in which Mabel confesses to Silverbridge her ambition in wanting to marry him: "Not think of it! Do not men think of high titles and great wealth and power and place? And if men, why should not women? Do not men try to get them;—and are they not even applauded for their energy? A woman has but one way to try. I tried" (chapter 73). This passage echoes Glencora's words in justification of her unwonted energy as political hostess: "And why should she not have her ambition in life as well as he his?" (*The Prime Minister,* chapter 32). The interrogatory form that both defensive speeches take is significant because they challenge masculine assumptions, questioning the grounds of male authority. Mabel's exasperated words indicate that she is Glencora's heir in her frustration with the confinements of woman's role, with conventional expectations of what is properly woman's "nature and mission."

Mabel is also heir to Glencora in her self-hatred, as she thinks of her willingness to betray the ideal of purity for Victorian womanhood:

> And what could she lose? The sweet bloom of her maiden shame? That, she told herself, with bitterest inner tears, was already gone from her. That bloom of her maiden shame, of which she quite understood the sweetness, the charm, the value—was gone when she had brought herself to such a state that, loving one man, she should be willing to marry another. The sweet treasure was gone from her. Its aroma was fled. (Chapter 59)

Mabel's anguished reflections echo Glencora's self-upbraidings, voiced to Alice in *Can You Forgive Her?*:

> She had loved a man and had separated herself from him and had married another, all within a month or two. "It is an unmaidenly thing to do, certainly . . . but one may be driven. One may be so driven that all gentleness of womanhood is driven out of one. . . . Oh, Alice, if you knew how I hate myself!" (*Can You Forgive Her?*, chapter 25)

It is, however, because Mabel is finally *not* able to be untrue to her love for Tregear, because she has misunderstood her own faithful nature, that she expresses contempt for herself. She is speaking to Silverbridge: "A jackal is born a jackal, and not a lion, and cannot help himself. So is a woman born—a woman. They are clinging, parasite things, which cannot but adhere; though they destroy themselves by adhering!" (chapter 54).

To Tregear, in her final, painful meeting with him, Mabel expresses the desperation of her passion in terms that are explicitly sexual, offering—although she knows it is impossible—to be his mistress in order to be true to her love. Part of Mabel's tragedy is that she has come to think of her essential, unwilling faithfulness as "wicked," because she judges herself by the canons of female purity: as a woman, she should not be sexually passionate, should certainly not long for a man who does not intend to make her his wife—who indeed no longer loves her. Her speech is one of the most moving in all of Trollope:

> "Frank, is it wicked that I should love you?" He could only shake his head in answer to this. "If it be so wicked that I must be punished for it eternally, still I love you. I can never, never, never love another. You cannot understand it. Oh God,—that I had never understood it myself! I think, I think, that I would go with you now anywhere, facing all misery, all judgments, all disgrace. You know, do you not, that if it were possible, I should not say so. But as I know that you would not stir a step with me, I do say so."
> "I know it is not meant."
> "It is meant, though it could not be done." (Chapter 57)

Again, Mabel is Glencora's heir in that she is forced to think of herself in the role of the most reviled of Victorian women, the "fallen woman."[7] Neither Glencora nor Mabel "fall"—but the sympathy with which sexual passion in women is treated in these two stories is subversive of conventional models of female purity and angelic sexlessness.

Although Butte claims that "Mabel inherits that bitterness in Glencora" which, because Glencora made the marriage Mabel finally could not, "left deeper scars" (712) in Glencora's psyche, I think he is wrong. The more tragic figure, the one with much less fulfillment, is surely Mabel, who is left with nothing *but* her scars. Glencora is to have some means of expressing her sexuality—she will, after all, engage in marital intercourse and bear four children—and she will see her passion for Burgo achieve a surrogate consummation in her daughter's love for Tregear.[8] Mabel, however, is to live a celibate existence with only Miss Cassewary as companion, as she jokes with assumed lightness to Frank, "two old maids together!" (chapter 77).

At the conclusion of Mabel's history, after she has told Silverbridge not only that she has never loved him, but that "to the end of time I shall love Frank Tregear" (chapter 73), Silverbridge's thoughts serve as chorus to the tragedy of Mabel's position:

> What a terrible story was that he had heard! The horror to him was chiefly in this,—that she should yet be driven to marry some man without even fancying that she could love him! And this was Lady Mabel Grex, who, on his own first entrance into London life, now not much more than twelve months ago, had seemed to him to stand above all other girls in beauty, charm, and popularity! (Chapter 74)

To assess his realization of her tragedy, one must compare Silverbridge's somber thoughts about Mabel's dilemma with the conventional, thoughtless attitude expressed in his earlier remarks to her. Mabel and Silverbridge are at a Matching dinner party, discussing his loss of an enormous sum of money at the Leger horse races. Mabel speaks first:

> "Your father has just paid seventy thousand pounds for you. My father has been good enough to take something less than a quarter of that sum from me;—but still it was all that I was ever to have."
> "Girls don't want money."
> "Don't they? When I look forward it seems to me that a time will come when I shall want it very much."
> "You will marry," he said. (Chapter 52)

One wonders if Silverbridge, pondering Mabel's fate as he leaves her amid the gloomy disarray of her dead father's house—a house that will not belong to her and which is at that very moment being dismantled—remembers Mabel's prophecy and his own thoughtless prediction and muses over their bitter irony.

While the possibility of a more tragic fate is visualized in Mabel's story, through Isabel and Mary the consummation of passionate love that Glencora was denied is realized. We have seen how Mary's love for Tregear somehow symbolizes her mother's abandoned love for Burgo Fitzgerald to both Glencora and to Palliser. As Butte points out, for the Duke, Silverbridge's prospective marriage to Mabel symbolizes his own proper marriage with the highly born noblewoman Glencora (716). Isabel, as an outsider, an American, at first seems to the Duke, with all his publicly espoused Liberal sympathies, to be an intruder in the private realms of English aristocracy.

The history of Mary's love for Tregear and her resemblance to her mother in both appearance and with relation to certain traits of her character—such as the "hot-headed obstinacy" (chapter 24) Lady Cantrip notes in exasperation—mark her as one inheritor of Glencora's history. However, it is Isabel Boncassen, who is to be the wife of Glencora's son Silverbridge, who not only most resembles Glencora in wit and spirit, but who finally seems to achieve the most perfect balance of self-realization within love and marriage of which Trollope can conceive.

Isabel is, first, heir to Glencora's vivacity, to her zest for life: "Isabel Boncassen was certainly a very pretty girl. . . . Her eyes . . . were full of life and brilliancy, and even when she was silent her mouth would speak. . . . It was, I think, the vitality of her countenance . . . that made all acknowledge that she was beautiful" (chapter 28). The very first thing we hear about Isabel is Mrs. Montacute-Jones's comment that she has inquired about Silverbridge in a spirit of "real downright fun" (chapter 28). And although it seemed to Glencora at last that there was no more fun in life—"I have never really enjoyed anything since I was in love, and I only liked that because it was wicked," she tells Mrs. Finn (*The Prime Minister,* chapter 72)—Isabel's fate will be more kind. Her sense of humor does not turn to sharp sarcasm because of disappointment and boredom, as does Glencora's. Isabel will achieve her love and retain her wit, including the ability to poke fun at herself: She can use Dolly Longstaffe's epithet for her, "pert poppet," to Lord Silverbridge, and even tease the formidable Duke about being "your scarlet coat and your cross-legged Turk" in her first formal interview with him (chapter 72). Only Isabel and Glencora have ever, in all the long history of the Palliser novels, dared the intimacy of raillery with this austere man. Isabel's gentle tone, however, accompanied by "a sparkle of mirth in her eye," now replaces the often acrid comments of Glencora, whose wit was her weapon, her frustrated defense against a man whose temperament was exasperatingly different from her own.

The even tenor of Isabel's sense of humor and her capacity for self-mockery tell of another of her qualities: self-respect, a sense of self-worth. This quality is manifested in several ways, each indicative of an independence and integrity of character of which the young Glencora was not yet capable. Even in her first encounter with Silverbridge, Isabel demonstrates this self-respect when she insists on abiding by "English ways" as to the proper conduct for young women, rather than desiring to be an exception because she is an American:

> "I needn't wear a hideous bit of cloth over my face in Constantinople because I am a woman. But when the discrepancies are small, then they have to be attended to. . . . Do you think that I don't understand that everybody will be making remarks upon the American girl who won't leave the son of the Duke of Omnium alone?" (Chapter 28)

Such language is reminiscent of another of Trollope's wisest heroines, Violet Effingham. One can hear the accents of Violet as she explains to Lady Laura why she must be careful of herself—and why Lord Chiltern is a risk:

> "When I was a child they used to be always telling me to mind myself. It seems to me that a child and a man need not mind themselves. Let them do what they may, they can be set right again. . . . But a woman has to mind herself—and very hard work it is when she has a dragon of her own driving her ever the wrong way." (*Phineas Finn*, chapter 10)

During Dolly Longstaffe's misconceived courtship of Isabel, when he tells her that "I can give you as good a position as any man without a title in England," Isabel answers indignantly: "Mr. Longstaffe, I rather fancy that wherever I may be I can make a position for myself. At any rate I shall not marry with the view of getting one. If my husband were an English Duke I should think myself nothing, unless I was something as Isabel Boncassen"(chapter 32). Readers of *The Prime Minister* surely cannot help but think at this point of Glencora's words, as at a much later age, she tries to define her sense of self to Mrs. Finn: "I am myself, too, Glencora M'Cluskie that was, and I've made for myself a character that I'm not ashamed of" (*The Prime Minister*, chapter 37).

But it is in her relations with Silverbridge that Isabel most clearly demonstrates her very strong sense of self, as she repeatedly insists that she must be assured of acceptance by the Duke before she becomes Silverbridge's wife. (In admiring this stance, I differ from Juliet McMaster, who feels that within the context of Mabel's and Mary's pain, Isabel's seeming willlingness to abandon her love is untenable, a throwback to Lucy Robarts and Grace Crawley of the Barsetshire series [*Palliser Novels*], 151–53). To Mary, Isabel states proudly of her wish to marry Silverbridge that "though it be heaven I will not creep there through a hole. If I cannot go in with my head upright, I will not go even there" (chapter 47).

The significance of Isabel's self-respect is brought into relief as a commentary on the self-hatred of so many of the other women in *Can You Forgive Her?*, *The Prime Minister,* and *The Duke's Children.* In part, Trollope means us to see self-respect as the manifestation of a loving family life: Mr. Boncassen is both affectionate and wise, and Mrs. Boncassen is a loving, nurturing woman. Further than this, Isabel has been taught not only by her family but by her country to be independent and to seek knowledge. Trollope obviously respects his fictional character's very American sense of independence (as he did his American friend Kate Field's), which Isabel, with her wisdom and charms combined, manages to use in the best possible manner.

Another aspect of Isabel's independence is exhibited in the symbolic scene in the Priory ruins. Since the scene is emblematic in nature, encompassing not only the story of Isabel, but also the stories of Glencora, Mary, Mabel and even Mrs. Finn, it is worth discussing at some length. The scene is introduced with Lady Mabel's bitter comment to Mrs. Finn that the lovemaking between Isabel and Silverbridge "means nothing":

> "If so, I am sorry for the young lady," said Mrs. Finn.
> "Don't you think that one always has to be sorry for the young ladies? Young ladies generally have a bad time of it. Did you ever hear of a gentleman who had always to roll a stone to the top of a hill, but it would always come back upon him?"
> "That gentleman I believe never succeeded." said Mrs. Finn. "The young ladies I suppose do sometimes." (Chapter 53)

In answer to Mabel's Sisyphus-like vision are, first, Mrs. Finn's characteristically sympathetic, rational replies. But the even more effective response is the scene of Isabel's and Silverbridge's lovemaking in the ruins, a point Trollope makes clear with the phrase "in the meantime," used as a transition between Mabel's disillusioned perception (with Mrs. Finn's commentary) and the sweet vision of the lovers:

> In the meantime Isabel and Silverbridge were among the ruins together. "This is where the old Pallisers used to be buried," he said.
> "Oh indeed. And married, I suppose."
> "I dare say. They had a priest of their own, no doubt, which must have been convenient. This block of a fellow without any legs is supposed to represent Sir Guy. He ran away with half a dozen heiresses, they say. I wish things were as easily done now."
> "Nobody should have run away with me. I have no idea of going on such a journey except on terms of equality,—just step and step alike." Then she took hold of his arm and put out one foot. "Are you ready?"
> "I am very willing."
> "But are you ready,—for a straightforward walk off to church before all the world? None of your private chaplains, such as Sir Guy had at his command. Just the registrar, if there is nothing better, so that it be public, before all the world." (Chapter 53)

Isabel's insistence on equality and openness in her sexual relations is indicative of both her independence and her pride of self. Her bantering declaration that she will have nothing to do with elopements or abductions resounds immediately; we think first of Glencora's thoughts of running off with Burgo, and then of Mabel's final, desperate statement to Tregear, her half-willingness even for that disgrace. Of course, for those familiar with *Can You Forgive Her?*, the symbolism of the scene is further marked: Glencora is buried in the Priory, and the ruins are the scene of her moonlight ramble with Alice Vavasor (*Can You Forgive Her?*, chapter 27) and the locus of romantic associations for Glencora.[9] In this place, where Glencora sought consolation amid the symbols of Romanticism (ruins, moonlight), Isabel walks in the light of day, rejecting the destructive romance of Sir Guy, insisting on the importance of reality, of public avowals of her love. The scene reverberates until the end of the novel; Isabel will walk in these ruins once again, as Silverbridge's wife, in the procession at Mary's wedding in the Priory. Thus Mary, too, is fulfilled in the place which symbolized discontentment and unsatisfied longing for her mother.[10]

Finally, the presence of Mrs. Finn, Glencora's most intimate friend, is significant. As Madame Max Goesler, she might well have thought her love for Phineas Finn was the effort of Sisyphus (in *Phineas Finn, Phineas Rudux*), but her perseverance ends not in defeat but in victory. Mrs. Finn was one of the young ladies who "do sometimes" succeed; her understated comment resonates with knowledge of her history.

That all these associations are conscious on Trollope's part, and accrete in the Palliser series as a whole, tells us much about his novelistic method. Perhaps he is not overtly a "symbolic writer," but to state, as some of his critics have, that he does not use symbolism, constitutes a serious undermining of his diverse powers as a fictionist.

In this same beautiful scene of Isabel's and Silverbridge's lovemaking in the Priory ruins, Isabel demonstrates another facet of her character that is much like Glencora's: she is passionate, and sexually responsive. Isabel longs to kiss Silverbridge, and tells him so—but again, her strong sense of her self-worth holds her back from any action that might even yet diminish her self-respect: " 'No,' she said. 'What is it but a trifle! It is nothing in itself. But I have bound myself to myself by certain promises, and you must not ask me to break them. You are as sweet to me as I can be to you, but there shall be no kissing till I know that I shall be your wife' " (chapter 53). To the twentieth-century reader, this may seem like mild stuff, but Isabel's "you are as sweet to me as I can be to you" is Trollope's means of expressing that feminine sexual longing is equal to that of men. We are a long way from the sexless angel of Victorian convention. And as Juliet McMaster points out, Isabel's exclamations to Mary about Silverbridge being "as handsome as a god" (chapter 47) are another means Trollope uses to express her sexual attraction to Silverbridge.[11] Finally, to Silverbridge himself, Isabel speaks passionately of her love: "Love you! Oh, my darling . . . From the sole of your foot to the crown of your head I love you as I think a man would wish to be loved by the girl he loves . . . " (chapter 52).

Thus there is a subversive element even in the comic resolution of the novel, particularly in Isabel's story. Her self-realization seems to me to be both more complex and more perfect than Mary's, although Trollope stresses that Mary's union with Tregear will be successful because "the wife thoroughly respected the husband, as did the husband the wife" (chapter 80). Moreover, the story of Lady Mabel provides a strong tension against this comic resolution, a powerful commentary on the plight of Victorian womanhood under a patriarchal system. Her history is that of a woman who is victimized not only by the culture's confused dictates for women,[12] but also much more intimately by her father and brother, the familial embodiments of the patriarchal society under which she is crushed.

Conclusion

At the beginning of this study, I quoted Michael Sadleir's statement that Anthony Trollope was the "Voice of an Epoch." In agreement with Sadleir, Raymond Williams cites Trollope's "smooth and recommending construction" as evidence that he is at ease with the conventions of his times. Williams states that the characteristic "unity" of a Trollope novel is evidence that Trollope lacks the "creative disturbance" that signals "where the life is" in the fiction of George Eliot and Thomas Hardy:

> What we have to emphasise, on the contrary, is the creative disturbance which is exactly George Eliot's importance. . . . That is where the life is, in that disturbed and unprecedented time. And those who responded most deeply, who saw most, had no unified form, no unity of tone and language, no controlling conventions, that really answered their purposes. Their novels are the records of struggle and difficulty, as was the life they wrote about. (85)

In this study of Trollope's Palliser novels, I have focused on the tensions in Trollope's work which embody his ambivalent response to the Victorian ideals for womanhood that lay at the heart of the "Woman Question" controversy. I suggest that this tension, rather than Williams's "smooth and recommending construction," is precisely the characteristic Trollopian form. This is the dialectic that makes Trollope's novels "records of struggle and difficulty," and signals Trollope's importance as a social historian of "that disturbed and unprecedented time" that was nineteenth-century Victorian England.

This dialectic seems to become more intense as the Palliser saga progresses. In *Can You Forgive Her?*, the comic closure is qualified in both Glencora's and Alice's stories, but neither the remembrance that Alice's marriage to John Grey is a retreat from freedom nor the contradictions inherent in Glencora's acceptance of her unsatisfying marriage with the birth of her son strains against the novel's essentially comic vision to the degree that elements subversive of comedy intrude upon the final images of happiness in the later novels of the series. In *Phineas Redux,* Phineas's marriage to Madame Max and Adelaide's to Gerard Maule, and the fertile union of Violet with Chiltern are shadowed by the final image of Lady Laura in wretched seclusion with the patriarch who has contributed to her misery. In *The Prime Minister,* the memory of the Wharton who is now "no better than a beggar brat" belies Willliams's dictum that to read Trollope is "to find the conventional happy ending where property and happiness can coexist and be celebrated, rather than an awkward stubborn unappeased resignation" (84–85). Finally, in the ending of *The Duke's Children*—the conclusion to the entire Palliser series—the image of the dispossessed Mabel in the ruin of her dead father's house remains powerfully with us, rising to the stature of the tragic even as the weddings of Isabel to Silverbridge and of Mary to Tregear suggest a new equality of love and respect in relations between Man and Woman.

The subversiveness which is inherent in this dialectic appears to be more deliberate than critics have heretofore acknowledged. Critics like Geoffrey Harvey and Peter Garrett have recently argued persuasively that Trollope is a much more conscious artist than has traditionally been allowed. I have found their work helpful as support for my contention that the structure of Trollope's Palliser novels consciously embodies his conflicting ideas about his culture's feminine ideals, as it undermines the traditional beliefs about women's nature and role that the conventions of romantic comedy embody.

Trollope's reservations about his culture's feminine ideals did not, of course, begin or end with the Palliser novels. Trollope creates angelic heroines that have his overt approval in an early work like *The Three Clerks* (1858) and in a novel written in the last year of his life, *Marion Fay* (1882). In *The Three Clerks,* the angelic Linda and Katie Woodward pale in comparison to Gertrude, their strong, passionate sister, who becomes a heroic emigrant wife. In *Marion Fay,* Trollope seems to be making a final attempt to glorify an angelic heroine who is dying a Romantic death from tuberculosis. However, by the time of her literal apotheosis, her goodness is depicted as an unnatural, perverse resistance to sexual fruition that seems far from ideal. She is upstaged by the witty, rebellious Lady Frances Trafford, who emerges as the voice of joyful sanity.

Trollope's explorations of the feminine ideal of self-sacrifice continue until his death. Two novels written at the end of his life, *Kept in the Dark* (1882) and *An Old Man's Love* (1884), come to different conclusions about the ideal of womanly self-denial. In *Kept in the Dark,* in which Trollope seems to be criticizing contemporary assumptions about male and female sexual roles, there is a conventional resolution which seems to negate the intent of the entire book. Cecilia Holt, the novel's heroine, at length insists that she alone is guilty for her past estrangement from her husband, despite evidence clearly implicating him. In contrast, in *An Old Man's Love,* Mary Lawrie rebels against the conventional expectation of self-denying female character, and she finds passionate fulfillment in marriage to the man she loves, John Gordon. It is Mr. Whittlestaff, the man who originally demands that she conform to the self-sacrificing ideal, who is himself compelled to suppress his desire.

The idea of the gentleman is at the center of Trollope's work. My study suggests that the "gentleman question" inherent in Trollope's response to the

"Woman Question" could be fruitfully investigated in a companion study that would examine Trollope's attitude toward Victorian cultural ideals of masculinity. Recent work on Victorian women writers by Kathleen Blake, Shirley Foster, Judith Newton, and Ann Shapiro suggest that a rigorous comparison of Trollope to major female novelists of his time would provide further insight into the extent of the subversiveness inherent in Trollope's attitude toward his culture's sexual ideals.

Pat Jalland's fine exploration of the lives of Victorian women in the world of high politics in *Women, Marriage, and Politics, 1860–1914* (1987) provides further evidence that many Victorian middle- and upper-class women eluded the constraints placed upon them and led freer, more active lives than has generally been supposed. This landmark work, based on the archives of seventy major political families, provides a crucial historical context for Trollope's fiction while it simultaneously calls for companion studies of lower middle- and working-class women that would further illuminate the influence of class upon Victorian ideals of womanhood.

Ultimately, Trollope's vision of women's rights is marital equality. And yet Glencora, the central heroine in the Palliser novels, is not satisfied with what Isabel calls the "terms of equality." She longs for equality with men in the public world, but she fails in her attempt to negotiate these more subversive "terms of equality," the terms that J. S. Mill calls for in *On the Subjection of Women.* The sense of comic fulfillment at the end of the series is undermined not only by the tragic fate of Mabel Grex, but by the memory of Glencora, whose dissatisfied ghost broods over the weddings of her children.

Notes

Introduction

1. See also Charles Blinderman, John Halperin, and David Aitken for additional support of this view. Blinderman, for instance, states that "Trollope helps define the mode in which the Victorian woman was stereotyped by society and by literature" (55). In his discussion of Alice Vavasor, Halperin insists upon Trollope's "distaste . . . for independent women" (*Trollope and Politics,* 38). He asserts that "women who want to become "independent" are portrayed by Trollope and Dickens as neurotic, confused, wavering, and unhappy—unfeminine in their aggressive hardness and, ultimately, embittered failures" (41). Aitken argues that "Trollope appears to subscribe unthinkingly" to conventional notions of woman's nature and role.

2. See Trollope, *An Autobiography,* (154–55): "To carry out my scheme I have had to spread my picture over so wide a canvas that I cannot expect that any lover of such art should trouble himself to look at it as a whole. Who will read *Can You Forgive Her?, Phineas Finn, Phineas Redux,* and *The Prime Minister* consecutively, in order that they may understand the characters of the Duke of Omnium, of Plantagenet Palliser, and of Lady Glencora? Who will ever know that they should be so read? On the plan to add *The Duke's Children:* "I have an idea that I shall even yet once more have recourse to my political hero as the mainstay of another story" (300).

3. See Ramona L. Denton, "*The Eustace Diamonds:* Trollope's Book of Odd Women" *(Kentucky Philological Association Bulletin,* 1977:7–13) for a brief but cogent analysis of "the extent to which the 'Woman Question' governs the novel's concerns" (8). Denton's article deals only with the two central female characters in the novel, Lizzie Eustace and Lucy Morris.

4. In this view I differ from Bill Overton, who states that "Trollope's official view is then reinforced . . . by his design in his novels" (6), and from Jean Kennard, who discusses Trollope's orthodox use of the literary convention she terms the "convention of the two suitors" (10–11). The argument made by Richard Barickman, Susan MacDonald and Myra Stark that Trollope's critique of sexual roles is reflected in the analogical structuring of his multiplot novels is closer to my view. They state that "counterpoint has become unresolved dissonance" (200). In "Emily and Nora and Dorothy and Priscilla and Jemima and Carry," Ruth apRoberts is concerned with the significance of the analogical pairings in *He Knew He Was Right* as a method of newly assessing "the ways of courtship and marriage" (87). She states that the "focus and common concern of all the stories is a sexual self-realization" (100).

5. James Kincaid was the first critic to discuss "a basic duality between the conventional comedy and the conventional narrator who is employed in highly unconventional ways" (17). Kincaid also argues that the form of "most Victorian fiction" is a "mixed form," that is somewhere in between the traditional closed form of the romantic comedy and the modern open form (18–23).

He speaks of this "opening of the closed form, a delicate operation for which Trollope had many instruments at hand: the action itself, the narrator, and the chronicle device" (28). Kincaid is particularly concerned with Trollope's "marked tendency to resist one of the major traditional requirements of romantic comedy, namely the full-hearted satisfaction women feel in anticipating marriage" (28). While Overton tends to view the narrator, who voices "explicit remarks in their [the novels'] telling" as a support to "Trollope's official view" (6). Kincaid argues that Trollope's "intrusive" (32), often ironic narrators are one of the devices he uses to open the closed form of his novels. I argue that Trollope's narrators are at times conventional and at times subversive, reflecting Trollope's own conflict in relation to Victorian ideals for women. Our understanding of Trollope's use of comic form is immeasurably deepened by Christopher Herbert's recent book, *Trollope and Comic Pleasure,* in which he analyzes the tension created between Trollope's realism and his use of the traditional formal patterns of Jacobean stage comedy.

6. Although the term "redundant" became current with W. R. Greg's 1862 *National Review* article, "Why Are Women Redundant?," the problem had been recognized by 1851, when Anna Jameson announced from the lecture platform that there was an excess of half a million women in England. Although Jameson was not entirely accurate (the census figures allow 365,159), she was right about the general proportions of the problem. But it was an 1859 article by Harriet Martineau in the *Edinburgh Review* which drew on the 1851 census figures that is often acknowledged to have focused public awareness on the problem of "redundant" women. See Lee Holcolme, *Victorian Ladies at Work* (Archon, 1973, 11–14) for a cogent discussion of Martineau's article.

7. See J. A. Banks, *Prosperity and Parenthood,* chapter 5; and Patricia Branca, chapter 3.

8. Trollope wrote to Kate Field in February of 1877: "All your points can be argued pro and con as to women lecturing;—but you do not I think catch the objections which are made;—that oratory is connected chiefly with forensic, parliamentary, and pulpit pursuits for which women are unfitted because they are wanted elsewhere;—because in such pursuits a man is taken from his home, and because she is wanted at home" (*Letters,* 2: 708-9).

9. See "The Telegraph Girl," *Good Cheer* (the Christmas number of *Good Words,* 1877) and "The Young Women at the London Telegraph Office," *Good Words* 17 (June 1877, 377-84). Trollope writes in a letter to Donald Macleod, editor of *Good Words:* "Some weeks since I went to see these young women at work, and being much struck with them, my imagination went to work and composed a little story about one. . . . Then Mr. Isbister suggested (on hearing my description of the girls' work and of the excellence of their conduct) that I should give some such description in a separate article. . . . I think you will be gratified at the success of this branch of female employment" (*Letters,* 2: 705-6).

10. Henry James's "Modern Women" (*Nation,* 7 [1868], 332-34) reviews *Modern Women and What Is Said of Them* (New York, 1868), an anonymously published collection of articles written by Linton and J. R. Green: the quotation from James's review is from 333, quoted in Helsinger, Sheets, and Veeder (1: 119).

11. One of the ways in which Trollope qualifies his sympathy is, interestingly, to portray Arabella as sexually frigid. While Ruth apRoberts recognizes this sexual coldness (*Moral Trollope,* 183-84), R. C. Terry believes that in Arabella, "amongst others, we sense human sexuality, rather than passionless purity" (107)

12. See James Hammerton, *Emigrant Gentlewomen,* chapter 3, for a good discussion of Taylor.

13. See Nina Auerbach, chapter 4, for an excellent discussion of real-life heroic old maids in Victorian England.

14. Michael Sadleir tells us that "Miss Todd is said to have been modelled on Frances Power Cobbe, a fat jolly lady who was prominent as a humanitarian and an antivivisectionist" (386n).

15. For an opposing view on Lily's choice, see Judith Weissman, who states that Trollope does not present her as "self-destructive or masochistic" (17). Weissman focuses on the originality of Trollope's conception of Lily Dale as a novel heroine, asserting that "Lily Dale is the first important heroine in the English novel who falls in love with someone who clearly does not deserve her, suffers, and neither learns some kind of lesson that enables her later to fall in love with the right person—like Dorothea Brooke or Amelia Sedley—nor comes to a tragic end— like Scott's Rebecca" (16-17). Weissman states that "Trollope is satisfied to see Lily become a woman like her mother or Lady Lufton or Monica Thorn [sic] or Lady Julia de Guest" (24) because her choice to remain an old maid vindicates the worth of integrity and individuality within the community of Barsetshire. Carolyn Heilbrun disagrees with me and with Weissman: "The question of why society should not provide saner outlets for the energies, abilities, and forcefulness of vital women is never asked by Trollope, whose conventional world leaves no room for such questions. Lily Dale may not marry, but her refutation of marriage wins for her, and for us, no new revelation of individual worth" (57). See also Sarah Gilead's fine essay, "Trollope's Orphans and the 'Power of Positive Performance,'" *Texas Studies in Language and Literature,* (27 [1985]: 86-105), in which Gilead discusses Lily's "symbolic orphaning" by Crosbie, exemplar of "the ruthless social-climbing ambitions of the middle-class urbanite" (90). Gilead asserts that "Lily's humiliation at having been jilted leads to her adopting the role of celibate martyr, an unrejectable role in a society seeking secular versions of the Christian myth of redemption by renunciation or self-sacrifice. . . . Lily's loyalty to the absconded Crosbie removes her from the victimized class of marriageable young women; as permanent daughter to her widowed mother, Lily becomes a spectator safely on the sidelines of the emotionally risky processes of generation" (90).

Chapter 1

1. In "Unity and Irony in Trollope's *Can You Forgive Her?,*" *Studies In English Literature* (8 [1969]: 669-80), David S. Chamberlain is also interested in the thematic unity of the three plots in the novel, arguing that the main theme is "that good marriage demands certain specific and different compromises by both men and women" (670). However, contrary to my perception of Arabella Greenow as a subversive figure, Chamberlain views the widow's "sensible compromise between romance and prudence" as "Trollope's main thematic control" (676).

2. In his controversial essay, "Can You Forgive Him?: Trollope's *Can You Forgive Her?* and the Myth of Realism," *Victorian Studies* (18 [1974-75]: 5-30), George Levine also discusses this scene, interpreting it as symbolic of Glencora's fate if she pursues romance (Burgo) rather than the pragmatic (Palliser): "The application to Glencora is almost too obvious, but we are reminded of it, more delicately, when she dances with Burgo later. 'Then she put up her nostrils,—as ladies do as well as horses when running has been severe and they want air' (II, 125)" (28). Nina Auerbach provides commentary on Burgo's relation to Glencora when she states that "we experience with Vronsky the aristocratic magnificence of [Frou-Frou] . . . foreshadowing his finely bred dream-mistress Anna. Through clumsy riding Vronksy betrays his eloquent horse" (178-79).

3. Women were born to be imperious queens who ruled all mankind through their unquestioned moral power, but they were also born to be perpetual children. In the vision of the Victorian angel, Woman possesses the "majestic childishness" (Ruskin, 90) that indicates her distance from the struggles of the male sphere of ambition—and of sexuality. The clearest example of this "majestic childishness" is in Patmore's *The Angel in the House:*

> He's never young nor ripe; she grows
> More infantine, auroral, mild,
> And still the more she lives and knows
> The lovelier she's express'd a child. (89)

The Victorian woman's ideal childlike sexual innocence was authenticated by medical authorities such as Willliam Acton, who denied that normal children and women felt sexual desire. For Acton, as for Patmore and Ruskin, woman's childlike purity was necessary to control "the chaos of sexual excess" (Helsinger, Sheets, and Veeder 2: 58) that might bring down civilization itself. (For crucial insight into Ruskin's own marriage with Effie Gray, see Phyllis Rose's fascinating book, *Parallel Lives*.) For other Victorians, such as the Tennyson of the *Idylls*, woman's moral superiority, which was due to the greater purity and spirituality of her feminine nature, made her worthy of the chivalrous love that exalted man above the beasts. As Carol Christ has shown in "Victorian Masculinity and the Angel in the House," Victorian men perceived themselves as both worshippers and desecrators of women's purity. Woman's childlike passivity called forth man's protective instincts, *and* excited his sexual desire.

4. In contrast to my view, Wijesinha states that "it is apparent that the actual motivation behind the care exercise [sic] on behalf of Glencora and her interests he [Trollope] regards with unqualified approval" (51).

5. Donald D. Stone discusses the Byronic aspects of George Vavasor. Juliet McMaster states that "in his depiction of the Satyrs, the wild men, Trollope is voicing the common-sense Victorian reaction to Romanticism. George Vavasor's scar, like his moody and violent behaviour, relate him to Cain and Ahab, and other Satanic heroes dear to the Romantic imagination" (24). John C. Kleis, in "Passion vs. Prudence: Theme and Technique in Trollope's Palliser Novels," (*Texas Studies in Language and Literature* 11 [1970]: 1405-14), discusses George's "Heathcliffian treatment of Kate" and other aspects of his behavior, character, and appearance that are those of "the superirrational hero" (1408). David R. Eastwood, in "Trollope and Romanticism" (*Victorian Newsletter* 52 [1977]: 1-5), stresses Trollope's undermining of Byronic Romanticism, but does not discuss *Can You Forgive Her?*

6. All of these feminine ideals, however divergent, were dependent on the doctrine of the "two spheres." The idea of distinct and separate spheres of influence and activity for the sexes was given its most influential early Victorian expression in Sarah Lewis's *Woman's Mission* (1839). Lewis helped to define some of the central terms in the "Woman Question" controversy: "Woman's mission," "Woman's sphere," and "Woman's influence." For Lewis, "Woman's mission" as moral teacher is defined by her innate moral superiority to Man because she has been chosen by God to be the vessel of maternal love. In her contented self-renunciation, Woman embodies the union of sacrifice and happiness exemplified by Christ. Women—especially mothers—were to exercise their moral influence within the shelter of the domestic sphere. For a complete discussion of Lewis's important text, see Elizabeth Helsinger, Robin Sheets and William Veeder, chapter 1.

7. Victorians of widely varying political views felt that woman's greater purity and self-sacrificing nature qualified her for the special mission of reforming man: early Compteans, the later followers of Comte led by Frederic Harrison and his fellow Positivists, who stated that "our true ideal of the emancipation of Woman is to enlarge in all things the spiritual, moral, affective influence of Woman" (*Realities and Ideals,* quoted in Burstyn, 32); women like Josephine Butler in England, who called for women to "elevate the moral standard of men" when she led the repeal of the Contagious Diseases Acts ("Address to Croyden" and "Address at Bradford," quoted in Helsinger, Sheets, and Veeder 2:163); apocalyptic feminists like American suffragettes Elizabeth Cady Stanton and Susan B. Anthony, who supported the Social Purity Reform Move-

ment which swept America in the 1880s; Eliza W. Farnham (author of a central text of apocalyptic feminism, *Woman and her Era*, 1864), or Frances Willard, American founder of the Woman's Christian Temperance Union.

8. The ideal of the Perfect Lady, the leisured ornament of society, could easily shade into the ideal of woman as delicate invalid. There were certainly elements in the life of an ornamental lady that might contribute to ill health: Victorian women often corseted themselves and their young daughters much too tightly in order to achieve a fashionable genteel figure; women's gowns were very heavy, involving as many as twenty yards of material, which was then often trimmed with stone such as jet; it was not considered appropriate for girls to engage in vigorous exercise after they reached puberty. For the controversy over "tight-lacing," see Deborah Gorham (69–70); for the restrictiveness of Victorian gowns, see Barbara Rees (chapter 8); for girls' exercise, see Gorham (70–72 and 94–97). Lorna Duffin tells us in "The Conspicuous Consumptive: Woman as Invalid," that "the image of the perfect lady, in time, became the image of the disabled lady, the female invalid" (26). For other good discussions of the ideal and reality of woman as invalid see Helsinger, Sheets, and Veeder (2: 72–75); Regina Morantz, "The Lady and Her Physician," and Ann Wood, " 'The Fashionable Diseases': Women's Diseases and Their Treatment in Nineteenth-Century America."

    Invalidism was a reality for some Victorian women, enhanced if not directly caused by the physical and mental constraints imposed upon them by cultural ideals of femininity. In "Sex and Death in Victorian England," Sheila Ryan Johansson cites the mortality rate of well-to-do Victorian females during girlhood and middle life—which was higher than that of middle-class males at corresponding periods—as evidence that "females employed as ladies, like men employed as copper miners, were engaged in a hazardous occupation that undermined their health and shortened their lives" (181). This reality was reinforced by the ideal of the perfect lady as invalid. In turn, the ideal of the ethereal "lady on a couch" may have provided many women with an escape from a repressive reality. Victorian women were confused by the "impossible duties and contradictory ideals" set forth by their society, and they "expressed through illness what otherwise would have remained repressed and destructive" (Helsinger, Sheets and Veeder 2: 74). They got sick instead of getting angry; the former was acceptable feminine behavior, but the latter was not.

9. On the ideal of woman as ornament of society, see especially the work of Gorham, Rees, and Leonore Davidoff.

10. Praz quotes this passage as an example of Trollope's "realistic, balanced point of view, which admits shades of difference and compromises. . . . This is the 'photographic' realism of Trollope, as opposed to the false, melodramatic moralizings of Dickens and the reticences of Thackeray" (300).

11. N. John Hall states that "certainly the present investigation into the original illustrations for Trollope is largely predicated upon the undeniable authority Trollope gave them: in many cases he selected the subject for illustration and, of Millais' work at least, voiced his very generous approval. The original plates were an integral part of the book, one may say of the text, on its first appearance" (2). See also Hilary Gresty, "Millais and Trollope: Author and Illustrator" (*Book Collector*, 30 [1981]: 43–60).

12. Garrett comments on this point that Alice's "potential for evading this conventional resolution has been dissipated much earlier, not only by her own limitations but by the multiplication of narrative lines. . . . She is completely assimilated by the conventional codes" (188, 189).

13. Lowry Pei argues that "Alice's power of self-punishment has at last been backed into a corner by a greater force. Suddenly it becomes clear that her desperately defended independence has been concealing a desire for a strong authority that she can give in to. She ultimately needs

Notes for Chapter 2

someone who can command her obedience and love—in other words, a father, since her actual father can do neither of these. And John Grey wins her by acting like a father" ("The Conquest of Separateness," 59).

14. In her article, "Henry James as Adapter: *The Portrait of a Lady* and *Can You Forgive Her?*" (*Rocky Mountain Review of Language and Literature* 38 [1984]: 35-43), Susan Hendricks cites Trollope's novel as a central source for James's book. Hendricks, in opposition to my view, stresses the unproblematical conventionality of Alice's and Glencora's stories, and the greater tragic realism in Isabel's stark fate.

15. The most provocative discussion of this characteristic of self-sacrifice in the women of *Can You Forgive Her?* is in Barickman, MacDonald, and Stark: "The only essential power they see for themselves is the power to devote themselves totally to the desires of a man. Each not only senses but describes this option as what it is—an act of self-annihilation" (24).

Chapter 2

1. In my textual citations, I will abbreviate *Phineas Finn* as *PF* and *Phineas Redux* as *PR*.

2. Juliet McMaster stresses that "Phineas has lived up mainly to that role of the boyish Telemachus, who must blurt out his triumphs and troubles to her, cost her what it might" (*Palliser Novels*, 55).

3. "Simply as an introduction into official life nothing could be more conducive to chances of success than a matrimonial alliance with Lady Laura. Not that he would have thought of such a thing on that account! No;—he thought of it because he loved her; honestly because he loved her. He swore to that half a dozen times, for his own satisfaction" (*PF,* chapter 5).

4. Robert Polhemus does not cite Madame Max's journey, but he states that "the course of the novel and its subdued ending seem to say that only love provides the sustaining base of value and meaning in society" ("Being in Love," 394).

5. Polhemus cites this passage as evidence of "the power of public opinion insidiously perverting her nature" (*Changing World*, 156).

6. Only Lowry Pei seems to comment on this quarrel in relation to Laura's subjugation by Kennedy: "Laura, like Bunce, refuses to submit to coercion, but the result of her demonstration is that she is thrown in jail for good. Coercion is everyhere, too, in the relations of parents and children: particularly between Lord Brentford and Chiltern" ("The Conquest of Separateness," 124).

7. For example, this is the reaction of the selfish aesthete, Maurice Maule: "I hope he'll be hung, with all my heart" (*PR,* chapter 48). Chiltern, the truest of Phineas's male friends, says stoutly, "I have never for a moment believed him to be guilty" (*PR,* chapter 51). Only Mr. Monk's acutely rational mind prevents him from telling Phineas during the trial of his belief in Phineas's innocence. As he tells Phineas after the trial: "I believed you innocent with all my heart. . . . But there was always sufficient possibility of your guilt to prevent a rational man from committing himself to the expression of an absolute conviction" (*PR,* 48). All of Phineas's close women friends believe in him. Madame Max, Laura, Violet and Mrs. Bunce (Phineas's landlady) have the deepest confidence in his innocence, although Glencora—who does not know him well—is also his enthusiastic advocate. As Madame Max thinks, upon first hearing of the murder: "What judge of character would any one be who could believe that Phineas Finn could be guilty of a midnight murder?" (*PR,* chapter 48).

8. See Juliet McMaster, *Palliser Novels* (172-73), for the best discussion of Trollope's metaphors for expressing sexual desire in women.

9. Andrew Wright states "there is irremediable physical aversion to Kennedy on the part of his wife" (101).

10. For a tougher vision of Lady Laura, see Ramona L. Denton's fine article, "'That Cage' of Femininity: Trollope's Lady Laura" (*The South Atlantic Bulletin*, 45 [1980]: 1–10). Denton perceives Laura's love as an obsessive adherence to the love religion she originally defied: "Her story is one of lost opportunity but not, as she believes, simply the lost opportunity for love. There was, Trollope seems to recognize, no place for a woman like Laura to begin with—no place she might fill that would do justice to her entire nature. She is 'unfeminine' initially, but Trollope indicates that she is finally almost inhuman in her obsession with unrequited love" (9). Denton sees Laura's love for Phineas as "a betrayal of selfhood occasioned by love" (9) and a failure in the development of "moral consciousness" (7).

11. In contrast to my view, James Kincaid states that "the contrasted stories of Lady Laura and Violet Effingham . . . indicate the alternate poles of this world, bad luck and good luck. . . . These affairs simply indicate the boundaries, mark out the range of possibilities in a world ruled by luck. One story holds out the promise of comic fulfilment; the other warns of horrible ironic bondage. They illustrate in a stylized, almost didactic way alternate varieties of absurdity: unexplained joy, unexplained torture" (196–97).

12. Cf. Richard Barickman, Susan MacDonald, and Myra Stark: "The heart of the difference between Violet's and Laura's rebellion is that Violet—like Glencora—refuses to abandon herself or to hope for fulfillment from a man, while Laura—rather like Alice Vavasor—hopes to live vicariously through either Kennedy or Phineas and thinks Violet might do the same through Chiltern" (221). Lord Brentford's role in Laura's life is not mentioned in this excellent but cursory analysis of the Phineas novels.

13. There is of course, much less risk with a "lion" like Chiltern, who is "nobel-minded" than with a "griffin" like the sexual predator, Sir Griffin Tewett (*The Eustace Diamonds*), whose hunting of the frigid Lucinda Roanoke literally drives her to madness on their wedding-day. For an interesting discussion of the motif of predation in *Can You Forgive Her?*, *The Eustace Diamonds*, and *The Prime Minister*, see Donna Stine Givens ("The Motif of Predation in Trollope," Ph.D. dissertation, University of Illinois at Urbana, 1975).

14. Polhemus sees Violet's need to "tame" Chiltern somewhat differently: "She has to try to tame him and punish herself for loving him before she can give way to his force" (*Changing World*, 162).

15. The census of 1851 documented the surplus population of women in England. The phrase "redundant women" to describe single women—women who married late, or not at all—derives from W. R. Greg's 1862 *National Review* article, "Why Are Women Redundant?" Greg, a liberal manufacturer and frequent contributor to periodicals, refuses to equate work with marriage as a solution to the problem of supporting women. Greg's solution to the problem of surplus women is tripartite: (1) emigration; (2) earlier marriage; and (3) male premarital celibacy. The problem of "redundant women" was the center of the mid-century controversy over women's work. For a good discussion of all aspects of this problem, see Helsinger, Sheets, and Veeder (2: chapter 3).

16. These societies were created to help alleviate the problem of "redundant women." Greg, for instance, suggests that half a million women be sent to England's colonies "where they are clamored for." See James Hammerton, *Emigrant Gentlewomen*, for an exhaustive discussion of these societies. Lady Baldock's emigration society is apparently a parody of the Female Middle-Class Emigration Society, which was founded in 1862 by the feminist "ladies of Langham Place."

17. Barickman, MacDonald, and Stark also think that this childhood incident suggests that Chiltern "might make a good husband for Violet" (223).

Notes for Chapter 3

18. Polhemus, citing this passage, views Violet's imagery in describing Chiltern as "sometimes startlingly sexual" (*Changing World,* 162).

19. The authors of *Corrupt Relations* state that "Chiltern's treatment of horses gives a clue to his personality and the social roles that distort its expression" (224). They stress his "gentleness with horses" (225), but they make no comparison to Burgo.

20. For me, it is a poignant moment in the reading of Trollope's letters when he writes to William Blackwood in March of 1878: "Alas—alas—my hunting is over. I have given away my breeches, boots,—and horses" (*Letters* 759).

21. See 74–80 for Shirley Letwin's valuable discussion of Madame Max.

22. In his astute essay, "Being in Love in *Phineas Finn/Phineas Redux,*" Polhemus focuses on Phineas's fulfillment, but he too views this marriage as a union of equals. In the movement from Mary to Marie, Polhemus perceives "hope in the progress of love for Phineas" (394).

23. Cf. Isabel to Silverbridge: "I needn't wear a hideous bit of cloth over my face in Constantinople because I am a woman. But when the discrepancies are small, then they have to be attended to. . . . Do you think that I don't understand that everybody will be making remarks upon the American girl who won't leave the son of the Duke of Omnium alone?" (*The Duke's Children,* chapter 28).

24. Kincaid also cites this passage as exemplifying Madame Max's "'sacrifice' thus desentimentalized" (211–12).

25. Polhemus states that "being in love is literally a quest for faith in Trollope" ("Being in Love," 391).

26. Kincaid states that Maule is "a darker version of Deportment Turveydrop" (211–12).

27. There are good discussions of this parallel by Polhemus (*Changing World,* "Being in Love in *Phineas Finn/Phineas Redux*") and Juliet McMaster. Polhemus states: "Along with the affairs of Phineas (Trollope deliberately makes their careers parallel), her climb to the top of the social ladder and her crisis of conscience dominate the last part of the novel" (Polhemus, *Changing World,* 157). McMaster cites Polhemus, adding that "they [Phineas and Madame Max] are both highly ambitious, and high scrupulous. Both find adaptability to be the secret of success" (*Palliser Novels,* 56). In "Being in Love in *Phineas Finn/Phineas Redux,*" Polhemus states that Phineas and Madame Max have in common "worldly ambition, doubt, a will to please, a passionate nature, a generous spirit, talent, style, and a need to find a center of sustaining faith" (391).

28. Polhemus closes his chapter on *Phineas Redux* with this passage, which he says "might seem almost nothing; and yet it is everything. In it Trollope sees the grace, the emotional intensity, the poise, and the will to communion and love on which civilization depends" (*Changing World,* 185).

Chapter 3

1. Juliet McMaster states that "a passage of conversation between her and Barrington Erle deserves quoting at length, because her tone and sentiments are evidently such as Trollope approves" (*Palliser Novels,* 178).

2. Elizabeth Helsinger, Robin Sheets, and William Veeder state that Lewis helped to define the terms "mission," "sphere," and "influence" (1: 5). The first chapter of this volume is devoted to an analysis of Lewis's *Woman's Mission,* and the fifth chapter is centered on a discussion of Ruskin's "Of Queens' Gardens."

3. Richard Barickman, Susan MacDonald, and Myra Stark refer briefly to a line from this passage

when discussing Glencora's need for a career of her own (216), but they do not make the connection with either the doctrine of the two spheres or with the code of chivalry and Trollope's idea of the gentleman.

4. See Shirley Letwin for a fascinating and exhaustive examination of this Trollopian ideal.

5. See Mary Poovey (21-26). Although Poovey is mainly concerned with the effect of the ideal of the "proper lady" on Mary Wollstonecraft, Jane Austen and Mary Shelley, her introductory chapter, which examines its historical origins, is illuminating for both male and female writers of the Romantic and Victorian periods.

6. A similar axis of comedy is evident in two of my favorite scenes from *The Duke's Children*. In the first scene (chapter 25), the austere Duke tries to educate his loving but irresponsible sons, Silverbridge and Gerald, about the value of money. In the second scene (chapter 65), the Duke lectures Gerald about the perils of gambling. For astute commentary on these scenes, see James Kincaid (227-28), and Christopher Herbert, "Trollope and the Fixity of the Self" (*PMLA* 93 [March 1978]: 228-39).

7. See Juliet McMaster's discerning discussion of the *Macbeth* theme in relation to the Duke and Lopez as well as to Glencora (*Palliser Novels*, 106-7).

8. Gerald, Silverbridge's younger brother, although not a major figure in *The Duke's Children*, seems likely to be similar in character to his brother, although one could not define him yet as an ideal gentleman. Lord Chiltern (*Phineas Finn, Phineas Redux*) is always a favorite with Trollope, but his early wildness is that of the Romantic hero, and he is never portrayed as immature. Despite his violence, his truth to Violet characterizes him as constant rather than capricious.

9. Kincaid states on this point that "it is not at all the same thing to Glencora. She must resist this sort of absorption" (224).

10. Barickman, MacDonald, and Stark, contrary to my view, cite this line of Violet's as blatant "evidence of antifeminism" (195) in Trollope's novels.

11. Another aspect of Trollope's fiction, pointed up by Huxley's phrase "musicalization," is discussed by Robert Polhemus in "Trollope's Dialogue." Polhemus stresses the intensely aural quality of the fiction. He writes about the way in which Trollope's discourse defines both character and meaning, and creates Trollope's communal vision. As with the resonances of Violet's jest throughout the Palliser novels, it seems to me that this aural quality of Trollope's novels serves as a structural principle of the fiction.

12. Violet's joke resounds beyond the Palliser series into other novels. In *He Knew He Was Right* (1869), written immediately after *Phineas Finn,* Dorothy Stanbury says: "A man who is a nobody can perhaps make himself somebody,—or, at any rate, he can try; but a woman has no means of trying. She is a nobody, and a nobody she must remain" (chapter 51).

13. These lines are quoted by Barickman, MacDonald, and Stark to support the statement that Glencora "has developed a strong sense of self" (216). To me it seems that the rest of the speech undermines Glencora's brave declaration of her identity.

14. Juliet McMaster comments on this point: "Trollope does not go into the details of the bedroom, but he gives us enough information to make it a fairly good guess that the Pallisers' sex life has more or less petered out" (*Palliser Novels*, 122).

15. Despite the supposed passivity of their true natures, one predominant ideal of Victorian womanhood exhorted women to make their daughters businesslike in their approach to housewifery, from child-rearing to the management of servants. In household manuals from Mrs. Beeton's *The Book of Household Management* (1861) for the comfortable middle class to Mrs. Eliza War-

ren's *How I Managed My House on Two Hundred Pounds A Year* (1864) for the less affluent, the Victorian woman was exhorted to be in thorough charge of an organized household establishment. Moreover, as J. A. Banks and Patricia Branca have shown, most middle-class families could afford only one servant, so the typical Victorian middle-class mother worked hard.

16. Many Victorian women rejected the passivity enjoined upon them by counselors like Sarah Ellis (*Daughters of England, Wives of England,* etc.) and sought to widen their sphere of activity through philanthropy. As F. K. Prochaska states in the best study of this topic, *Women and Philanthropy in Nineteenth-Century England* (Oxford, 1980):

    > One is struck by the way so many women, and not only of the middle and upper classes, led independent lives despite the weight of convention. There were pressures on them to 'suffer and be still,' . . . but this should not lead us to conclude that they necessarily did so (1).

17. Trollope's portrait of Griselda is his most extended treatment of this ideal. In each of the four works in which Griselda figures, Trollope's strategy is to compare her to his heroines. In *Framley Parsonage,* Griselda hopes to marry Lord Lufton, who wisely chooses the quiet strength and subtle wit of Lucy Robarts instead. Griselda then makes a splendid match with the aptly named Lord Dumbello. We next encounter Lady Dumbello when she has embarked upon her career as ornament of society in *The Small House in Allington,* in which she is implicitly compared to the lively, passionate Lily and Bell Dale. As the new Marchioness of Hartletop in *The Last Chronicle of Barset,* she is implicitly compared to the poor, learned Grace Crawley. Grace's true aristocratic beauty, in a neat ironic pattern, is recognized immediately by the Archdeacon, the Marchioness's father, and by her brother Henry, who falls in love with Grace and marries her. Finally, as the grandly beautiful, coldly perfect ornament of society in *Can You Forgive Her?,* the Marchioness is compared to Glencora, whose fallible humanity, imaged in the dishevelled loveliness of her wild hair and in her animated face, is clearly preferred by the narrator.

18. Most often cited are the letter (perhaps written to Trollope's American friend Adrian Joline, although this is uncertain) in which Trollope states that the "supremacy of men over women" is "as certain to me as the eternity of the soul" (*Letters,* 2: 821), Trollope's 1868 lecture on the "Higher Education of Women," and the epigram in *North America:* "The best right a woman has is the right to a husband."

19. One wonders whether Henry James had this passage in mind when he wrote the scene in *The Portrait of a Lady* in which Isabel sits in the dark in misery over her marriage to Osmond (2: chapter 42). There is a parallel scene in *Phineas Finn* (chapter 23) in which Lady Laura sits in the dark, in misery over her marriage to Kennedy: "Then she sat alone first in the dusk and then in the dark, for two hours, doing nothing. Was this to be the life she had procured for herself by marrying Mr. Kennedy of Loughlinter?" (*PF,* chapter 23). There is also a similar scene in *Phineas Redux* (chapter 69), after Phineas visits Lady Laura for the first time since his acquittal for the murder of Mr. Bonteen. Holl's illustration of this scene depicts Laura bent in despair in front of the fireplace at Saulsby. The caption reads: "She sat weeping alone in her father's house."

20. See Polhemus for a sensitive discussion of Palliser's thoughts subsequent to this scene (*Changing World,* 108–9).

21. See Hector Whistler's modern illustration of this scene in the Oxford edition of *The Prime Minister* for an accurate interpretation. There were no illustrations in the original publications of *The Prime Minister,* either in its serial form (eight monthly parts, November 1875 to June 1876) or when published as a four-volume book by Chapman and Hall in May of 1876. N. John Hall tells us that "of the eight novels published serially in parts, all but one, *The Prime Minister,* were illustrated" (*Trollope and His Illustrators,* 26).

22. Cf. Barickman, MacDonald, and Stark: "Marrying an insider and not marrying an outsider seem to be the major options available to her for asserting that she is not simply a subordinate part of the clan" (218).

23. Cf. Henry James's *The Portrait of A Lady:* "The real offense, as she ultimately perceived, was her having a mind of her own at all. Her mind was to be his—attached to his own like a small garden plot to a deer-park" (2: chapter 42).

24. My analysis directly opposes that of Barickman, MacDonald, and Stark: "In the Lopez plot of *The Prime Minister,* the social outsider's fraudulent sexual and economic dealings are overshadowed by the coercive, exclusive, snobbish power of the respectable establishment" (232-33).

25. Letwin discusses the four cardinal attributes that combine to produce the integrity of the gentleman: discrimination, diffidence, courage, and honesty (68-71).

26. There are, however, some dissenting voices among the critics. Barickman, MacDonald, and Stark, for example, look upon Emily's actions subsequent to her husband's death as unconsciously coercive; the Fletcher-Wharton clan is gradually compelled by her continued refusal of their cherished Arthur not only to forgive her for her defection in marrying Lopez, but to act as supplicants. In terms of consequences, this perception is true:

> But, through it all, there was present to the hearts of most of them a feeling that much more was to be effected, if possible, than this simple and cosy marriage, and that the fate of Mary Wharton was hardly so important to them as that of Emily Lopez (chapter 59).

However, I think that this analysis oversimplifies Emily's motivation for her apparently morbid and perverse behavior, despite its accuracy with respect to the result of Emily's actions. The reasons for Emily's self-punishment and in particular, for the prolonged wearing of excessive mourning garb by which it is manifested, are rather more complicated.

27. It also seems quite possible that Emily is grieving for her dead infant as well as for her own lost purity. Glencora's description of Emily as a "Niobe" perhaps has more truth in it than the Duchess intended. The death of her child is scarcely mentioned by critics other than Juliet McMaster, who states that Emily had "so hated him [Lopez] that she was glad their baby died" (118) and Polhemus, who states "Emily rejoices at her baby's death" (200). In truth, Emily is grief-stricken by the child's death, but she is not allowed much expression of that pain at the time. When she begs her husband to "speak one kind word to me now," he repulses her, and there is "not much show of mourning in the house." (This cold gesture to a wife at a child's death recalls Sir Hugh Clavering, another tyrannical husband in Trollope's novels [*The Claverings,* chapter 20, "Desolation"].) Emily's grief can be given only private expression until Lopez dies:

> The poor mother would sit gloomily alone day after day. . . . [S]he would look at all the preparations she had made—the happy work of her fingers when her thoughts of their future use were her sweetest consolation,—and weep till she would herself feel that there never could be an end to her tears (chapter 54).

Chapter 4

1. George Butte and Lowry Pei also discuss this aspect of Glencora's attitude toward Tregear. However, the focus of both essays is the Duke's psychology, rather than the efforts of Glencora and her "descendants" to achieve self-realization.

2. Although neither critic mentions this circumstance, Butte and Pei focus on the ways in which Mary is a painful reminder of Glencora to the Duke.

3. Pei also cites the Duke's final line as evidence that "in Mary's marriage to Tregear he reconciles himself to Glencora's first love for Burgo, letting that pass away from him so that he no longer sees Tregear as an adventurer (a new Burgo) but as a worthy, if bold, young man" ("Reflection and Reconciliation," 301).

4. The question of how much the Duke has really changed at the end of *The Duke's Children* (and thus at the conclusion of the entire Palliser series) has provoked a good deal of critical controversy. The most rigorous analyses of the question are those of John Hagan, Butte, Juliet McMaster, Christopher Herbert, and Pei. Hagan views the change in the Duke as profound and permanent, an exorcism of "the ghosts of his past forever," and an emergence into "the broad daylight of justice, good sense, rationality, love, and intellectual conviction" (20). Butte's emphasis is on the Duke's partial healing of his psyche through his ultimate acceptance of his children's lovers. McMaster's focus is also on the Duke's new "flexibility," on his ability to adapt to the present despite the psychological burdens of the past. Herbert, whose essay focuses on Trollope's perceptions about "the persistence of character over time" (236), stresses that although "there is no reason to think that his difficult character has fundamentally changed. . . . [A]t the end of *The Duke's Children* the stress does fall less upon the permanent liabilities of the Duke's character than upon the adjustments that this supposedly inflexible man is able to make to enable life to go on" (237). Pei, who is interested in the theme that he terms the "conquest of separateness, becoming one with the process, entering or, often, reentering the human race" ("Reflection and Reconciliation," 302), states that "there is still that in Palliser which must dwell on his sufferings, but we feel at the end that he has made new 'links between him and the world'"(301).

5. Despite his public pronouncements to the contrary ("The Higher Education of Women," *North America*), in Trollope's novels, as early as his depiction of the learned Grace Crawley (*The Last Chronicle of Barset*), Trollope exhibits his admiration for a genuine course of study for women. (See Coral Lansbury's discussion of Henry Grantley's attraction to Grace because she *is* an intellectual [214–15].) In his life, Trollope's closest female friend was the well-educated American, Kate Field (Snow, 117–28). It seems clear in this passage that Trollope sees the Duke's vision of Mary's genteel "quarantine" as a tool of oppression. There are dissenting voices to my assessment: Simon Gatrell, for instance, in his article "Jealousy, Mastery, Love and Madness: A Brief Reading of *He Knew He Was Right*," states that Priscilla Stanbury is "the nearest to an unsatirised [sic] intellectual woman in Trollope's major fiction; he was not fond of intellectual qualities in women" (99).

6. J. Hillis Miller, in his discussion of *Ayala's Angel*, emphasizes Trollope's focus on falling in love as the primary constituent of "authentic selfhood" (123).

7. A woman who succumbed to male desire was abruptly knocked off her moral pedestal. She became The opposite of the feminine angel: the fallen woman. The popular vision of the fallen woman changed during the nineteen century from moral outrage at the temptress of man to pity for the victim of man's lust (Helsinger, Sheets, and Veeder 2: 152), but in Victorian feminine ideology, the nature of a fallen woman was divided by a gaping abyss from the pure angelic nature of the undefiled woman, the virgin girl or the married woman. For the middle-class woman whose chastity was the emblem of her family's respectability, the fall was irremediable. In paintings such as Augustus Egg's dramatic 1858 trilogy, *Past and Present* ("Misfortune," "Prayer," "Despair") depicting the fall of a middle-class wife, the fallen woman is portrayed as a social outcast whose lot is an inevitable downward spiral to isolated destitution. In *Victorian Narrative Painting*, Raymond Lister quotes Samuel Redgrave as stating that "the painter's treatment of the subject was too painful to please, and it remained on his walls until

his death." See also Helene E. Roberts, "Marriage, Redundancy or Sin: The Painter's View of Women in the First Twenty-Five Years of Victoria's Reign," 45-77. Nina Auerbach's discussion in *Woman and the Demon* focuses on the subversive counter-myth of the fallen woman's power. She discusses both Egg's trilogy and George F. Watts's painting, "Found Drowned" (1848-50).

8. After years of reading books and articles on the Palliser novels, I thought that I was somehow the only critic who had remarked that there had once been (in *The Prime Minister*) a little Lady Glencora. However, I now find that George Butte mentions this fact in a footnote in which he surmises that even as early as *The Prime Minister*, "one daughter was marked as Glencora's heir" (710).

9. Donald D. Stone touches on Romanticism in *Can You Forgive Her?* only in his discussion of the "Byronic" figure of George Vavasor.

10. John Kleis, in his fine essay, "Passion vs. Prudence: Theme and Technique in Trollope's Palliser Novels," states: "The cycle ends where it began—at Matching Priory; for others too, if they dare face the dangers, the affirmation of romance wins out over sinister anarchy. Glencora, who tries so hard to reconcile passion and prudence, is buried here, having conquered her 'self-devotion' (*CY*, II, 363) as much as she can and thus having found some peace in her marriage; and even though Palliser experiences some of her destructive confusion in his dealings with Mme Max, he can overcome it. Silverbridge and Isabel find peace in the ruins when they visit them in broad daylight at the end of *The Duke's Children*, having reached the integration which eludes Mabel. Finally, Mary weds Tregear in the Priory church, Tregear having cast off those qualities which remind Glencora of Burgo in favor of outgoing love and responsibility. Mabel fails, the others win; for those who can become aware of the well of irrationality within and around them, and more important, can balance it with an equally great prudent restraint, positive affirmation of life is possible" (1414).

11. This discussion of the sexuality of Trollope's women is both original and thorough. In *Trollope and Comic Pleasure*, Christopher Herbert brilliantly explores the sexuality of female characters such as Lucy Robarts (*Framley Parsonage*) and Ayala Dormer (*Ayala's Angel*) as an element of charm, that essential ingredient of comic pleasure. There is also a good discussion of the flamboyant American beauty, Mrs. Hurtle, in R. D. McMaster's article, "Women in *The Way We Live Now*," in *English Studies in Canada*, 7 (1981): 68-80.

12. Pei states that "she has been the victim of her class and of her particular family: from them she inherited both the idea of absolute spontaneous love and 'the grinding need for money, the absolute necessity of luxurious living . . .'" ("Reflection and Reconciliation," 293).

Bibliography

Acton, William. *The Functions and Disorders of the Reproductive Organs.* London: n.p., 1857.
apRoberts, Ruth. "Emily and Nora and Dorothy and Priscilla and Jemima and Carry." In *The Victorian Experience: The Novelists,* edited by Richard A. Levine, pp. 87-120. Athens: Ohio University Press, 1976.
──. *The Moral Trollope.* Athens: Ohio University Press, 1971.
Auerbach, Nina. *Woman and the Demon: The Life of a Victorian Myth.* Cambridge, Mass.: Harvard University Press, 1982.
Banks, J. A. *Prosperity and Parenthood.* London: Routledge & Kegan Paul, 1954.
Bareham, Tony, ed. *Anthony Trollope.* London: Vision Press, 1980.
Barickman, Richard, Susan MacDonald, and Myra Stark. *Corrupt Relations.* New York: Columbia University Press, 1982.
Blake, Kathleen. *Love and the Woman Question in Victorian Literature: The Art of Self-Postponement.* Totowa, N.J.: Barnes and Noble, 1983.
Blinderman, Charles. "The Servility of Dependence: The Dark Lady in Trollope." In *Images of Women in Fiction: Feminist Perspectives,* edited by Susan Koppelman-Cornillon, pp. 55-67. Bowling Green, Ohio: Bowling Green University Popular Press, 1972.
Branca, Patricia. *Silent Sisterhood.* Pittsburgh: Carnegie-Mellon University Press, 1975.
Butte, George. "Ambivalence and Affirmation in *The Duke's Children.*" *Studies in English Literature* 17 (1977): 709-22.
Chamberlain, David S. "Unity and Irony in Trollope's *Can You Forgive Her?.*" *Studies in English Literature* 8 (1969): 669-80.
Christ, Carol. "Victorian Masculinity and the Angel in the House." In *A Widening Sphere: Changing Roles of Victorian Women,* edited by Martha Vicinus, pp. 3-29. Bloomington: Indiana University Press, 1977.
Cockshut, A. O. J. *Man and Woman: A Study of Love and the Novel, 1740-1940.* London: Collins, 1977.
Davidoff, Leonore. *The Best Circles: Society Etiquette and the Season.* London: Croom Helm, 1973.
Denton, Ramona L. "*The Eustace Diamonds:* Trollope's Book of Odd Women." *Kentucky Philological Association Bulletin* 1977: 7-13.
──. "Female Selfhood in Anthony Trollope's Palliser Novels." Ph.D. dissertation, University of Kentucky, 1977.
──. "'That Cage' of Femininity: Trollope's Lady Laura." *South Atlantic Bulletin* 45 (1980): 1-10.
Duffin, Lorna. "The Conspicuous Consumptive: Woman as Invalid." In *The Nineteenth-Century Woman: Her Cultural and Physical World,* edited by Sara Delamont and Lorna Duffin, pp. 26-57. London: Croom Helm, 1978.
Eastwood, David R. "Trollope and Romanticism." *Victorian Newsletter* 52 (1977): 1-5.
Foster, Shirley. *Victorian Women's Fiction: Marriage, Freedom and the Individual.* London: Croom Helm, 1985.

Garrett, Peter. *The Victorian Multiplot Novel: Studies in Dialogical Form.* New Haven, Conn.: Yale University Press, 1980.
Gatrell, Simon. "Jealousy, Mastery, Love and Madness: A Brief Reading of *He Knew He Was Right.*" In *Anthony Trollope,* edited by Tony Bareham. London: Vision Press, 1980.
Gilead, Sarah. "Trollope's Orphans and 'The Power of Adequate Performance.'" *Texas Studies in Language and Literature* 27 (1985): 86–105.
Gilmour, Robin. *The Idea of the Gentleman in the Victorian Novel.* London: George Allen and Unwin, 1981.
———. "A Lesser Thackeray: Trollope and the Victorian Novel." In *Anthony Trollope,* edited by Tony Bareham. London: Vision Press, 1980.
Gindin, James. "Anthony Trollope." In *Harvest of a Quiet Eye: The Novel of Compassion,* pp. 28–56. Bloomington: Indiana University Press, 1971.
Givens, Donna Stine. "The Motif of Predation in Trollope." Ph.D. dissertation, University of Illinois at Urbana-Champaign, 1975.
Gorham, Deborah. *The Victorian Girl and the Feminine Ideal.* London: Croom Helm, 1982.
Gresty, Hilary. "Millais and Trollope: Author and Illustrator." *Book Collector* 30 (1981): 43–60.
Hagan, John. "The Divided Mind of Anthony Trollope." *NCF* 14 (1959–60): 1–26.
Hall, N. John, ed. *The Letters of Anthony Trollope.* 2 vols. Stanford, Calif.: Stanford University Press, 1983.
———. *Trollope and His Illustrators.* New York: St. Martin's Press, 1980.
Halperin, John. "Trollope and Feminism." *The South Atlantic Quarterley* 77 (1978): 179–88.
———. *Trollope and Politics: A Study of the Pallisers and Others.* New York: Barnes and Noble, 1977.
———. "Trollope's Conservatism." *South Atlantic Quarterly* 82 (1983): 56–78.
———, ed. *Trollope's Centenary Essays.* Hong Kong: MacMillan Press, 1982.
Hammerton, A. James. *Emigrant Gentlewomen: Genteel Poverty and Female Emigration, 1830–1914.* London: Croom Helm, 1979.
———. "Feminism and Female Emigration, 1861–1866." In *A Widening Sphere: Changing Roles of Victorian Women,* edited by Martha Vicinus. Bloomington: Indiana University Press, 1977.
Hartman, Mary S. *Victorian Murderesses.* New York: Schocken, 1977.
——— and Lois Banner, eds. *Clio's Consciousness Raised.* New York: Harper and Row, 1974.
Harvey, Geoffrey. *The Art of Anthony Trollope.* London: Weidenfeld and Nicolson, 1980.
Heilbrun, Carolyn G. *Toward a Recognition of Androgyny.* New York: Knopf, 1973.
Helsinger, Elizabeth K., Robin Lauterbach Sheets, and William Veeder. *The Woman Question.* 3 vols. New York: Garden Publishing, 1983.
Herbert, Christopher. "*He Knew He Was Right,* Mrs. Lynn Linton, and the Duplicities of Victorian Marriage." *Texas Studies in Language and Literature* 25 (1983): 448–69.
———. *Trollope and Comic Pleasure.* Chicago: University of Chicago Press, 1986.
———. "Trollope and the Fixity of the Self." *PMLA* 93 (March 1978): 228–39.
Holcombe, Lee. *Victorian Ladies at Work: Middle-Class Working Women in England and Wales, 1850–1914.* Hamden, Conn.: Archon, 1973.
Jalland, Pat. *Women, Marriage, and Politics, 1860–1914.* Oxford: Clarendon Press, 1986.
Johansson, Sheila Ryan. "Sex and Death in Victorian England: An Examination of Age and Sex-Specific Death Rates, 1840–1910." In *A Widening Sphere,* edited by Martha Vicinus, pp. 163–82. Bloomington: Indiana University Press, 1977.
Kennard, Jean E. *Victims of Convention.* Hamden, Conn.: Archon, 1978.
Kincaid, James R. *The Novels of Anthony Trollope.* Oxford: Clarendon Press, 1977.
Kleis, John C. "Passion vs. Prudence: Theme and Technique in Trollope's Palliser Novels." *Texas Studies in Language and Literature* 11 (1970): 1405–14.
Lansbury, Coral. *The Reasonable Man: Trollope's Legal Fiction.* Princeton, N.J.: Princeton University Press, 1981.

Letwin, Shirley Robin. *The Gentleman in Trollope: Individuality and Moral Conduct.* Cambridge, Mass.: Harvard University Press, 1982.
Levine, George. "Can You Forgive Him? Trollope's *Can You Forgive Her?* and the Myth of Realism." *Victorian Studies* 18 (1974-75): 5-30.
Lister, Raymond. *Victorian Narrative Paintings.* New York: Clarkson N. Potter, 1966.
McMaster, Juliet. *Trollope's Palliser Novels: Theme and Pattern.* London: MacMillan, 1978.
―――. "Trollope's Country Estates." In *Centenary Essays,* edited by John Halperin. London: Macmillan, 1982.
McMaster, R. D. *Trollope and the Law.* New York: St. Martin's Press, 1986.
―――. "Women in *The Way We Live Now."* *English Studies in Canada* 7 (1981): 68-80.
Miller, J. Hillis. *The Form of Victorian Fiction.* Notre Dame: University of Notre Dame Press, 1968.
Morantz, Regina. "The Lady and Her Physician," In *Clio's Consciousness Raised,* edited by Mary S. Hartman and Lois Banner. New York: Harper and Row, 1974.
More, Paul Elmer. "My Debt to Trollope." In *The Demon of the Absolute,* New Shelburne Essay, Vol. 1, pp. 89-125. Princeton, N.J.: Princeton University Press, 1928.
Newton, Judith Lowder. *Women, Power and Subversion: Social Strategies in British Fiction, 1778-1860.* London: Methuen, 1985.
O'Connor, Frank. "Trollope the Realist." In *The Mirror in the Roadway: A Study of the Modern Novel.* New York: Knopf, 1956.
Overton, Bill. *The Unofficial Trollope.* Sussex: Harvester Press; and Totowa, N.J.: Barnes and Noble, 1982.
Page, Frederick, ed. *The Poems of Coventry Patmore.* London: Oxford University Press, 1949.
Pei, Lowry. "Anthony Trollope's Palliser Novels: The Conquest of Separateness." Ph.D. Dissertation, Stanford University, 1975.
―――. "*The Duke's Children:* Reflection and Reconciliation." *Modern Language Quarterley* 39 (1978): 284-302.
Polhemus, Robert. *The Changing World of Anthony Trollope.* Berkeley: University of California Press, 1968.
―――. "Being in Love in *Phineas Finn/Phineas Redux:* Desire, Devotion, Consolation." *NCF* 37 (1982): 383-95.
―――. "Trollope's Dialogue." In *Trollope Centenary Essays,* edited by John Halperin, pp. 95-108. Hong Kong: Macmillan Press, 1982.
Poovey, Mary. *The Proper Lady and the Woman Writer.* Chicago: University of Chicago Press, 1984.
Praz, Mario. "Anthony Trollope." In *The Hero in Eclipse in Victorian Fiction,* edited by Angus Davidson, pp. 261-318. London: Oxford University Press, 1956.
Prochaska, F. K. *Women and Philanthropy in Nineteenth-Century England.* Oxford: Clarendon Press, 1980.
Rees, Barbara. *The Victorian Lady.* London: Gordon and Cremonesi, 1977.
Roberts, Helene E. "Marriage, Redundancy or Sin: The Painter's View of Women in First Twenty-Five Years of Victoria's Reign." In *Suffer and Be Still,* edited by Martha Vicinus, pp. 45-77. Bloomington: Indiana University Press, 1972.
Rose, Phyllis. *Parallel Lives: Five Victorian Marriages.* New York: Knopf, 1984.
Ruskin, John A. *Sesame and Lilies.* New York: Lovell, Coryell, n.d.
Sadleir, Michael. *Trollope: A Commentary.* New York: Farrar, Strauss, 1947.
Shapiro, Ann R. *Unlikely Heroines: Nineteenth-Century Women Writers and the Woman Question.* Westport, Conn.: Greenwood Press, 1987.
Smalley, Donald, ed. *Trollope: The Critical Heritage.* New York: Barnes and Noble, 1969.
Snow, C.P. *Trollope: His Life and Art.* New York: Charles Scribner's Sons, 1975.
Stone, Donald D. *The Romantic Impulse in Victorian Fiction.* Cambridge, Mass.: Harvard University Press, 1980.

Terry, R. C. *Anthony Trollope: The Artist in Hiding.* Totowa, N.J.: Rowman, 1977.
Thale, Jerome. "The Problem of Structure in Trollope." *NCF* 15 (1960): 147–79.
Thomson, Patricia. *The Victorian Heroine: A Changing Ideal, 1837–1873.* London: Oxford University Press, 1956.
Tracy, Robert. *Trollope's Later Novels.* Berkeley: University of California Press, 1978.
Trollope, Anthony. *An Autobiography.* Berkeley: University of California Press, 1978.
Vicinus, Martha, ed. *Suffer and Be Still: Women in the Victorian Age.* Bloomington: Indiana University Press, 1972.
———, ed. *A Widening Sphere: Changing Roles of Victorian Women.* Bloomington: Indiana University Press, 1977.
Weissman, Judith. "'Old Maids Have Friends': The Unmarried Heroine of Trollope's Barsetshire Novels." *Women and Literature* 5 (1977): 15–25.
West, Rebecca. *The Court and the Castle.* New Haven, Conn.: Yale University Press, 1957.
Wijesinha, Rajiva. *The Androgynous Trollope: Attitudes to Women Amongst Early Victorian Novelists.* Washington, D.C.: University Presses of America, 1982.
Williams, Raymond. *The English Novel from Dickens to Lawrence.* New York: Oxford University Press, 1970.
Wood, Ann Douglas. "'The Fashionable Diseases': Women's Complaints and Their Treatment in Nineteenth-Century America." In *Clio's Consciousness Raised,* edited by Mary S. Hartman and Lois Banner. New York: Harper and Row, 1974.
Wright, Andrew. *Anthony Trollope: Dream and Art.* Chicago: University of Chicago Press, 1983.

Index

The American Senator, Arabella Trefoil in, 5; Trollope on, 5
apRoberts, Ruth, 2
Austen, Jane, *Emma*, G. Knightly in, 40
Autobiography: on *The Last Chronicle of Barset*, Lily Dale in, 6; on *Phineas Finn* and *Phineas Redux*, 40; on *Phineas Finn* and *Phineas Redux*, Lady Laura in, 43; on Plantagenet Palliser, 88
Ayala's Angel, Aunt Rosina in, 5

Barchester Towers (1857): Monica Thorne in, 5; Stanhope family, 73
Barickman, Richard, Susan MacDonald, and Myra Stark, *Corrupt Relations:* on *Can You Forgive Her?*, title of, 9; on Lady Mabel Grex, 129; on John Grey, 26, 28; on Trollope, and sexual relations, ambivalence toward, 2
Beale, Dorothea, 6
The Belton Estate (1866): Clara Belton in, 3–4; Will Belton, 4; marriage in, 4
The Bertrams (1859): Lionel Bertram in, 77; Miss Todd in, 3, 5
Bodichon, Barbara Leigh Smith, 87
Brontë, Anne, *The Tenant of Wildfell Hall*, Helen in, 98
Brontë, Charlotte, 6, 100
Buss, Frances Mary, 6
Butte, George, on Lady Mabel Grex, 129, 132

Can You Forgive Her?, 2, 39
—Mr. Bott, 14; and Alice, 17–18; and Lady Glencora, 15, 61
—Cheeseacre in, 43
—comic closure of, 137
—comic subplot, and subversiveness in, 9–11, 19
—convention of the two suitors, 86
—conventionality, Levine on, 21
—courtship plot, disrupted, 40
—Burgo Fitzgerald in, 11; and Lady Glencora, 11–12, 15, 17, 20, 27; and prostitute, 9, 13; and treatment of horse, 66
—Miss Grant, George Vavasor and, 13
—Arabella Greenow in, 3; and Bellfield, 43; and Cheeseacre, rejection of, 43; marriage, 10; marriage, to Bellfield, 11; marriage, to Greenow, 10; sexuality of, 9–11
—John Grey in, 3, 7, 92; Alice and, 23, 25–29; Barickman et al., on, 26, 28; character of, 27–28; chivalry of, 116; in Parliament, Overton on, 31; jilted, 9; Kincaid on, 26, 28; Letwin on, 26, 29; Levine on, 26; McMaster on, 26; Overton on, 26–27
—Henry James's review of, 8
—Jane (George's mistress) in, 7–9; as "fallen woman," 36, 38; George's use of, 13, 36, 38; self-sacrifice of, 36, 38
—Mrs. Marsham, 14; and Alice, 14; Lady Glencora and, 14–15, 61
—Matching Priory ruins, 16–17, 22, 24, 135
—Lady Midlothian in, 15–16
—narrative, divergence from convention of the two suitors, 10–11
—narrator, and events, disparity of, 33, 35
—Lady Glencora Palliser in, 3, 7, 60; and Alice, 15–16; and Mr. Bott, 15; and Burgo, 7, 9, 11–12, 15–17, 20, 24, 27, 85, 114; and Burgo, love, characterized, 121–22; and Mrs. Marsham, 14–15; and Lady Midlothian, 15–16; and Plantagenet, proposal scene, 67, 84; as child, 14–15, 17; independence of, and language, 61; love dilemma of, 11, 20; marriage, 7, 10, 126, 137; marriage, money and, 11, 13, 20; marriage, mutual affection in, 20–21, 100–101; marriage, worthy man and, 11–12, 15, 20; moonlit walk, 16–17, 22, 24, 135; narrator's ambivalence toward, 19–20; on single operatives, 4; orphan, 13, 25;

pregnancy, and motherhood, as resolution, 20–24; self-hatred, 12–13, 16–17, 22, 24, 63, 131; struggle for self-realization, 11, 21–22, 24; Trollope's treatment of, as new ideal, 18–19
—Plantagenet Palliser in, 9–11; marriage, accommodation in, 20–21; marriage of, 11, 15, 20; treatment of Lady Glencora, 17
—Taylor's illustrations for, 21–22, 24
—text, and illustrations, tension between, 33, 35
—title: Barickman et al., on, 9; critics on, 8–10; Kincaid on, 8–9; Letwin on, 9; McMaster on, 8; Overton on, 9; treatment of female purity and, 9–10
—Alice Vavasor in, 3, 21–22, 60, 87; and Mr. Bott, 17–18; and her father, 14; and George, 13, 24, 25, 27–29, 35, 36, 107; and George, her self-sacrifice, 35, 36; and Lady Glen, 15–16; and John Grey, 13, 15, 24, 25–27, 114; and John, his treatment of her, 28–30; and John, love, characterized, 121–22; and John, marriage, 10, 137; and John, proposal scene, 32–33, 67–68, 84; and John, resolution, contradictions in, 31, 33; and Jeffrey Palliser, separation from, 12; and Kate, 36; and Lady Macleod, 13–14, 25–26; and Mrs. Marsham, 14; and Lady Midlothian, 26; as jilt, 35; character of McMaster on, 25, 28; convention of the two suitors and, 24, 25; critics on, 8–9; her mother and, 25–26; Letwin on, 30; narrative, disrupted courtship and, 25; purity of, 32, 35; search for selfhood, 7; wedding, and illustrations for, 33, 35
—George Vavasor in, 7, 9; Alice and, 27–29; and Jane, his use of her, 13, 36, 38; and Kate, his use of her, 13, 36–37; exploitation of women, 13; Romanticism and, 13
—Kate Vavasor in, 7, 9; and Alice, 36; and George, 13–14, 36–37, 94–95; and George, her self-sacrifice, 36–37; and her grandfather, 14; Kincaid on, 36; orphan, 13, 25; self-hatred, 36–37
—womanhood, Trollope's ambivalence toward, 25–26
—womanhood, ideal of in: as child, 12, 14–15, 17; delicate lady, 17–18, 29; Lady Glencora and, 16–17; martyr and, 16–17; moral teacher and, 19; purity and, 12, 19–20, 30–31; self-sacrifice and, 16–17, 20–21, 36, 38
—women in: and roles of, disruption in, 7, 13; lack of parental care, 13–14
Chivalry. *See under* Gentleman, idea of
The Claverings, 48

Cobbe, Frances Power, 6
Cockshut, A. O. J., on Trollope, conventionality of, 1
Collins, Wilkie, 2
Courtship, and marriage, Trollope's attitudes toward, Wijensinha on, 1

Dickens, Charles, 2, 100; *Hard Times*, Louisa Gradgrind in, 97–98; *Little Dorrit*, 18
Doctor Thorne, 92, Kennard on, 25
The Duke's Children, 2
—Isabel Boncassen in, 3, 119, 132–33; and Silverbridge, 133–34; and Silverbridge, equality of, 83, 135–36; and Silverbridge, Lady Mabel on, 135; and Silverbridge, Madame Max on, 135; and Silverbridge, McMaster on, 136; and Silverbridge, Mrs. Montacute-Jones on, 133; and suitors, 127; family life of, 129, 134; independence of, 134–35; influence of Lady Glencora on, 133; Lady Mabel compared to, 129–30; marriage of, 8, 39, 138; McMaster on, 134; on Dolly Longstaffe, 127; passionate, 136; self-worth of, 133–36
—Lady Cantrip, 123
—Miss Cassewary in, 125–26
—comic resolution, subversion of, 136
—critical response to, 122
—Phineas Finn in, 92
—Lord Gerald in, 128
—Madame Max Goesler in: and Duke, 70, 125; and Duke, McMaster on, 123–24; and Phineas, 136; as alter ego to Lady Glencora, 124–25
—Lady Mabel Grex in, 3, 8, 48, 64, 119; and Miss Cassewary, 129, 132; and Lord Grex, 128–29; and Silverbridge, 55, 122–26, 129–31; and Silverbridge, Butte on Duke and, 133; and Silverbridge, refusal of, 128; and Tregear, 55, 125–26, 130–31, 135; and womanhood, conventions of, 129–32; as "fallen woman," 131–32; as ornament, 128; as tragic, 125–26, 128, 131–32; Barickman et al., on, 129; Butte on, 129, 132; compared to Isabel, 129–30; family life, Gindin on, 128–29; isolation of, 8, 94–95, 138; McMaster on, 126; patriarchy, effects of on, 128–29, 136; self-hatred, 131; Silverbridge on, 132; Wijensinha on, 129
—Lord Grex, and Mabel, 128–29
—Dolly Longstaffe in, 127; and Isabel, 127, 134
—Matching Priory ruins, 136
—Lady Glencora Palliser in, 3, 7–8, 131–32; and Madame Max, as alter ego to, 124–25; Hagen on, 119, 122; influence of Lady

Mary and Tregear, 98, 104, 119–20, 122; marriage of, 119; struggle for self-realization, continued, 119
—Lady Mary Palliser in, 3, 119; and Lord Popplecourt, 121, 123; and suitors, 127; and Tregear, 132–33; and Tregear, Duke's resistance to, 122–124; and Tregear, Lady Glencora's encouragement of, 119–20, 133; and Tregear, wedding, 136; characterization of, 120–21, 123; marriage of, 8, 138; on Lord Popplecourt, 127
—Plantagenet Palliser (Duke of Omnium): and Lady Glencora, marriage, resolution of, 122; and womanhood, ideal of, ownership and, 122–24; and womanhood, ideal of, purity, 124
—Lord Percival, 127–28
—Lord Popplecourt, 122, 127; Lady Mary on, 127
—McMaster on, 122
—Silverbridge in, 8, 92; on Lady Mabel, 132
—Francis Tregear in, resemblance to Burgo, 119–20, 124
—Trollope's critique of patriarchy in, 127–28
—Victorian society, male power in, 128
—young men in, 127

Eliot, George, 100; Dorothea, and Casaubon, 53; Williams on, 137
The Eustace Diamonds, 2, 141n.3; Lady Glencora in, and Lizzie Eustace, 98

Fawcett, Millicent Garrett, 87
Feminism (*see also* Women's rights), 87; Trollope's opposition to, 94
Field, Kate, 134, 142n.8; and Trollope, 4; Trollope to, on careers of single women, 4
Foster, Shirley, 139

Garrett, Peter, on Trollope, 138
Gentleman, idea of: and civilization, 105, 110; chivalry and, 88; in Trollope's works, 19, 26–27, 29, 52, 89, 138–39; Letwin on, 27, 29, 109; perfect, Trollope's depiction of, 26–27, 88; Gilmour on, 52
Gilmour, Robin, *The Idea of the Gentleman in the Victorian Novel*, 52
Gindin, James, on Trollope's motherless women, 48
Greg, W. R., on redundant women, 4

Hagan, John, on *The Duke's Children*, Lady Glencora's influence in, 119, 122
Hardy, Thomas, 137
Harvey, Geoffrey, on Trollope, 138
He Knew He Was Right (1869): Arabella French in, 5; Camilla French in, 5; Col. Osborne in, 77; Dorothy Stanbury in, 5; Jemima Stanbury in, 5; Priscilla Stanbury in, 5; Wallachia Petrie in, 5
Heilbrun, Carolyn, on Trollope, conventionality of, in *Toward a Recognition of Androgyny*, 1
Herbert, Christopher, 2
Holl, Friedrich, illustrations, for *Phineas Redux*, 55, 58–59
Huxley, Aldous, 95

Is He Popenjoy? (1878), 73, 117; Baroness Bannman in, 5; Olivia Q. Fleabody in, 5; Tracy on, 117

Jalland, Pat, *Women, Marriage, and Politics, 1860–1914*, 139
James, Henry, 107, 146n.14, 150n.19; review of *Can You Forgive Her?*, 8; review of Linton's essay, "Girl of the Period," 5; *The Sacred Fount*, 115

Kennard, Jean: on convention of the two suitors, in *Victims of Convention*, 10, 23, 25, 40; on *Doctor Thorne*, 25
Kept in the Dark (1882): and male-female roles, assumption of, 138; Francesca Altifiorla in, 5
Kincaid, James, 2, 114; on *Can You Forgive Her?*, title, 8–9; on John Grey, 26, 28; on Kate, 36
Kleis, John: on Palliser series, 153n.10; on Trollope's use of setting, 31

Ladies of Langham Place, 147n.16
The Last Chronicle of Barset (1867), Lily Dale in, 6
Letters, on *The American Senator*, Arabella in, 5
Letwin, Shirley, 2; on Alice Vavasor, 9; on *Can You Forgive Her?*, title, 9; on John Grey, 26; on Madame Max, as perfect gentleman, 69, 125; on perfect gentlemen, Trollope and, 27; *The Gentleman in Trollope*, 109
Levine, George: on *Can You Forgive Her?*, conventionality of, 21; on John Grey, 26; on Trollope, conventionality of, 1–2
Lewis, Sarah, 93; *Woman's Mission*, 88
Linton, Eliza Lynn, "Girl of the Period," James's review of, 5

Marion Fay (1882), angelic heroine of, 138
McMaster, Juliet, 2; in *Trollope's Palliser Novels*, on *The Duke's Children*, 122; on

Can You Forgive Her?, title, 8; on Emily, financial ignorance of, 110; on John Grey, 26; on Isabel, 134; on Isabel and Silverbridge, 136; on Lady Mabel, 126, 129; on Madame Max, and the Duke, 123–24; on place, and Trollope's characters, 22, 24; on Trollope, and women's rights, 87; on Trollope, sympathy for landed gentry, 116–17

Mencken, H. L., on Trollope, on single women, in *Quotations*, 4

Mill, John Stuart, 87; *On the Subjection of Women*, 93, 139; on women's rights, 64–65

Millais, John, illustrations, for Trollope, 145n.11

Miss Mackenzie (1865): John Ball in, 3; Lady Glencora in, 7; marriage in, 3; Miss Todd in, 3, 5; Miss Todd, modeled on F. P. Cobbe, 6

More, Paul Elmer, on Trollope, and landed gentry, 116

Narrative: commentary, Trollope's use of, 2; convention of the two suitors, Kennard on, 10, 23, 25, 40; disruption of, 3; intent and resolution, Trollope and, 2; Trollope's disruption of (*see also* individual works), 2

The Nation, James's review of *Can You Forgive Her?* in, 8

National Review, W. R. Greg in, on redundant women, 4

Nightingale, Florence, 6

North America, Trollope in, on single women, 4

O'Connor, Frank: on "heart," in Trollope's characters, 52; on Trollope, use of narrator, 33

An Old Man's Love (1884), 138

Overton, Bill: on *Can You Forgive Her?*, title, 9; on John Grey, 26–27, 31; on Trollope, attitudes toward women, in *The Unofficial Trollope*, 2

Philanthropy, 99

Phineas Finn (1869), 2
—Mr. Appledon in, 42
—Augusta Baldock in, 4, 64
—Lady Baldock in, 42, 59; Violet and, 59, 61, 63
—Mr. Bonteen in, 74
—Mrs. Bonteen in, 74
—Earl of Brentford in, 46, 48; and Lord Chiltern, 48–49
—Lord Chiltern in, 42, 48; and Violet, 49; characterization of, 65–66, 68; Kennedy compared to, 66–67; Laura on, 65; Phineas on, 65; proposal scene, 67
—convention of the two suitors in, 40–43
—courtship plots, disruption of, 40–41
—Violet Effingham in, 2–6, 39–40, 45; and Lady Baldock, 59, 61, 63; and Lord Chiltern, 49, 58, 60, 63; and Lord Chiltern, marriage of, 39, 42, 65, 68; and women's rights, 64–65, 94; characterization of, 59–61, 63; compared to Mary, 68–69; conventions, recognition of, 61, 63–64, 134; courtship, disruptions in, 41–42; independence of, 61, 63; Mary compared to, 60; Madame Max on, 60–61; on Phineas, as suitor, 67–68; on women as saviors, 97
—Lord Fawn, 42
—Phineas Finn in, and Lady Laura, 45–46, 52; and Mary, 45–46; and Mary, marriage, 42; and Madame Max, 68–70; and Madame Max, marriage, 42; and Violet, 42; as suitor, Violet on, 67–68; on Lord Chiltern, 65; reputation of, 78
—Aspasia Fitzgibbon in, 4, 64
—Madame Max Goesler in, 3, 39–40, 45; and Lady Glencora, 69; and elder Mr. Maule, 42; and Phineas, 71, 136; and Phineas, marriage of, 39–40, 55; and Plantagenet, 42, 69–75; as ornament of society, 73–74; as perfect gentleman, Letwin on, 69, 125; courtship, disruptions in, 42; on Violet, 60–61; Trollope's ambivalence toward, 70
—Mary Flood Jones in, 40; and Phineas, marriage of, 40, 42, 45; compared to Lady Laura, 81; compared to Madame Max, 81; compared to Violet, 60, 81; juxtaposed with Lady Laura, 43, 45–46
—Mr. Kennedy in, 40–41; and Lady Laura, patriarchy in marriage of, 50, 52, 53; and womanhood, ideal of as efficient domestic manager, 53; attempted murder of Phineas, 52; characterization of, 66–67; Chiltern on, 66–67; compared to Chiltern, 66–67; religion and, 53
—Gerard Maule in, 77
—Maurice Maule in, characterization of, 75, 77; on Plantagenet, 74–75
—Adelaide Palliser in, 44
—Lady Glencora Palliser in, 39–40
—Plantagenet Palliser (Duke of Omnium) in, 74; as ornament of society, 73–75; characterization of, 72–74; compared to Duke of St. Bungay, 73–74; Maurice on, 74–75
—redundant women in, treatment of, 4
—resolution, compared to *Phineas Redux*, 39–40
—Saulsby Wood, Violet and Chiltern in, 65, 67

―Lady Laura Standish in, 2–3, 39–40, 45; and Mr. Kennedy, 40–41, 67; and Mr. Kennedy, marriage of, 46, 48, 50, 52–53, 63; and patriarchy, effects of on, 48, 50; and Phineas, 40–41, 45–46, 48, 53, 55; characterization of, 45–46; courtship, disruption of, 41; juxtaposed with Mary Jones, 43, 45–46; marriage, frustration in, 39; Trollope on, 43
―Trollope on, 40
―womanhood, ideal of in, Trollope's ambivalence toward, 40, 43
―women in, characterization of, 43

Phineas Redux, 2
―Augusta Baldock in, 64
―Mr. Bonteen, Emilius' murder of, 50, 52
―Earl of Brentford: and Lord Chiltern, 49–50; and Lady Laura, 49–50; and Phineas, 49–50; characterization of, 49–50
―Lord Chiltern in, 42
―comic subplot of, 42–43
―Violet Effingham in, 2; and Chiltern, 42, 137; and Chiltern, equality of, 67–68
―Mr. Emilius, and Lizzie Eustace, 50, 52
―Phineas Finn in, 49–50; and Earl, 49–50; and Lady Laura, 41; reputation of, 78
―Madame Max Goesler in, 41, 70; and Maurice Maule, 71, 75, 77; and Phineas, marriage of, 92–93, 136–37; and Phineas, proposal scene, 83–84; and Phineas, reversal of conventions, 79, 81–83
―Holl's illustrations for, 55, 58–59
―Mr. Kennedy in, marriage of, 49
―Adelaide Palliser in, 3; and Gerard Maule, 42–43, 64; and Gerard, marriage of, 125, 137; and Mr. Spooner, 42–43; courtship plot, disruption in, 40, 42–43
―Lady Glencora Palliser in, 39; and Adelaide, 98
―resolution, compared to *Phineas Finn*, 39–40
―Lady Laura Standish in, 3, 94–95; and Duke, 137–38; and Earl, 49–50; and Kennedy, marriage of, 49–50; and Phineas, 41; on Parliament, 87–88; patriarchy, effects of on, 55; Trollope on, 43
―Trollope on, 40
―womanhood, ideal of in, Trollope's ambivalence toward, 40, 43
―women in, characterization of, 43
Polhemus, Robert, 2; on Lady Glencora, and prostitute, parallels, 13
Poovey, Mary, *The Proper Lady and the Woman Writer*, 89
Praz, Mario, on Trollope, conventionality of, 1

The Prime Minister, 2
―courtship plot, disruption of, 85–86
―Barrington Erle in, 78
―Arthur Fletcher in, 106; and Emily, 106–8; and Silverbridge election, 108; as gentleman, 109, 114–15
―John Fletcher in, 117
―Mrs. Fletcher in, 105
―gentleman, idea of in, 117
―Madame Max Goesler, and women's rights, 78
―landed gentry: sympathy for, 117; sympathy for, and iniquities of, 117, 138; narrator and, 116–17
―Ferdinand Lopez in, 8; and Arthur, 108; and Emily, marriage of, 52; and Emily, marriage, his domination of, 107–11; suicide, 111
―Lopez payment controversy, 89
―marriage, focus on, 85–86; importance of, narrator on, 105–6
―men and women in, roles of, 88–92; Trollope's ambivalence toward roles, 92–93
―narrative, subversion in, 85
―narrative structure, of parallel careers, 106
―Lady Glencora Palliser in, 7, 39, 78, 85; ambitions and career of, 85–86, 93–96, 104, 130; and Emily, 8, 98; and Emily, romance with Ferdinand, 98–99; and Emily and Arthur, 98–99; and Plantagenet, marriage, mutual affection in, 100–101, 104–5, 107; and Plantagenet, marriage of, 88–90; and Plantagenet, parallel careers of, 86–92; as child, 91–93; characterization of, 90–91, 93; on herself, 134; philanthropy, 99; struggle for self-realization, 85–87, 93, 95–97, 99, 104
―Plantagenet Palliser (Duke of Omnium) in, 86; and Lady Glencora, marriage of, 88–90; as perfect gentleman, 88, 105; domestic illusion of, 96–97
―Mrs. Parker, 110
―plot, convention of the two suitors, altered, 86
―Silverbridge election, Lady Glencora and, 89–90, 92, 108
―Duke of St. Bungay, on Lady Glencora, 96
―Wharton heir in, 73
―Abel Wharton in, 105, 108; and Lopez, money and, 108, 110
―Sir Alured Wharton in, 116
―Emily Wharton in, 3; and Arthur Fletcher, 106–7, 111–13, 125; and Arthur, marriage of, 85–86, 105, 114; and Arthur, proposal scene, 67, 84; and Ferdinand Lopez, 85–86, 125; and Ferdinand, marriage, money and, 108–10; and Ferdinand, marriage, reasons

for, 105–7; and Everett Wharton, compared, 115; as child, 108; as counterpart to Lady Glencora, 8; as Ferdinand's possession, 111; as widow, 111–13, 151; self-realization, attempt at, 113
—Everett Wharton in, 106, 108; and Mary Wharton, 106; characterization, and attitudes toward women, 115–16; inheritance, 116–17; success of, 115–16
—whip, as symbol in, 108
—womanhood, ideal of: and ambivalence toward, 85–86, 88–89, 92; and Lady Glencora, self-sacrifice, 97; Angel-in-the-House, Emily and, 115; as child, reversed, 91–92; efficient domestic manager, and Lady Glencora, 96, 98; moral teacher, subverted, 91; ornament of society, Lady Glencora and, 99–100; ornament of society, Griselda Grantley and, 99–100; purity, Emily and, 112–13
—women's rights in, 86–87

Ramée, Marie Louise de la, *Ouida*, 100
Romanticism, 144n.5; oppression of women and, 13; George Vavasor and, 13
Rossetti, Christina, 6
Ruskin, John, 93; "Of Queens' Gardens," 88, 90, 143n.3

Sadleir, Michael, on Trollope, conventionality of, 1, 137
The Small House at Allington (1864): Lord de Courcy in, 128; Johnny Eames in, 92; Griselda Grantley in, as ornament of society, 18; Lady Glencora Palliser in, 7; Lady Glencora, and Burgo, 7
Society, Victorian: conventions of, 77–78; male children, importance of, 22; male power in, 13, 20–21, 50; sexual power, imbalance of, 22
Stone, Donald, *The Romantic Impulse in Victorian Fiction*, 13, 144n.5

Taylor, E., illustrations, for *Can You Forgive Her?*, 21–22, 24, 32, 35, 36–37
Taylor, Harriet, 87
Taylor, Mary, 6
Terry, R. C., 2
Thackeray, William, 2, 100
Thale, Jerome, on Trollope's works, thematic structure, 95
Thomson, Patricia, on Trollope, and women, submissiveness of, in *The Victorian Heroine: A Changing Ideal*, 1
The Three Clerks (1858): angelic heroine of, 138; Gertrude Tudor in, 6

Tolstoy, Leo, *Anna Karenina*, 11, 143n.2
Tracy, Robert, on *Is He Popenjoy?*, 117
Trollope, Anthony
—and feminism, opposition to, 94
—and Kate Field, 4
—and sexual relations, ambivalence toward, 2
—and Woman Question, 3, 39, 89
—and womanhood, Victorian ideal of, ambivalence toward (*see also* individual works), 2
—and women: recognition of sexuality of, 55; redundant, 3–6
—and women's rights, 86–87
—as feminist, West on, 1
—as social historian, 137
—Barsetshire series: Grace Crawley, 134; Griselda Grantley, 18; Lady Glencora Palliser, 7; Lucy Robarts, 134
—characterization, ambiguous, 2
—conventionality of: Cockshut on, 1; Heilbrun on, 1; Levine on, 1; Praz on, 1; Sadleir on, 1
—courtship and marriage, attitudes toward, 1,6
—Garrett on, 138
—gentlemen, idea of, 19, 26–27, 52, 109, 138–39; Letwin on, 27, 29
—Harvey on, 138
—illustrations, and text, tension between, 2
—landed gentry, sympathy for, 116–17
—marriages, equality in, 100
—McMaster on, 116–17
—men, treatment of horses and women in, 66
—More on, 116
—narrative structure: disruption of, 2; intent and resolution in, 2
—on single women, 4
—Overton on, 2
—Palliser series (*see also* individual works): comic end of, subverted, 139; Madame Max Goesler, as perfect gentleman, Letwin on, 125; Lady Mabel Grex, isolation of, 139; Lady Mabel Grex, McMaster on, 129; Kleis on, 153n.10; Matching Priory ruins in, 135–36; narrative conventions, disruption of, 3; Lady Glencora Palliser in: ambition of, 139; as matchmaker, 98, 125; central to series, 39; extended characterization of, 3, 7; family and, 129; narrative and, other women as complements to, 7; struggle for self-realization in, 7; Plantagenet Palliser in, as perfect gentlemen, 109; redundant women in, ambivalence toward, 4; structure, and conflict of ideals of womanhood, 138; Trollope's conception of, 2, 141n.1; women in, self-hatred of, compared to Isabel, 134
—Phineas saga: Violet Effingham in, and Chiltern, equality of, 79, 84; Madame Max

Goesler in: and Phineas, as parallels, 77–79; and Phineas, equality of, 78–79, 81, 83; as perfect gentleman, 79, 81; suitors and, 71; Phineas in, and Madame Max, 77–79
—place, characters and, McMaster on, 22–23
—proposal scenes, as characterization of marriage, 83–84
—"Republican Browning," spinster in, 5
—setting, Kleis on use of, 31
—spinsters in; feminist, 5; kind, 5
—"The Telegraph Girl" (1877), 4
—thematic structure, Thale on, 95
—womanhood, ideal of in: and Trollope's ambivalence toward, 78, 85–86, 88–89, 92, 105–7, 137–38; as child, ambivalence toward, 91–93; delicate lady, 111–12; efficient domestic manager, perceptions of, 98; marriage, equality in, 100; ornament of society, 99–100; purity, ambivalence toward, 9–10, 19–20, 113; self-sacrifice: ambivalence toward, 97–98; exploration of, 138
—women in: motherless, Gindin on, 48; sexuality, recognized, critics on, 2; submissive, Thomson on, 1; treatment of: and Lady Glencora, as new ideal, 18–19; critics on, 1–2; unconventional, critics on, 2
—women's rights: and marital equality, 139; McMaster on, 87; perception of, and Madame Max, 78
—"The Young Women at the London Telegraph Office" (1877), 4

The Vicar of Bullhampton (1870): Col. Marrable in, 77; Miss Marrable in, 5

The Way We Live Now (1875): Dolly Longstaffe in, 127; Georgina Longstaffe in, 5
West, Rebecca, on Trollope, as feminist, 1
Wijensinha, Rajiva, on Lady Mabel, 129, on Trollope's attitudes toward courtship and marriage, in *The Androgynous Trollope*, 1
Williams, Raymond, on Trollope, 137–38
Woman Question (*see also* Women's rights), 64, 89, 137; and gentleman question, 138–39; redundant woman and, 3; tensions of, 2; Trollope's reaction to, conflict in, 3; Trollope's treatment of, 39
Womanhood, ideal of: and male power, 85, 88; Angel-in-the-House, 53, 69, 138, 143–44n.3; as child, 12, 14–15, 17, 61, 110; as child, Trollope's ambivalence toward, 91–93; delicate lady, 29, 88–89, 145n.8; efficient domestic manager, 53, 149–50n.15; efficient manager, Trollope's perception of, 98; martyr, 16–17; moral teacher, 19, 144–45n.7; nature and mission of, 95; ornament of society, 18, 73–75, 99–100; purity, 86, 88, 143–44n.3; purity, Trollope's ambivalence toward, 19–20, 113; self-sacrifice, 77, 86, 93, 138; Trollope, and marriage, equality in, 100; Trollope's ambivalence toward, 2, 78, 85–86, 88–89, 97–98, 105–7, 137–38
Women (*see also* Woman, redundant): emigration of, 4; "fallen," 16–17, 20, 36, 55, 152n.7; nature and mission of, 2–3, 6; repression of, and Romanticism, 13; role of, James on, 95; sexuality, Trollope's recognition of, 2; submissiveness of, Thomson on, 1
—Trollope's treatment of: critics on, 1–2; unconventional, 2
—vulnerability and exploitation of, 13
Women, redundant, 64, 142n.6, 147nn.15,16; and Woman Question, 3; Greg on, 4; Trollope's ambivalence toward, 3–6
Women's rights (*see also* Feminism): and marital equality, Trollope's views of, 139; Trollope's limits on, 86–87; Trollope's perception of, 78; Violet and, 64–65